Mean Feat

A 3,000-mile walk through Portugal,
Spain, France, Switzerland and Italy

JOHN WAITE

The Oxford Illustrated Press

© John Waite, 1985
Printed in Great Britain by J. H. Haynes & Co Limited
ISBN 0 946609 19 5
The Oxford Illustrated Press, Sparkford, Yeovil, Somerset, England
Distributed in North America by Interbook Inc.,
14895 E. 14th Street, Suite 370, San Leandro, CA 94577 USA

British Library Cataloguing in Publication Data

Waite, John
Mean feat: a 3000 mile walk through Portugal,
Spain, France, Switzerland and Italy.
1. Europe—Description and travel—1971-
I. Title
914'.04558   D923

ISBN 0-946609-19-5

All maps and line illustrations drawn by the author
Front cover photo: Images Colour Library Ltd

For all those people in Portugal, Spain, France, Switzerland and Italy
who helped me along the way with their kindness and hospitality, or
simply a smile.

'The moon is set and the Pleiades are gone,
Midnight is near, the hours pass
and I sleep alone.'

Sappho

Acknowledgements

I should like to thank the staff of the Cambridge University Library
for their help in my researches, Jane Marshall for such attentive,
thoughtful editing, Nicholas Rankin for unfailing help and much needed
encouragement, Alison Beattie for her continuous support,
Louise Hashemi, Colin Hayes, Piers Corke, my mother and my father
for their suggestions after reading bits of the original drafts, the
Hildyard family for their help with Mas Bas, Allen Halls for the title,
the Studio School of English for allowing me time off from teaching
and Mrs. Elizabeth Wamsley for the cottage on Valance Farm where I
found the peace, quiet and horizons to settle down for a while
and write this book.

Contents

Introduction

PART ONE The Iberian Peninsular

Portugal

Spain

PART TWO From the Pyrenees to Grenoble

France

PART THREE The Alps

France

Switzerland

Italy

PART FOUR Southbound

Italy

Epilogue

Bibliography

Index

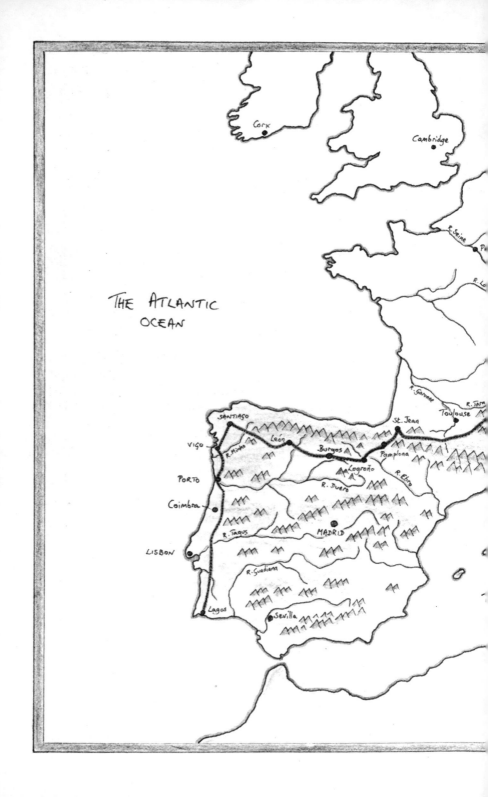

A WALK THROUGH SOUTH WESTERN EUROPE, 1981

Day	JAN.	FEB.	MAR.	APR.	MAY	JUN.	JUL.	AUG	SEP.	OCT.	NOV.
1			Amarela	Ponte da Barca	Logroño	"	"	Col de Jaman	"	Lake Trasimene	Albero-bello
2			Santa Clara	Minho	Allo	Zoo	"	Lac d'Hongrin	"	Perugia	The Adriatic Coast
3			São Martinho	Vigo	Villa-fuerta	Langue d'oc	"	Gstaad	Plan	Assisi	Brindisi
4			Alvalade	Santiago	Pamplona	Ariège	"	Adelboden	Corvara	Sasso-vivo	
5			Ermidas Sado	Ledesma	"	Canal du Midi	Lodève	Kandersteg	Pelegrino	Visso	
6			Vale de Guiso	Borra-jeiros	"	Bassin de Lampy	Cévennes	Eiger	Rifugio Mulaz	Monte Utero	
7			Alcácer do Sal	Miño	"	Montagne Noire	Mont Aigoual	Grindelwald	Levetti	Gran Sasso	
8			São Lourenço	Samos	"	Dolmen	Mimente	Meiningen	Monte Grappa	Assergi	
9			Vendas Novas	Pío Pájaro	"	St. Martin du Froid	Tarn	Lake	Bassano	Pópoli	
10			Frades	Castro-petre	"	Bédarieux	Villefort	Jochpass	Padua	Sulmona	
11			Coruche	El Bierzo	"	Mas Bas	Les Vans	Altdorf	"	Monte Genzana	
12			Chouto	Ponferrada	"	"	Ardèche	Suworow Weg	"	Scanno	
13			Abrantes	Acebo	Erro	"	Rhône	Flims	"	Cerro al Volturno	
14			Pine Woods	Astorga	Ron-cesvalles	"	Dieulefit	Rhine	"	Isernia	
15			Vila de Rei	León	St. Jean	"	Forêt de Saoul	Chur	Colli Euganei	Matese	
16			Fondada	Mansilla de las Mulas	Iraty	"	Saillans	Sunden Pass	Este	Sepino	
17			Lousã	Sahagún	Larrau	"	Plan de Baix	Davos	Po	Tammaro	
18			Penacova	Carrión	Pic d'Arlas	"	Gorges de la Bourne	Adige	Medicina	Pompei	
19			Bucaco	Pisuerga	Bedous	"	Vercors	Merano	Imola	Naples	
20			São João	Hornillos del Camino	Larons	"	Autrans	Bolzano	Monte Battaglia	"	
21			Caramulo	BURGOS	Col d'Aubisque	"	Grenoble	Padua	Appenine Ridgeway	"	
22			Sejnes	"	Lugagnan	"	Col de Coq	"	Paso Muraglione	"	
23			Arouca	"	Bigorre	Le Puech	St. Michel	"	Camaldoli	Mud	
24			PORTO	"	Banios	"	Isère	"	La Verna	Apice	
25			"	"	Lortet	"	Le Châtelard	"	Uncle Tom's Cabin	Grotta-minarda	
26			"	"	"	"	Lac d'Annecy	"	Arezzo	Monte Volturo	
27		LAGOS	"	Snow	Garonne	"	Le Bornand	"	Siena	spring beds	
28		Monchique	"	Valmalá	Montjoie	"	Romme	"	"	Acerenza	
29			"	Rioja	St. Girons	"	Col de Coux	"	Sta. Maria	Irsina	
30			Guimarães	Ebro	"	"	Abondance	"	Cortona	Matera	
31			Citania de Briteiros		"		Montreux	"		Puglia	

● Nights on ground / Walking days ○ Bed □ Hostel or guest house

Route Calendar

Introduction

The train trundled across the cool, flat countryside of Andalucía, old 'Al Andalus', a low mist clinging to the hollows beneath almond trees in blossom, vivid streaks of bloody gold glowing on the horizon. A cloudless sky slowly turned the lovely, pale blue of morning.

We changed trains to an old *Ferrobus* with sides of shiny corrugated iron. The driver, mate and inspector all sat together at the front chatting, paying little attention to the few passengers or the tracks that led to the border at the river Guadiana, where a red and yellow ferry took us over to Portugal.

'Portucale' first became an independent Christian kingdom in 1140, slowly expanding southwards over the Tagus, forcing back the Moors, who were finally driven out of 'Al Gharbi' (The West), at the end of the thirteenth century. At this point Alfonso III became King both of Portugal and the Algarves.

February was drawing to a close. The windows of the train to Lagos were open to the soft, warm flow of the Gulf Stream, which allows spiky pointed agaves, carob, fig and olive trees to grow. Oranges blinked from lush, dark green orchards, while a mass of yellow flowers covered the embankment, closing into little bells as evening approached. The train followed the coastline, affording glimpses of the same calm, unruffled sea below that tempted Prince Henry the Navigator to turn his back on the rest of the peninsular and send his ships beyond the boundaries of the known world, round the coast of West Africa in search of the fabled Kingdom of Prester John. They reached Madeira, the Azores, the mouth of the Gambia river, Guinea and the Cape Verde Islands. Prince Henry died in 1460, but exploration continued to the mouth of the Congo and Angola. By 1487 Bartolomeu Dias had rounded the Cape of Good Hope, but his crew were so terrified of the unknown monsters that lay in wait for them that he was forced to turn back. Ten years later the intrepid Vasco da Gama rounded the Cape, sailed north to Mozambique and then across the Indian Ocean to Malabar, proving

1

the 10,000-mile journey possible, returning a profit of 600% and laying the ground for the expansion of the Portuguese Empire.

Lagos is a fishing village and tourist centre selling sun and sea, pots of Marmite, Bovril, Bird's Custard and Bath Olivers to proudly monolingual British pensioners. A chapel near the centre is dedicated to Saint Anthony, who was born in Lisbon in the twelfth century. The Patron Saint of Portugal, he is an honorary Captain in the Portuguese Army, while his statue in the chapel once sported the sash of a British Field Officer awarded to him during the Peninsular Wars of the nineteenth century.

We stayed at the campsite, lit a fire, cooked supper and lay back in the womb-like red light of the tent. Back in Spain, an important parliamentary debate was being broadcast on television when suddenly two hundred Civil Guards in patent leather tricorn hats under the command of a certain Lieutenant-Colonel Antonio Tejero crashed in through the doors, spraying the ceiling with bullets from their sub-machine guns. The people of Spain saw their terrified politicians dive for cover before the television screens went blank. The papers were full of it, a timely reminder that, for some at least, the Spanish Civil War was not yet over. Fortunately, the coup was ill-prepared and fizzled out within a few days when the proudly unrepentant Tejero was led off to prison.

In the morning, I checked my equipment, all to be contained in a capacious Karrimor rucksack with a light aluminium frame and a belt to distribute the weight. On my feet, I would have Trickers boots, bench made, tough but pliant, with commando soles that could be replaced when they wore out. When walking, I would need little more than shorts, a vest and a shirt, but I was not sure what to expect and had to cater for extremes of cold and wind. The clothes worked on the layer principle, so I could wear them all at the same time if necessary: 4 pairs of socks, two thick, two thin, 1 pair of thick trousers, 1 pair of shorts, 3 pairs of underpants, 1 pair of longjohns, wool, 1 sleeveless vest, 1 short-sleeved vest, 1 long sleeved vest, 1 shirt, Viyella, 1 short-sleeved pullover, 1 pullover, 1 down waistcoat, handmade from my old sleeping bag, 1 scarf, 1 woolly hat, 1 old 'Space Blanket', 1 cagoule, with hood.

Then there were washing things: a plastic bag containing tooth-paste, toothbrush, a soap tin (Savon de Marseilles was best for it could be used for washing both body and clothes), Germolene ointment as a general antiseptic cream, and half a towel, a concession to weight saving.

A budget of £100 a month would be enough for food and the occasional night in a cheap boarding house or hotel, but most of the time I would be sleeping rough. My camping equipment included an

2

'A' frame, stormproof, snowproof, rainproof tent with a fly sheet, inner tent, aluminium poles and pegs. I had bought a Karrimat to sleep on, which would keep away the ground chill, and a good quality Black's Icelandic 'mummy' sleeping bag that would keep me warm enough even if the temperature dropped below freezing. This had an inner cotton lining that could be washed, so the sleeping bag itself should not get into too filthy a state. I was also carrying a sheet of polythene to go under the tent to protect its somewhat delicate-looking groundsheet.

As I refused to live on a diet of cold food and the budget did not stretch to more than the occasional meal in a restaurant, cooking equipment was an absolute necessity. The 'kitchen' consisted of an Optimus petrol stove with light aluminium pans and burner paste for starting the thing off, a petrol bottle (one litre), a water bottle (one and a half litres), mess tins, tin opener, sponge and scourer, rag, knife, fork and spoon, a tin mug and matches carefully wrapped in a plastic bag so that they would not get damp.

In addition to this, in various pockets, were needle and thread, string, dubbin, glasses case with spare glasses, passport, cheque book, wallet, diary, address book, pen, book, compass, cigarettes and, most important, maps. The weight would be considerable since I had yet to include basic provisions, but it was a price I was prepared to pay for independence.

Piers and I were good friends, having known each other for fifteen years. He had decided to come with me on the first part of the walk, though quite when he would set off home was as yet undecided. We had everything we needed except maps of Portugal. I took a train to Lisbon and found the Instituto Geográfico e Cadastral, the only place in the whole country where you can buy decent maps. It was pouring with rain in the capital and I stayed only long enough to buy the maps before taking the next train back to Lagos. The plan was simple: to walk the length of Portugal, heading due north to the border with Spain. The first half across the Alentejo would be flat, a trial period for warming up and getting fit. North of the Tagus, it would become more hilly, even mountainous at times, as we crossed the provinces of Beira, Douro and Minho. If we walked some twenty miles a day, this first leg would take about a month. From the Spanish border, we would continue north to Santiago de Compostela, then turn east for the Pyrenees, France, the Alps, Switzerland, Northern Italy and so across to Istanbul, the planned destination. As we were starting from the south-western corner of Europe, it didn't seem impossible to cross to the other side, yet the distant, domed mosques of Istanbul were little more than a faint, hazy mirage on the horizons of my imagination. There was no time limit. I had no illusions about the journey. The walk would be a challenge needing patience, stamina, determination. It would involve days of hard slog, blisters, aching shoulders, fatigue, despair and solitude. I had only walked long distances once, for a few weeks in the high Andes in Peru, but that one experience had given me the appetite for more. Walking was, in retrospect, so much more worthwhile than travelling by bus, train or car. There is no waiting, no timetable to consult, nothing that cuts you off from the people you see and the places you are travelling through. Then, too, the slower you travel, the more time you have to digest the experience fully. On foot, you can go where you want when you want, stopping at will and reaching places where no other form of transport will take you, not even the bicycle. After months of planning and preparation in the warmth and comfort of my sitting-room, the time had come, at last, to emerge and see what lay outside.

PART ONE

The Iberian Peninsular

'Caminante, no hay camino:
Se hace el camino al andar.'

(Traveller, there is no road ahead:
it unfolds beneath you as you walk.)
(Antonio Machado, 1875-1939)

'From Spain neither a good wind, nor a
good marriage.'
(Portuguese Saying)

'No one should ever dream of making a walking
tour in Spain . . . walking is the manner by
which beasts travel, who have therefore four
legs; those bipeds who follow the example of
the brute animals will soon find they are
reduced to their level in more particulars
than they imagined or bargained for.'
(Richard Ford, *Gatherings from Spain,* 1846)

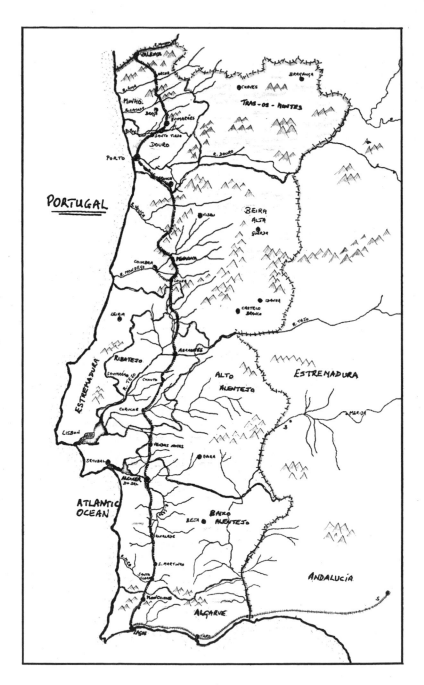

Portugal

The old woman wore black with a headscarf and a soft trilby to protect her from the sun. She talked lovingly of her country, especially of the Algarve, as her stout shoes scrunched on the dirt road.

'I walk up here every day,' she said. 'It keeps me fit and happy.'

It was the last day of February, 1981. Greeted by a rainbow as we set out, the sky was now clear, the day dry, warm and promising, an occasional puff of white cloud scudding by in the breeze. Two friends from the campsite had decided to come along on our first day: Michel, who could scarcely believe the weight of our packs and Annie, who had made us some marmalade over the fire in the campsite.

The woman turned off into her orchards. The track soon became a path up into the wooded slopes of the Serra de Monchique, the soft ochre earth and green pastures giving way to scrub and woods of chestnut, cork, scented eucalyptus, all dotted with periwinkle, forget-me-not and the light, pearly blue of wild rosemary. The climb was hard work and we were tired already, stopping to rest and lunch beside the murky waters of a stream, trying not to think too much about having to carry the packs for the rest of the day and admiring the first grapefruit tree I had ever seen instead. The fruit seemed incongruously large for such a small tree.

On the outskirts of Casais, gazing out over the hills rolling down to the sea, two men were sitting on a tree trunk, while their pigs snuffled about in the undergrowth. They set us on the right track to Monchique and watched us go. By the corner of a stone-walled field we said goodbye to Annie and Michel, who were taking the road back to Lagos. Walks are normally circular or there and back; it was one of the best things about this particular walk that there was no need to turn back, that it was always forward, always new. We picked our way round the occasional puddle and past a group of men who had been watching Piers change into his sandals. We were slightly

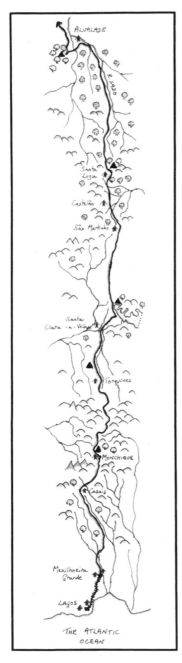

nervous, vulnerable at this stage to all new impressions, and felt vaguely threatened by their stares. Later, a woman washing clothes in the water from a spring refused to let us quench our thirst until she had fetched a glass from her house, then stood back and watched with a smile as we drank. This simple gesture was reassuring.

By early evening we reached Monchique. Piers' boots had given him blisters, the soles of my feet were sore, our backs and shoulders ached. The barman in the cafe on the main square brought over two bottles of beautifully cold beer, setting them down on the marble-topped table with a bang. The village men-folk had nothing much to do except scratch and stare at anything remotely out of the ordinary. My sense of anxiety caused me to see malice where there was only an innocent curiosity.

It was a Saturday, which meant buying provisions for the next day. Groups of women were preparing supper, braising peppers in the courtyards of their stone houses off the steep cobbled streets and alleys. Everything was shut. Enquiries eventually led us through the low doorway of a dimly lit shop, where a solitary man at the counter was quietly drinking spirits from a small glass. There were some cakes in a dusty, glass-topped wooden box, and some shelves stacked with tins of sardines, but little else. The portly, slow-moving proprietress produced rolls of bread from a sack on the floor and climbed laboriously onto a chair to reach for the sardines. Our

8

Sunday lunch would not be much of a feast.

Light was fading rapidly from the woods on either side of the quiet evening road out. The last thing we wanted was to be caught by the dark and have to grope around in the woods for somewhere to pitch the tent, so we camped hurriedly on the first suitable spot as night fell. We had not found anywhere to fill the water bottles, so I went back to the nearest house and knocked. The door opened, a shaft of light blinding me for an instant. A young woman was looking at me quizzically.

'I'm sorry to disturb you at this time of night, but could I have some water, please?'

I held an empty water bottle in either hand. Her mother called from another room.

'Who is it?'

'A stranger wants some water.'

'Well, give it to him, then.'

'Yes, Mama.'

She let me in through the hall of the modern bungalow to a bright, clean kitchen with blue

'Whitewashed adobe'

lino on the floor. I was instantly conscious of the mud on my boots and tiptoed in embarrassment to the tap to fill the bottles, thanked her and left, turning my back on that comfortable electric world of television and hot baths.

The soup we made was good and hot. By the light of the paraffin lamp that Piers had brought I wrote some notes, while he lay back in his sleeping bag. I was glad I had a companion: without him it would have been a lonely, uncertain moment.

'Are you asleep?'

'Almost,' he said.

We had started.

A goat herd came by as we packed up in the morning after a good breakfast. There hadn't been enough rain that winter and the grass hadn't grown, so the milk yield was down. He kept the goats away from the tempting nourishment of the tent as he talked.

'We suffer as much as the animals,' he said, as he continued on his way through the undergrowth, his goats frisking about him.

Sleep had come instantly the night before and we took to the road feeling refreshed. It was the first day of March, and mimosa was cascading in bursts of bright yellow besides the road that wound over the Serra da Brejeira and through woods that were a mass of wild flowers. From the track that took us out of the Algarve we caught glimpses through the trees of the Mira basin below, a countryside of small streams with hillocks bobbling off into the distance and scattered with groups of long, low houses, some brightly whitewashed, others of simple adobe that blended in with the sparse brown vegetation. This was the beginning of the Alentejo, 'the other side of the Tagus', looking from the Christian north.

In the yard of a house in one of these tiny settlements six men were sitting round a table having lunch and, as we approached, we saw a woman bringing out a large casserole, about to set it down. All movement froze as seven puzzled faces turned towards the apparition at the gate, the casserole remaining poised in the air.

'Excuse me, is this Yellow?'

'Yes, it is.'

'Ah, thank you very much.'

It is difficult to convey how ridiculous it felt to ask such a question. According to the map, the name of the place was *Amarela*, which translates as 'yellow'. I backed out apologetically, feeling foolish. At least we were on the right track.

Too tired to go much further without a rest, we sat down by a stream, rolled up our trousers, took off our boots, peeled away socks and immersed our aching, blistered feet in the clear, numbing water. Afterwards, we shared a lunch of olives, bread and cheese, sardines, almonds and the few remaining figs. As we were resting our backs against the trunk of a tree later that afternoon, studying the maps, working out a route to the lake at Santa Clara, a man came over to say hello and pass the time of day. He looked at the map as a man looks for the first time at an abstract painting, shaking his head a little as if to focus properly. Illiteracy is high in the south—up to 40 per cent of the population in rural areas can neither read nor write, signing their names with a personal mark. We asked if he knew Sabóia, the place we were aiming for.

'Oh, yes, just follow this road and you'll get there.'

He wandered off. At Torquines we quenched our thirst with cool, sweet water from an arched well set into the bank at the side of the path. A woman approached to fill a water jug, and we asked her about life in the village.

'This year hasn't been a good one for us,' she said. 'The oranges that we rely on for our income have all been caught by a frost and now we haven't enough money to pay for the flour we need.' She also told us how difficult it was to cultivate the land when they still used oxen to pull the plough.

She shrugged her shoulders in a gesture of resignation and joined her sisters washing clothes on the boulders of the stream below.

We never reached Sabóia. Looking for a place to spend the night, we climbed a rounded hillock to find a wiry, middle-aged woman in a thin grey dress feeding her pigs and chickens.

'Would it be all right if we spent the night here, *Senhora?*'

She eyed us up and down in silence.

'We won't be any trouble, honest ...'

'Huh,' she said, 'I know that I am honest, but how can I tell that you are?'

She stalked back to her house a few hundred yards away without another word. There were ant holes everywhere and too strong a smell of pigs and chickens for comfort, so we moved nearer the river, dined meagrely on what was left of the provisions and stretched out to sleep through our second night. In the morning my tent was dripping with dew whereas Piers, who had slept under a tree, was barely touched. I decided that the next night I would try the same.

Santa Clara-a-Velha lies beside the Mira river, which has been dammed for irrigation and hydro-electricity. Crossing over the bridge into the cobbled high street, past a cafe opposite a fish market selling sardines at twopence a pound, we were confronted by a disturbingly red pillar box set against a bright whitewashed wall, silent testimony to the Old Alliance between Portugal and Britain, 'an inviolable, eternal, strong, perpetual and true friendship'. Most of the day before had been spent thinking what we could get rid of so as to lighten the load. The woman in the post office apologised for not being able to handle packages of more than a kilo at a time, but kindly found us some sugar paper, scissors and string. The sandals, book, address book, a vest and the short sleeved pullover were the first to go. In all we made up five parcels and sent them home. Emerging into the sunlight five kilos lighter, we headed for the cafe to celebrate with a tot of *Modronho,* a clear, fiery spirit distilled from the strawberry trees *(Arbutus Unedo)* that were so common in the area. A young man propped nonchalantly on the bar watched as the barman poured the drinks and passed comment on the size of our packs.

'I may look like a donkey with all this baggage, but even donkeys can be intelligent,' I commented.

He laughed. It was good to make a joke in Portuguese, however lame; it meant a growing confidence. They were delighted to find a foreigner who spoke their language, and happily gave us lengthy instructions on the best way to get to the lake we were aiming for. Either we had misunderstood or their directions weren't very good, for we were soon tramping across the scrub on a compass bearing. A shepherd tried to send us back onto the road, saying there was no way through, but eventually conceded there was a track. It took us

11

down into a hollow and up again for our first sight of the lake, at which point we decided it was time for lunch.

A herd of goats went by. The bright little supermarket in Santa Clara had provided wine and other supplies, including tea, which we had originally forgotten to bring with us, an oversight much regretted in the mornings and late at night. We lazed away the afternoon in the sunshine before heading for a knoll overlooking the lake on the other side, where we would camp and relax a little more. A family down at the water's edge greedily pored over the map but were sadly disappointed to find their house was not marked. They told us the water was good to drink. It was certainly good for a wash. We climbed the knoll, pitched camp under a tree and collected wood for the fire.

We had only come a few miles that third day. We needed the rest. The cairns that dotted the western hills were silhouetted against the pale blue sky as a purple cloud moved away to the north. Piers wrote a letter while I lay back and listened to the tinkle of bells that rose from the gully below, the fire bumbling in the breeze while the cicadas started their nightly washboard song. A bat looped through the half light as I looked up to watch a shooting star streak across the sky.

'How do you spell "conscience"?' asked Piers.

The only lights in sight now were those of the dam reflected in the dark, still waters of the lake. This was the life! Time for grilled fish with lemon and a good, warming cup of tea.

The shallow river valley headed conveniently north, the track the colour of cinnamon. The blister on the ball of my foot had shifted to the arch, where it received less weight. About the size of a Victorian penny, it only hurt badly when starting off again after a rest.

I had gone ahead scouting and returned to find Piers talking French to a woman with a baby and a large Alsatian dog, which tried to take a chunk out of one of my ankles. She was amused and flattered when I asked what part of France she came from, since she was pure Portuguese; her family had emigrated to France to find work and higher pay. She showed us the watercress in the river before taking us to the house of some friends who let us feast on oranges straight from the trees, though many of them had been blighted by the frost. One of the younger women brought out a tray of small, sugary doughnuts onto the terrace, where we stood making conversation in a mixture of French and Portuguese. With a last sweet mouthful and a bag of oranges we took our leave, following the track winding on up the valley through the mixed woods that they called the *deserto*.

A man in a soft trilby appeared behind us shortly after, walking fast to catch up, a cigarette sticking out between his lips under a thin black moustache.

'That's my house up there,' he said, but we passed it by. A few yards further on he turned off right, beckoning us to follow down some steps, through the doorway of another house. It was the local bar, a small, bare room with a few bottles and tins of sardines on the shelf behind a wooden counter. A tiny woman came in to serve us each a tot of *Modronho*, which, we discovered, was made in that very place. A group of men came in through the inner doorway; one of them was remarkably tall with fair hair and bright blue eyes, which was surprising since the average height of a Portuguese man is five foot six and almost everyone is dark haired, the few exceptions being found in the north. He held a ruddy-faced child in his arms which everybody obviously adored.

'Say *"bom dia"*.'

'Bodá.'

'Eh, bravo, bravo!'

Amidst the happy laughter a girl slipped out from behind her father's legs to join her mother behind the bar, wearing the same patterned jersey as her brother. The incongruously Nordic-looking father good naturedly agreed to show us his distillery.

What little light there was came through chinks in the tiles, shafts of sunlight catching drifts of smoke from the well-stoked fire beneath an old pot still. A condenser ran from the top of the still to a receiver, into which spring water flowed from a niche in the wall. At the base of another tank stood three pottery jars to catch the precious liquid dripping slowly into them. There were two more large tanks along the wall, but I never did fully understand the process despite his painstaking explanations. Heath Robinson would have been proud of such a display of ingenuity, but he would never have pictured the thick layer of ancient dust, soot and grime that coated the works, giving it a special magic, worthy of an alchemist's dream. In an even dimmer alcove stood a row of enormous pottery jars the size of septic tanks, which contained a brown sludge of fermenting berries that would later be transferred to the still.

On returning to the real world we tasted another sample of the brew while the child entertained us by telling everybody's name.

'Who's that?'

'Titi.'

'Yes. And who's this?'

'Zé'.

'Bravo! Muito bem! Very good!'

We asked how long it would take to get to São Martinho.

'A woman should get there in an hour and a half,' they said, laughing as they waved goodbye.

The menu for lunch was established when the eggs fell out of the pack on the long hill down into São Martinho. Two old men with a wry twinkle in their eyes materialised out of nowhere to watch the bizarre antics of these two strangers, accepting some of our almonds with pleasure, exclaiming in wonder as the cooker was assembled and the eggs poured out of the brown paper bag.

'What's that?'

'It's the cooker, made in Sweden, very clever. The stove fits into the pan and then this larger pan fits over the smaller one and the frying pan acts as a lid for the whole thing.'

'What does it burn?'

'Just about anything: petrol, alcohol, whisky, *Modronho* even.'

'Where are you going?'

'North, to Alvalade. What do you do here?'

'We're farmers. This is our land. We work it as best we can, but we're old now and there will be no one to look after it when we die. Nobody comes to work in the countryside any more, not if they can help it. They prefer to go to the towns where the pay is better and they can have fun in the evenings. You can't blame them, really. It means there's just us old men now, though.'

We finished lunch and headed down into the village. Two clowns wearing pointed hats, with white stockings over their faces and bells around their ankles, were knocking on people's doors, shaking a tambourine, playing dumb and banging their victims on the head with a harmless plastic hammer. It was the pre-Lent carnival. In the village we sat outside the cafe watching the somewhat forlorn celebrations: a guitar and harmonica provided the music. There was much hopping and desultory clowning by a small group of men in plastic masks and heavy workmen's boots. Villagers watched half-heartedly until they moved on.

The road to the station ran beside a straight line of flowering mimosa. Groups of unemployed seasonal labourers huddled together talking by the buildings or simply watching the world go by. We crossed the railway track and cut through the woods, evening drawing in as we walked over a swathe of green pasture to the crossroads outside Santa Luzia. The cafe there was closed. A young woman with dyed blond hair came out of a dark blue house with a red door opposite the cafe, carrying a bucket of water. She let us fill our bottles from it, telling us the cafe would be open from 9.30 till 2 a.m. for the festivities.

We camped close by on a knoll among olive trees, the sky blue as only Dalí can paint it. Looking south past an abandoned windmill we could just make out the ridge of the Serra da Brejeira in the distance.

We had come all that way on foot, a good feeling. We never made it to the party, as we were sound asleep before the doors even opened.

The low lying mist had cleared from the plain as we came over the last of the southern hills. The Alentejo stretched out in front of us, flat plain as far as the eye could see. The average population density of the province is 52 people per square mile, though the figure is far lower away from the rivers where the soil is poor, dry, light and infertile with virtually no natural vegetation bar a thin pasture for transhumant flocks of sheep. 'The Alentejo has no shade save that which falls from above.' Geographically, it is an extension of the tablelands of Spanish Estremadura. The hot sun began to turn the backs of our legs a fine shade of salmon pink as we humped our loads over a monotonous landscape of holm oak, olive, eucalyptus and mile after mile of cork plantations. Tufts of green were trying hard to survive the drought where the earth had been ploughed and harrowed around the trees, flocks of sheep and some bullocks were gleaning what they could from the parched land. It would not have been surprising to see a herd of elephants or antelopes go by.

We stopped for lunch when we reached the river Sado which flows north to Alcácer do Sal, the 'Fortress of Salt'. A group of labourers, mostly women, were spreading polythene sheets over wicker arches in readiness for a crop of tomatoes to be irrigated by the river. They wore no hats, a sign of their low social status, but were otherwise well wrapped in sweaters, shawls and headscarves, as they had the peasants' natural suspicion of baring flesh to draught and light. In only our shorts, we presented a curious contrast. They drifted over in dribs and drabs as we ate our sardines, asking if we were going to swim, probably thinking that our shorts were in fact swimming trunks.

The morning had been hard, rest stops much appreciated, but in the afternoon a new energy seemed to flood through my muscles. I paced along happily while Piers followed, muttering every so often about the dogs that invariably set up a chorus of barking whenever we passed one of the hillock settlements they call *montes*. Roughly two thirds of the farms in Portugal are over one hectare, or two and a half acres, but of these 500,000 farms three quarters are under five hectares. Only one per cent are over a thousand hectares, yet this one per cent accounts for nearly half the agricultural land. They call these great estates the *latifundios* and they are all in the south of the country. The *montes* are the centres of the estates with the master's house, barns, stables, bakeries, lodgings for permanent workers and their families and rougher accommodation for seasonal labourers. The system has been operating unchanged since the time of the

Romans. The Moors swept in from Africa, and they, in turn, were driven out by the Christian Kings of the north, who gave the estates to their crusading knights as a reward for their support. Masters changed, but the people had no say in their own history. The Church and State have never done anything for them and nothing is expected. Parts of the Alentejo remain missionary areas, godless, the people showing little interest in the formalities of marriage or other Christian principles. Expropriation of property during the revolution in April 1974 did help to redistribute the land in some places near the cities but often resulted in chaos, while the good news never reached the remoter areas. They remain poor, backward and badly educated.

A factory siren wailed as we approached Alvalade, passing a gypsy encampment on the outskirts, some of the 100,000 in Portugal who make their living from begging, buying and selling animals, fortune-telling and, according to popular belief, violence, theft and smuggling. Their tents were interesting affairs made of large sheets of polythene, using the trunks and branches of trees as their main support, with stones to hold down the sides. It was good enough protection from the elements in this land where it so seldom seemed to rain.

Impish little boys clustered round laughing and teasing with cries of *'tem calor?'*, (are you hot?) at the sight of our shorts, which seemed to cause a stir almost all the time. Thirst and a keen desire to sit down drove us into a cafe full of men from the local factory which employed 360 people, according to the barman who served us a sausage sandwich with the chilled beer. A man who had been there most of the day judging by the wobble in his neck and his slurred speech, started to make fun of us in incomprehensible *fala meridional* till a policeman playing cards with the local councillors dressed in pin-striped suits came to our aid, telling him sharply to shut his mouth and leave us in peace.

Darkness caught us glued to the adverts on television. A football match was about to start, and men and boys began drifting in from the street corners for the excitement of the day. We left reluctantly, walking out of town down the long, lamplit street, finding a place to camp not far out. It was an effort to cook supper: all we really wanted to do was lie down and sleep away the fatigue.

Ermidas Sado had a supermarket and a coffee shop. We tucked in to a selection of sweet cakes, custard pies and milk before heading on. The countryside was unchanging, the same flat fields of eternal cork of which Portugal produces 200,000 tons a year, two thirds of the world supply. The bark is stripped off the trees in rotation, once every ten years or so, in July and August. Sometimes we passed

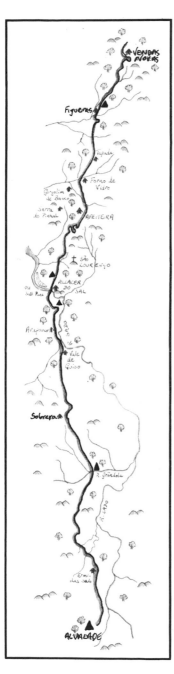

enormous piles of the stuff packed and ready to be transported to the coast where it is processed.

I remember the shocked look of one mother and her children when we appeared out of the wilderness to ask the way on, for we were never quite sure that the road we were on was the one marked on the map. It seemed a natural thing to us, but from their point of view the experience was traumatic, fraught with danger. After all, who were these wild, unshaven men, cloaked in dust and dirt, carrying some kind of contraband on their backs across the middle of nowhere? We could have been bandits, thieves, outlaws, murderers, escaped convicts, spies, rapists . . . for one with a fertile imagination the list was endless.

It began to pour with rain that afternoon. We were lucky to find a deserted schoolhouse in a nameless village the other side of the river Grândola in the early evening. Officially, there is free education for children from the age of six to fourteen, but after the revolution many teachers too closely associated with the old regime were removed from their posts, and history books were rewritten and replaced. In some cases it meant the children were left with neither textbooks nor teachers. Perhaps this was what had happened to this school.

There was an old plastic bucket on the terrace in which we collected water from the leaking gutters and poured it gleefully over our sticky bodies. A herd of placid cows came plodding by through the grove of umbrella pines opposite, on their way

17

to the river to drink. I asked the cowgirl if there was anywhere we could get fresh water and she directed me to an ingenious well on the far bank: sides of cork bark had been sunk half a metre into the ground through which the water was filtered, the cover being made of a single piece of bark kept in place with a flower pot.

'*Agua boa, sim*' (good water), she said, as she drove the cattle home through the finely falling drizzle.

Strange flying beetles with twitching red antennae arrived as night fell, attacking the paraffin lamp and diving into the frying liver. We sat at desks on the veranda of the school listening to the cicadas and the distant rumble of a major road, tucking in to liver, buckwheat, cabbage, bread, butter, cheese and the last of the chocolate washed down with a cup of tea. Almost a week had passed since we left Lagos. Physically, we were standing up well to the strain, our pace was improving, the blisters were turning into thick calluses and the packs were no longer such a burden. It was a comforting feeling to lie back full bellied and listen to the light rain falling, safe and warm on the tiled floor of the first of many abandoned buildings to give shelter for the night.

It was still raining. Without a compass we would have been led a merry dance, for there were few landmarks. The cork trees were now interspersed with pines, many of them gashed at the base where foresters had stripped off the bark and strapped a conical cup to the trunk to collect the resin which goes to make pitch and turpentine. In a clearing a man was walking methodically up and down his field fertilizing it by hand with the same rhythmic motion he had used in sowing. At a crossroads another man, chopping wood, directed us down a tarmac road to a cafe with no coffee, but the proprietor fetched three glasses of wine and a plate of delicious smoked ham. He told us widespread emigration had caused a shortage of labour and the landlords had been forced to increase wages. The average labourer now earned some 7,500 escudos a month, the equivalent of £65, which was enough to support a family, though he added that they would be lost if it weren't for the chickens, goats and pigs that they kept to supplement their earnings on the little plots of land expropriated during the revolution. We took the *caminho velho*, the old road, towards Vale de Guiso. Unreadable milestones showed that it had once been an important thoroughfare, but it was now little more than a sandy track used by carts and the occasional tractor.

The sandy paths, usually soft and a drain on our energy, had been hardened by the rain and we made good time. We were averaging about twenty miles a day, though the days were still short, the sun rising at half past seven and setting at half past six. At least it gave us time for healing sleep to wash away the fatigue.

Vale de Guiso was a charming village. A long terrace of whitewashed houses, with their doors and windows picked out in various blues, lavenders, greens and yellows, looked out over a line of ramshackle wooden sheds that housed all manner of animals. Beyond, on a stretch of pasture sloping down to the river Sado, horses, donkeys and goats were grazing peacefully. We spotted a water tap and stumbled towards it like travellers in the desert. As we drank, a young German woman appeared to show us to the faded green double doors of the local shop.

'Do you have any oats?' we asked the man behind the counter.

'Oats? What do you want oats for?'

'To eat.'

'You eat them?' he asked in amazement. 'We only feed them to the pigs and chickens.'

I began to explain to him how we boiled them with water and a touch of salt, but broke off when I saw a look of nausea slowly spreading across his face. They presumed we were friends of the German woman and found it difficult to believe that we were just passing through on a trek to the north. I had had to modify 'Istanbul' to 'north' as the concept of such a long walk was so alien, and later I had to modify it further still to the name of the next big town. It lessened the number of looks of blank incomprehension that we received.

On the wall of the shop were various letters from Germany. *'Nossos amigos'* (our friends), they started. Beside them were photographs of the villagers out in the fields harvesting, the men working in a row scything down the corn while the womenfolk, well-wrapped in headscarves and sweaters even in mid-summer, followed in their wake, gathering it into sheaves. After drinking a litre of milk which came in a sealed plastic bag, something I had not seen before but quite common in that area, we followed the river Sado out of the village.

A look of guileless innocence did not fool the cowherd and his wife who turned the corner from Arapouco just as we were about to nip over a barbed wire fence to a pleasant looking campsite. Both his wrists were heavily bandaged and I couldn't help wondering what had led him to try and take his life. We explained what we were doing but he said it was impossible and led us, unwilling, away. When he left, we doubled back on a track to where we wanted to be and camped. It was here that we found some really long, thick bamboo canes lying in the undergrowth and we each cut ourselves a stick. I cut mine to almost six feet, like a staff, thinking it would prove useful. If nothing else, it would be something to do with my hands.

It would certainly keep the dogs away.

Alcácer do Sal is so named because of the ancient salt pans that line the river out to sea, though we never actually saw them as we were more interested in the promise of a good meal in a restaurant. It was Saturday and the town, the biggest we had so far seen, was busy, noisy and full of traffic. The meal we had there is memorable for the quantity rather than the quality—six courses washed down with a litre of red wine followed by double helpings of pudding and a tot of brandy to round things off, all for little more than the price of fish and chips in England. It was extremely difficult to get up and on the road again but we somehow staggered out of town to a track that led us to a clump of trees on a knoll among rolling pastures. We should have known better than to pick some prickly pears with bare hands and taste them without first carefully scraping off the fine hairs. They caused irritation to my lips and tongue for some days.

The sound and feel of raindrops woke us in the early hours of the morning. Dawn broke to reveal the countryside wrapped in a wet mist. All morning we walked through completely deserted bush, getting frustratingly lost before eventually, and with relief, sighting an isolated farmhouse. Two children were playing outside: the elder sister was too shocked by our arrival and appearance to do anything but stare, but her young brother seemed more self-possessed. He showed us where we were and the way on. Shortly we came to a wide tarmac road that headed north, much to our surprise since it was not marked on the map, but then this had been printed in 1936 and never revised. There was a village at the end of it and a bar. As it was Sunday there was a noisy group of men drinking away their idle hours as their wives presumably cooked their lunch.

'Do homen, a praça, da mulher, a casa.' (For the man the square, for the woman the house.)

They were merry and curious but the atmosphere positively crackled when we spread out the map on the counter so they could help us find the way ahead. They crowded around.

'Hey, look, there's Tapada and there's Forno de Vidro and it's even got Gorgolim de Baixo! This map has everything!'

A diminutive, bandy-legged man who never took off his leather crash helmet collared Piers and talked to him rapidly, while Piers nodded his head wisely.

'Sim... sim... certo... sim... então... não séi...'

We escaped, finding shelter that night in an abandoned hovel near the washing lines of a gypsy caravan, where we slept comfortably on a warm bed of straw.

20

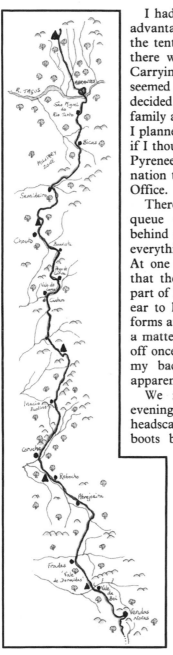

I had been having serious doubts as to the advantages of carrying the tent. If it rained, the tent got wet and heavy and if it was dry there was no real need to use it, anyway. Carrying all that weight for no good purpose seemed silly, and so after much thought I decided to send it off to the De Suso Mata family at Burgos in the north of Spain, whom I planned to meet later. I could collect it there if I thought that it would be necessary for the Pyrenees. At Vendas Novas, our first destination that day, I made straight for the Post Office.

There was only one woman serving a long queue while her colleagues chatted away behind a partition. In her rush she could find everything but the price of parcels to Spain. At one point she even tried to persuade me that there was no parcels service from that part of Portugal to Spain, but I turned a deaf ear to her protestations and kept filling out forms and declarations until the job was done, a matter of a long hour. After a meal we set off once more, and as I pulled the pack onto my back, the difference was immediately apparent; it felt almost light!

We reached Vale de Boi in the early evening, where a tiny woman in a green headscarf with a flat black hat and rubber boots beneath her tight, knee-length skirt welcomed us with a toothless smile, showed us the well and bid us help ourselves. It was very deep and we had difficulty getting the water into the bucket, so she showed us the trick which was to flick the rope just before the bucket hit the water, so it submerged. Leaving the dogs to bark at us, she went off to fetch some greens and came back with a whole armful of cabbage, which I stuffed into my pack with appropriate cries of delight and thanks. She refused any kind of payment and the whole

21

family gathered on the level crossing to wave goodbye: an old man, a woman in mourning with a young child in her arms and herself. I noticed the grandfather held his hands tightly to his side to try and stop the tips of his fingers from shaking uncontrollably.

We left our packs on the railway bridge in the twilight, washing in the river below, which smelt faintly of sewage but was cool and refreshing after the heat of the day. For the first time relations between Piers and myself became a little strained over a petty thing concerning the ratio of cabbage to rice in the soup. I ended up feeling miffed, sulking quietly on one side of the fire.

We had been having breakfast as soon as we got up but we adopted a new routine the next day, one which I was to follow faithfully for the rest of the journey: no breakfast until we had been on the road for a good while and our stomachs began to rumble. It was good for morale to get five miles or so behind us in the early hours when both the body and day were fresh and untried, and when the promise of an approaching cup of hot tea and breakfast was something to look forward to. Otherwise our routine remained unchanged, walking for about an hour or more, a ten minute rest and then on, though neither of us was carrying a watch.

Frades turned out to be a pleasant place; the details picked out in yellow on the long white houses made a change from the more common blues. A fine, arched gateway led into a spacious courtyard with a terrace of workers' houses on the left opposite the farm buildings. From one of the open doorways where a fly screen was moving lightly in the breeze, a woman directed me down to the covered well, which looked rather like a whitewashed dog kennel. I scooped some water out with the cork bowl left there for the purpose. It was cool, sweet and tasty. Even the beehives we saw in rows in the woods from time to time were made from cork bark. On the way out we passed the landlord's solid two-storey house with steps leading up to the front door, a little veranda looking out over the fields. It was closed up; I doubt if he lived there for more than a few weeks in the summer when he came to inspect that everything was being looked after properly for him. The doves from the picturesque dovecote above the cowshed had long since gone. A man was coming out of a field on his tractor.

'Is there anywhere around here we can buy cigarettes and a drink?'

It seemed there was, some five miles away. The thought gave us new momentum but once again we got lost amongst the bewildering mass of tracks and paths. Feeling hot and sticky, we finally found ourselves stirring up the dust in an unknown village high street. The lunch bell went as we sat resting outside the local school, and immediately a happy, gabbling crowd of pupils poured out to join a boy who had been sent out for misbehaving. We sauntered down to the cafe for a beer, the children pestering us to show them the map and compass while they, in turn, showed us where we were: Carapeções, not exactly where we had calculated but near enough to make no difference.

Armed with a loaf of fresh, crusty bread for lunch, we took the dirt road to Abrejoeira, where we met a young couple who talked of the revolution of April 1974. They painted a romantic picture of the crowds in Lisbon on the day Caetano was overthrown by a military junta, the

The landlord's house

people out on the streets marching up and down patting soldiers on the back, sticking carnations in the barrels of their guns, swarming over the tanks shouting 'Portugal is free, Portugal is free'. The revolution was virtually bloodless and there were no executions or reprisals. For the first time in almost forty years censorship of the press was lifted, factories were taken over by the workers, estates expropriated in the south and as many traces of the old regime as possible eradicated. Yet by the end of 1975 over 80,000 skilled workers, technicians, professionals and business people had left the country, mainly for Brazil. The fall of the dictatorship led to a massive flight of private capital before financial regulations were brought in by the provisional government to halt the flow, estimated by the Bank of Portugal at over a billion escudos, most of which went to deposit accounts in Switzerland. Our friends said it had done quite a lot for the people—*povo* is a stronger word—dividing the land so that everyone had a plot big enough to keep a few domestic animals and run an allotment, but added ruefully that some of the big estates had remained.

When I asked if there was anywhere we could get a little wine to go with our lunch, the man took one of our water bottles, disappeared round the corner and came back with it filled to the brim with his own brew. Lunch was a merry affair as a result. We pounded out the alcohol on the way to Rebocho, talking nineteen to the dozen about friends, love, hate, even architecture, the almond trees on

23

either side of the road in full bloom. The wine dried us out, so we were happy to reach the cafe at Rebocho, where we took on the local lads at table football while downing quantities of fizzy lemonade.

The sun was just beginning to dry the dew from the wild asparagus. In the corner of a field, three women were bent over, working the ground with their mattocks while a male supervisor stood behind them with his arms crossed over his bulging stomach, watching. One of the women unearthed a large stone and carried it to the side of the field. He waited until she was on her way back before stopping her with a shout.

'Hey! I don't want that stone there, I want it over there!'

He was pointing to the other side of the field. The woman did as she was told, obediently, without a murmur of complaint, then bent to her work once more. The other two women hadn't even looked up.

'Ah, she is truly beautiful, my wife. She works from first light until dusk in the fields and never utters a word of complaint as she prepares supper in the evening.'

This was rice-growing country, and the effects of the drought were clearly visible as we crossed the eight bridges over the river Sorraia into Coruche: the reservoirs were almost dry and the paddy fields below us were cracked and dusty.

The inhabitants of the town were very kind, helping us in our search for meths and paraffin among the narrow streets that led onto the wide, airy main square. After shopping we had toasted cheese and ham sandwiches in a sleazy cafe by the bus station, but a sudden urge to defecate had us moving quickly out of town with convenient bushes in mind. It was so much more healthy than sordid, ill-lit holes in the backyard—there were not many diseases to be caught from grass and leaves, even if one did run the risk of the occasional insect bite.

A man on an old black bicycle with 28-inch wheels stopped to greet us in a friendly way as we were polishing off our lunch by a fountain. I had just washed my hair for the first time since we started off and felt much better for it. He had seen us earlier in the day and was curious to know where we were going, setting us on a good dirt road to Inácio Paulino, where we were lured into the local bar for a drink of wine. To avoid the dehydration that we had suffered from on the road to Rebocho we cut it half and half with lemonade, which made a concoction that was both refreshing and fortifying. A quick drink became a rather longer session as the three men at the counter insisted on each buying a round. It was a curious place, both bar and shop, full of everything the local people could possibly need: beautifully decorated saddles for mules or donkeys, harness and

24

tackle to match, pulleys, ropes, torches, knives, candles, boxes of all kinds stacked against the walls, and sardines, of course.

For the first time in what seemed like a month we climbed a hill to follow a wooded ridge, resting the eye on distant views that were an almost forgotten pleasure. A trailer load of pine cones went by. One or two fell off; they were sticky, scented with resin, about the size of a large pear, but so hard it proved impossible to get at the pine nuts inside. A little later we came across a couple that had been crushed by a passing lorry, so we extracted a few. They looked like maggots, oily things full of calories with a rather soapy taste.

Our rice bubbled away on the evening fire in a eucalyptus wood. Seeing the man on a bicycle had sparked off a longing in Piers to get one himself, to move a little faster and further each day, as well as to get the weight off his feet and shoulders. Such thoughts were best expressed, since it was obvious that he was not very happy. The plain had been getting him down. It was monotonous for us both, but for me this was only a warm-up. I would get my fill of hill and mountain soon enough. Piers, who wasn't intending to travel that far, didn't have that consolation. Conversation with the people had made up for any tedium in the actual walking but it can't have helped Piers not to understand the language, and I fear I was a lazy, reluctant interpreter. We decided we should look for a bicycle in Abrantes.

I woke feeling tired and listless after a night spent hiding from drops of rain, a feeling that persisted throughout the day. My mood was not improved by the fact that we found no water till past midday and had to make do with bread and cheese for breakfast, postponing the delights of tapioca, which we had bought as a substitute for porridge oats, until we reached a tap at Vale da Lama. A worker from the nearby farm came up to get a drink.

'Does your government pay you to do this?'
'No. We do it purely for pleasure.'
'Are you spies?'
'No, no, just tourists.'
'How can you afford to travel when you're not paid to do so?'
'We saved up the money.'
'You're lucky.'
'I know.'

I asked him about the situation at the farm. It appeared that most of the land around, as far as the eye could see, belonged to the absentee landlord who lived and worked in Coruche. The large, empty house on the other side of the river was his but he never used it and it was slowly falling into decay. I asked if the revolution hadn't changed all that, but he shrugged his shoulders.

25

'It didn't come here, mate.'

Pego da Curva, a little further down river, could have been the model for one of the glazed tiles or *azulejos* that you see on important buildings in the big cities. It had the same faded blues, an air of quiet, peaceful decline. It was certainly picturesque, with terraces down two sides of the street and an old palm tree at the end. As we trudged north the spring was coming with us: the woods were full of blooming gorse, purple heather, bright yellow, pink and dark blue flowers, with wild rosemary, pines and eucalyptus scenting the air. But even all this beauty was not enough to snap me out of my melancholy. It took the shopkeeper in Chouto to do that.

We arrived earlier than expected with about twenty miles behind us, the church clock standing at twenty past five. A young boy led us proudly to his father's grocery. Senhor José Franklin Duarte Bareto was his name. With a splendid smile he asked about the journey and our impressions of Portugal while neatly wrapping in paper every item that we bought before tying it neatly with string. It felt like Christmas. Children ran everywhere.

'Do you have any olives?'

'Well, as a matter of fact, I don't, but wait . . . Hey, Zé, go down to your mother and get some olives for the Englishmen!'

He gave us a card with his name and address as we left. On the back it had a calendar of the year. It was the 12th of March, almost a fortnight since we set off. He had taken such care, he was so warm and friendly, that we left the village with a deep glow in our hearts that made my former disgruntled mood seem pathetic.

That night the owls screeched closer than ever before as they hunted in the bright moonlight which was beginning to cast shadows. Once I even jumped at my own shadow, thinking some intruder had come to do us evil.

The next day, if all went well, we would reach Abrantes, crossing the Tagus into a completely different Portugal. It meant we were about half-way to the Spanish border.

By noon we had reached a crossroads in the middle of a sandy red nowhere scattered with shrub and patches of trees.

'I'm sorry, but you can't continue on this road. There's a military exercise in progress.'

There was nothing marked on the map about military zones, but you don't argue with a soldier carrying a sub-machine gun. I did try to persuade him we were only taking the shortest route between Semideiro and Bicas, promising that we wouldn't get in the way, but to no avail. It appeared the British Army had been invited to show off their skills in artillery bombardment as part of a N.A.T.O. exercise, so we would have to make a wide, tiresome-

circumambulation of the area.

We consulted the map while the soldier looked on, decided to turn right and walked away until we were out of sight, before cutting across the scrub. The crump of exploding shells came from a distance, fighter planes zoomed overhead drowning the song of the first cuckoos. Later, we came across another soldier but this time he was lying on his back in the grass fast asleep. He woke with a start as we approached, so I squared my shoulders and gave him a naval salute at which he simply stared, nonplussed.

We reached the Tagus late that afternoon, which at 1000 kilometres is the longest river in the Iberian Peninsular. The water beneath the high, modern bridge that swayed and pitched under the heavy traffic was surprisingly low, full of filth and snaking whirls of scum. Above us lay Abrantes, its fortified castle standing out above the town, where the Duke of Wellington had had his headquarters for a while at the start of the Peninsular Wars. One of his aides, August Schaumann, described the town as 'a truly magnificent spectacle with its convents, churches and old Moorish castle which frowned menacingly into the valley'. The menace had gone. We climbed up into the centre, choking on the fumes of roaring buses, lorries and cars, and booked into the Pensão Alliança.

The hotel was cheap but very clean. The beds had no head or foot boards which meant that I would be able to stretch out fully and bask in my first bed for six weeks. I sat on the well-sprung mattress waiting for my turn in the bath down the corridor where Piers was singing merrily, and tried to ignore the embarrassing smell of feet and socks that would normally have been taken away by the wind. After bathing we went out on the streets and found an ill-lit restaurant up an alley where we were the only customers. A mangy dog strolled in past our table to see what was going on in the kitchen, where we could see the balding cook, all belly and buttocks, slapping our greasy chops onto a plate with rice and potatoes.

We gazed sleepily at the television after eating, while finishing the wine. It was way past our bed time. Inserted among the adverts came a government broadcast about the results of the ten-year census. At the time we were there the population stood at about the nine million mark, though the trend was negative due to massive emigration during the sixties and early seventies. About a million Portuguese had left the country during that time, mostly young men from the north where the majority of the population live along the coastal band between Lisbon and Porto. This meant that the population was ageing, particularly in rural areas where there were usually more women than men.

The woman announcer stared uncompromisingly at the camera,

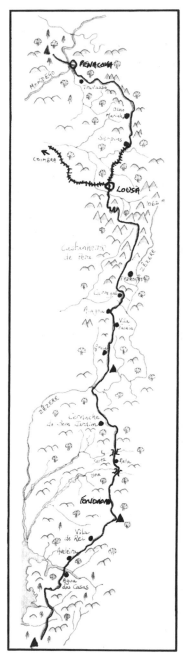

speaking very slowly so that everyone would understand exactly what they had to do. Coming out of the backwoods as I had, the exercise seemed pointless and remote. I would have sympathised heartily with any peasant who decided to avoid the tethers of a distant bureaucracy in a country where those who made the laws or governed did so to further their own interests rather than those of society as a whole. They would only tax me if I told them who I was, how many children I had, the number of acres of land that I possessed in the middle of the *mato* and I would get little or nothing in return for what they took.

We returned wearily to bed, slipping befuddled between the clean white sheets. In the morning we rose late and went looking for a second-hand bicycle for Piers, but had no luck in our search. They were hard to come by, and the new models were too expensive. The frustration of the fruitless search had a demoralising effect since Piers was forced either to continue when both of us knew his heart was not in it, or to find a more conventional means of transport. I was unrepentantly happy to get back onto a quiet track through blossoming countryside. We camped that night in a pine wood, grilling sausages over the fire before settling down on a soft bed of pine needles and burrowing into the warmth of our sleeping bags.

We found frost in the hollows in the morning and got off to a shaky start, not finding out where we were for quite some time, though the views

28

of pine-covered slopes and occasional glimpses of the lake of Castelo do Bode to the west compensated for everything. Two men in a battered Ford gave us a lift down to Agua das Casas, where we were rowed across the inlet by a boatman paid to do so by the hydro-electric dam people. Dams in the south are mainly for irrigation, but here in the north they are principally for electricity, generating three quarters of the total output. The sun was hot and strong by then, so we swam briefly in the lake before continuing to Vila de Rei. In the cafe there a mixed bag of young and old were watching the gyrations of a pop singer in a glittering, skin-tight, turquoise dress. Outside in the sun a man in a cloth cap romanticised about the fantastic life that he had led in Paris, showing off his thick French accent in front of an admiring crowd.

That evening, just before we camped, we were asked if we would like some soup at the house where we had gone to collect water. I'm not sure why we turned the offer down since it was an opportunity to talk to people and it was the first time we had been offered hot food. Perhaps the invitation lost spontaneity in translation.

Back once more on the wild, seldom-trodden tracks, we had breakfast by an old water mill on the bank of the river Isna, the water running fast and clear, still turning the wheels of the mill. The grass was lush around the olive trees growing at the base of the gully. From there we continued to Rolã, a tiny village where we were given a drink of wine by a couple, the wife gabbling so fast I had no idea what she was saying, concentrating instead on her carious teeth, noticing for no good reason that her trousers were undone. Everyone was more than happy to instruct us on the path ahead, so much so that I began to wonder if it would not be better to keep quiet.

We came to another gully. The bridge over the last had been humpbacked, probably Roman, but this one was flat with a double arch, the grass growing thickly over the surface of the old road like a green carpet. On the way up we met a strange man bustling busily down the path with a briefcase in his hand.

'Are you smugglers, criminals or outlaws?', he asked, scuttling away without waiting for the reply.

On our last day together we went over a thousand metres for the first time, walking along the spine of the Serra da Lousã, a lark twittering madly in the sky above, the slopes covered in purple heather, villages down below just dabs of red and white among the trees. A chilly Atlantic wind had us quickly putting on our trousers and jumpers: the Serra da Lousã runs east into the Serra da Estrela, with the highest mountain peak in Portugal at 1991 metres.

29

Together they form a line of condensation for clouds brought in on the Atlantic wind. We could expect a lot more rain from now on.

We were now crossing the province of Beira, a transitional zone between the south and the Douro/Minho area, one of the wettest in Europe with an average rainfall of up to eight inches a year, the land lush, fertile and much more mountainous. The south grows wheat, barley, olives, oranges, almonds, figs and cork while the north grows maize, rye, potatoes, beans and grapes. It is a land of tiny farms, the *minifundios*, worked by tenant farmers or peasants, very traditional by nature, with four to five hundred people per square mile. The Beira has a mixture of both north and south, the best of both worlds.

It took an age to twist down from the Serra to the town itself. I have only hazy recollections of a long, lamplit street with a bridge at the end of it, but we must have stayed the night in a *pensão* somewhere. I do remember the train station where we waited for our separate trains the next morning. The train to Coimbra arrived first. Piers heaved his pack on, we shook hands firmly and a moment later I was alone with my pack and stave, maps, thoughts and dreams. It was the 17th of March.

The train to Serpins headed away from the populous area around Coimbra to a line of ridges running roughly north, cut by the Mondego river at Penacova, at the base of the Serra do Buçaco. Outside the station a woman in black passed with a bundle of greens under one arm, the other balancing a bulky sack of hay on her head. Below the road an older woman was sitting in the shade of a vine that was trained over a large well on a strong iron frame, guarding a few sheep grazing among the wilting sprouts in her garden. I was off again, getting pleasantly side-tracked in the sunny woods of the second range, stopping to ask the way of a group of women resting under a tree in one of the walled fields at its base. They beckoned me to sit down and share their tea, offering wine from a large, earthenware flask and small, sugary doughnuts of which I ate quite a few without much prompting. We chatted about the journey until they made signs of wanting to get back to work planting potatoes, so I headed off up the road with a promise to immortalise them as the 'Good Ladies of Travasso', light-headed from the wine, touched by their kindness, happy at their open hospitality. As I turned to wave one last time, I saw a figure running towards me. It was one of the girls with my stave.

'You forgot your stick. You must have drunk too much wine!'
'Thank you. You shouldn't have troubled to run after me.'
'That's all right. What's your name?'
'John, Joãozinho to my friends. What's yours?'

30

'Rosa.'

'A beautiful name.'

She looked down at her feet shyly.

'Well, I'd better get back to work, I suppose.'

A little silence.

'Goodbye, Joãozinho. Good luck. *Boa viagem.*' (Have a good journey.)

She smiled wanly.

'Goodbye, Rosa, and thank you, *Adeus.*'

I had feared that with the departure of Piers I would be left in a vacuum with nothing to think about, so that first day I made careful plans on how I was to occupy my time so that I would not get bored, but I needn't have worried, for there was plenty to see and enjoy. Off the ridge beside the Mondego the earth was the colour of rich plain chocolate, crossed with bubbling streams, with lush, heavily cultivated plots hedged with vines and olive trees. The low bungalows had disappeared and stone houses were now more common. The mellow chimes of a local church bell carried in the still, afternoon air. By the side of the road a cross marked the spot where José had died at the age of seventeen. The inscription gave no reason for his death, simply offering a short prayer to God to take care of his soul.

A stone house

When my eyes grew tired of observing the gradually changing countryside, I found myself turning inwards to thoughts of my friends, loved ones, impressions of people I had met, my plans for the future, or more prosaically where I would be that night, whether there would be a shop in the next village, or if I would find water before the hour was up. Sometimes I would force myself to go a little further than I really wanted just to heighten the pleasure of stopping. At other times I would relax, with my pack still on, against the trunk of a tree in the middle of a silent wood, listening, studying the map, munching chocolate to give energy for the next lap. The mental effect of prolonged walking is similar to that inspired by meditation once you have grown accustomed to the weight of the pack and the sores on your feet. You become a part of what you are going through, lulled into a state of peace by the rhythm of the walking that can be likened to the effect of a mantra. Then you float along regardless until a rock or unobserved root causes you to stumble back into the world.

I camped on the other side of Penacova on the southern slopes of the Serra do Buçaco. The evening fire had just taken when a man appeared from the trees with a knife at the ready. My heart missed a beat or two. He came closer cautiously, asking me what I was up to. It turned out that he was as frightened of me as I was of him, and he went on his way with a harmless grunt when I had explained my presence. Only once in my life have I been confronted with a real aggressor, but that was on the outskirts of Paris at two o'clock in the morning when a revolver had been pointed at my stomach.

I turned in for a peaceful first night alone with supper still warming my guts, and watched the embers of the fire gradually dim before drifting off into a deep sleep. It was the first and last time I built a fire. Being on my own now, I was more vulnerable, and I did not want to attract attention to myself.

★ ★ ★

The British and Portuguese troops were allowed no fires either on 26th September, 1810. On that night they were drawn up along the length of the very same ridge I was sleeping on, looking down on the fires of the French army below.

Napoleon had invaded three years earlier, 'liberating Portugal from British economic domination' as he put it. When the Spanish turned against him, a British expeditionary force of 10,000 men that was on its way to attack the Spanish colonies in South America was diverted to Northern Portugal. The course of South American history might have been rather different if this had not happened, for the commander of the expedition was Viscount Wellesley, soon to become Lord Wellington, Napoleon's 'White Leopard'. He had prepared the position at Buçaco in advance, building a track along the ridge just below the crest so that he could keep his troops out of sight. It was a very strong position, for the French would be unable to bring their artillery to bear on the British and Portuguese as they attacked up steep, broken ground.

Masséna's plan was simple: they would advance with 14,000 men. As soon as these reached the crest and wheeled right to mop up the flank, another Corps of 22,000 would advance on the Monte Novo road to clear the way to Coimbra. Another would stay in reserve.

I woke early, watching the sky lighten from the warm cocoon of my sleeping bag, counting the chimes from a distant church in Penacova. Seven o'clock: by that time the Battle of Buçaco was in full swing.

★ ★ ★

32

The first three-pronged attack came through San Antonio at four in the morning under cover of a heavy morning mist, but the British and Portuguese front line sent the French reeling back. Wellington cantered up to one of his commanders:

'Upon my honour, Wallace, I never witnessed a more gallant charge!'

Another attack followed, but the main body of his infantry, unseen behind the ridge, was ready for them and charged. The rout was complete. Skirmishing continued, but the French were demoralised, having lost 4500 men to an allied 1252. The Portuguese fought with great courage under the command of William Carr Beresford, a huge, one-eyed man who remained in Portugal as Regent until 1822, when João VI reluctantly returned from Brazil to take his place as King.

By mid afternoon the battle was over, the dead were stripped of their clothes and possessions while troops from both sides came to draw water from a stream at the base of the ridge, watching each other cook, chatting together as if nothing had happened.

Wellington then withdrew to the Lines of Torres Vedras, two main lines of defence that stretched from the Tagus to the sea north of Lisbon, on which ten thousand Portuguese peasants had been working for almost a year. Masséna pursued, maintaining his position in front of the lines for four weeks before pulling back. He held out until March 1811, when sickness and lack of food forced a general retreat. The chase was on: just over three years later, Wellington entered Toulouse in triumph, Napoleon had abdicated and the Peninsular War was over.

* * *

There was no shrieking or moaning among the boulders on the hillside as I followed the track originally laid by Wellington. The woods were very quiet, a mass of yellow flowering mimosa, the only clue to the battle being the monument to the Duke of Wellington at the other end of the track.

From Cruz Alta, a large cross overlooking the western plains, I was able to plot my course to the Serra do Caramulo which lay to the north east. As I followed the path downwards, I passed benches for the elderly to rest beside shrines with life-size statues inside. A forest of beeches, oaks, limes, elm, poplar, magnolia, maple, cedar of Lebanon, sycamore, cypress and palm surrounded me; the famous forest of the Convent of Buçaco. At the end of the path, I came face to face with the Palace Hotel, a white 'neo-gothic piece of confectionery' completed in 1909, which still retained its sweeping

33

stairways, imposing doors, a long, arched balcony, towers and gables. It was here that Manuel II, the last King of Portugal, held his rendezvous with Gaby Deslys, star of the French Music Hall, before the collapse of the monarchy in 1910 forced him into exile in England, where he died at Twickenham in 1932.

It was a pleasant day, as I walked the hills above the plain from one isolated village to another. At Aljaraz, I left the road and picked my way down to the square through a straw-littered tunnel that smelt of animals and dung. To my surprise the shop had modern plate glass windows and easily-cleaned formica surfaces inside. The owners must have spent some time abroad. I bought cheese, jam and a bag of figs, which I paid for dearly the next day.

In Junqueira a small child took one look at me before running with a squawk to the safety of his mother's skirts. Perhaps he thought that I would catch him, take him away into the mountains and eat him. A rather more courageous boy pointed at my pack.

'What's that?'

'My house, *jovem*. I carry it on my back like the snail.'

It was no wonder they thought I was a monster if they had never seen a rucksack before.

In Fontemanha I stopped at the public fountain to wash a pair of socks and the crusted remains of porridge from my pot. Children immediately gathered round to watch my every movement. I asked if they went to school. They told me they did, but that after primary school they went to work. A curious, somewhat anxious mother approached.

'What are you selling?' she asked.

I camped just outside the village, but my sleep was disturbed when a downpour in the early hours forced me to build a makeshift tent. I modelled it on those I had seen the gypsies use outside Alvalade, tying one end of my stave to a convenient tree and propping the pack against the other end. This formed a steady ridge pole over which I threw the plastic sheet, and then I secured the base with stones.

I woke properly to the sound of a tractor. Some men were coming to investigate the strange construction in the woods, but when I told them that I was English everything seemed to be explained. They left me to dubbin my boots, pack up and set off. The tendon above my left ankle was painful, but a liberal application of Germolene ointment and loosening the boot laces helped. It was no further trouble.

Catraria, where I had hoped to find water, turned out to be just a couple of deserted houses among wet, dripping woods. I could find no spring or conveniently leaking gutter, nor could I find the route on. I felt wet, lost and utterly miserable as I sat down to a breakfast of cold bread and cheese. There were too many paths to choose from and mist had reduced visibility to twenty yards: twice in an hour I came full circle back to those two houses, both times with an equal sense of shock and bewilderment, beginning to wonder if this were some Olympian joke. The one path that I hadn't tried headed south but it was well used, so I took it. It wound round to the north-east eventually. It was a great relief to be back on the right track—and the day had only just begun.

At least a quarter of Portugal is covered with forest but there were no trees on the cold, deserted, windswept ridges of the Serra do Caramulo, although the Forestry Commission was breaking up the slopes in preparation for the planting of pine saplings. This meant the track was difficult to follow, at times unrecognisable. I was hoping to catch a glimpse of the cross at Buçaco, perhaps even the sea, but the mist slowly closed in on all sides as I climbed higher, while the morning drizzle became a hard rain that the biting wind slowly drove through all my clothes. It was unwise to stop for too long in such conditions, as my tired muscles would seize up in the cold, but I took shelter briefly in a gully, ate some sardines and smoked a soggy but comforting cigarette, wondering desperately what I was doing. It could well have been the middle of Dartmoor —there was nothing for it but to head on, hoping that I was going in the right direction. My self-confidence was low after the morning fiasco. All sense of time disappeared as I trudged on, feeling very much alone, holding on to my compass gratefully.

The sound of an engine throbbing powerfully somewhere over to the right quickened my pulse with a new hope. I stumbled over the uneven ground in what I prayed was the right direction, the noise growing louder. My deliverance came in the form of a monstrous, mud-bespattered bulldozer which loomed out of the mist, grinding and clanking over the earth like a ship in a heavy swell. It stopped. With misted glasses and an insane grin I climbed up onto the caterpillar tracks to conduct a shouted investigation into my whereabouts over the noise of the engine. I was on the right track, which was all I wanted to know. I bellowed my thanks and skipped on through the mist singing 'On Ilkla moor baht 'at' to keep up my flagging spirits.

A path tempted me off the ridge to Boi, a small village in the valley below. As I descended, the mist thinned and a sudden ray of sunlight broke through to reveal lush green carpets of clover, munching cows, waterfalls and bubbling brooks. I asked the way on to Teixo and São João do Monte of a pretty young woman I passed on the path.

'Do you see that woman holding the white flowers?'

'Yes.'

'She's going that way.'

It was good to have company after my recent experiences on the ridge. We walked through the woods above the river while she told me of her relatives who had emigrated to Brazil. They were doing very nicely and would never come back, which saddened her as she wanted to see the children before she died. She asked why I was walking and I made a real effort to explain, telling her of my travels in Central and South America, hitching rides on the back of lorries, jolting through the jungle in old American 'Bluebird' buses, lurching round sharp corners on the Pan-American Highway, or crowded into trains for long, finally tedious hours. Of course it can be fun and you meet a lot of very different people but they tend to be other travellers rather than the people of the place that you are passing through, particularly if language presents a problem.

The speed at which you travel is very important as well, for it seems to create its own momentum. Travelling by car, for instance, it is easy to persuade yourself that you will stop if you see something interesting, but generally you don't. You have to brake, there may be another vehicle behind and there is only a split second in which to apply the brake before what was of interest has passed. Very few people will stop and reverse unless they have seen something really spectacular like Krakatoa exploding. In a train or bus you do not even have this option.

36

The camera is well suited to this kind of travel, for you can make up for the fact that you can't stop, or that you only have a little time to do so, by clicking away through the glass that separates you from the world. Then, when you get home, you can have a look at what you saw.

I rambled on. It was good to talk to her. She seemed to understand that you didn't have these kinds of problem when walking, because the pace was so slow anyway. There was no waiting, no queuing for tickets, no fighting for a seat, no sitting except to rest. You have to be very patient and it is hard physical work but you get used to it and the tiredness it produces is a healthy exhaustion, a reward for your efforts, whereas the tiredness that you experience on a long-distance journey in a motor vehicle is a stagnant, sluggish one. When walking you are happy to rest a while before moving on; travelling by bus, car or train you are overjoyed to be able to stretch your legs for a while before returning to limbo and ennui.

The bicycle is an excellent method of travelling and it has all the advantages of walking plus that of greater speed for the impatient, but it will still not get you to the top of a mountain or through the undergrowth on leafy paths.

That walk in the Andes had been so much more memorable than any other part of the journey, so much more rewarding

A 'thick, stone-walled house'

in retrospect. It was a different world, peaceful and harmonious, which left a far more lasting memory. All other methods of transport now seemed boring and superficial.

We were silent for a while as we walked along together through the pine woods.

'Anyway, that's why I'm walking,' I concluded.

'I understand,' she said.

I was glad that she did.

We parted on the large paving stones of a narrow lane in the tiny, remote village that had been her home all her life. She directed me on, then ducked through the low doorway of the thick, stone-walled house and disappeared.

The scenery changed again as I climbed out of the valley onto pasture-land scattered with great outcrops of smooth, rounded granite like the shoulders of a buried grey giant. The houses and low walls were made of the same stone, contrasting vividly in the subdued, cloudy light with the bright, springy green grass. I steamed into the shop-cum-bar in Teixo for what I felt to be a well-deserved drink. Here I made short shrift of the first glass and a whole horseshoe of strong, garlicky red sausage and a loaf of bread, while making faces and playing peekaboo with three young girls who were ordered out of the shop for disturbing the grown-ups.

The proprietor sported a very fine set of waxed 'Battle of Britain' whiskers and what could only have been a French golfing hat in a bright, garish tartan. He talked to me in a very special mixture of all the languages that he knew, proudly pointing to his missing left leg.

'I lost it in an accident on a motorcycle in Switzerland, but I'm going to get back, crutches or no crutches. You can make good money there, unlike in this country.'

I stomped away with a wink at the still-tittering girls. I had really walked quite far enough for the day, but the name São João do Monte attracted me and I had hopes there might be something resembling a *pensão* there. The cows were being led home through the soggy fields, an old widow bent over the ground picking wild herbs, singing softly to herself. I marched into an ill-lit tavern in Valeiroso to down a quick shot of spirits while making illogical conversation with the locals.

'*Ai, que sacrificio,*' they sighed, wishing me a safe journey, thinking I was on my way to Fátima to visit the shrine, where a vision of the Virgin Mary had come to three rural children on May 13th, 1917—a convenient time for the Portuguese Church as faith was slipping badly.

In the bar at São João I ordered another shot of spirits and wiped the steam from my glasses to watch the table football. I asked the wife of the barman if there was any chance of a room for the night and she said they didn't have rooms, but that a woman down the road sometimes took lodgers. Eavesdropping locals soon took up the subject, all expressing their views on the matter, succeeding in confusing me thoroughly. A friendly looking man in a red polo neck sweater came forward and ordered another beer for me.

'I'm staying at a *pensão* down the road from here at Guardão. If you want, I'll give you a lift there and arrange matters with the landlord.'

It was completely dark outside by now. The idea seemed as good as any. My clothes were almost dry with all the walking, but my poor boots squelched noisily on the way to the car.

'There's a restaurant on the way where I often have supper,' the man said. 'If you want we can stop and have a bite to eat.'

I accepted readily. We pulled in under a large neon sign and the owner came forward to welcome us.

'*Como vai, Padre?*' (How are you, Father?)

I had been rescued by the parish priest. The fact that he was a priest came as a surprise since he wasn't wearing a dog collar. He explained that things had changed with the coming of the Republic, that the Republicans hated the clergy and all they represented and so they were forbidden to wear vestments.

The owner gave us a table by the fire, brought soup, wine, a dish of meat, chips and rice. A feeling of exhausted well-being was further enhanced by Padre Antonio's refusal to let me pay for any part of the meal. Memories after that become blurred: the *pensão* was neat and tidy, the full moon hidden behind thick banks of cloud cast a ghostly, pallid light on the balcony outside my room. I drifted off the moment my head touched the pillow.

The Padre took me up the Caramulo itself the next morning but we couldn't see anything because of the mist, so returned to town for a drink in his local bar, where a friend invited us to lunch. Norberto and his wife Maria were really kind. As the wine began to circulate, Norberto launched into an exposition of the fate of Portugal since the revolution, that they simply referred to as 'The 25th April'.

'Did you know that there were six provisional governments and two attempted coups in the first two years after the revolution? To say nothing of the demonstrations, the strikes and riots. Portugal is going to the dogs, you know, and it's all the fault of the bloody communists. Life was all right in the time of Salazar, but now . . . '

Maria looked at me apologetically, steering the conversation away only to see it return after a sortie into religion and the present lack of moral discipline and fibre. Norberto's attitude was understandable, for he had spent fifteen years working for the government in Portuguese Guinea. Salazar had encouraged emigration to the colonies, which he saw as provinces of a greater Portugal, completely ignoring the United Nations Declaration on Colonialism that called for the Imperial Powers to hand back their territories. It is true Salazar did a lot for Portugal in the first years of his dictatorship, particularly in putting to rights a financial situation that was in chaos when he came to power, but his policies depended entirely on the 'Provinces' and ignored the people of Portugal itself, despite the fact that he came from a peasant background. There was no growth of a trade-based middle class in Portugal as there was in other imperialist countries like Great Britain. New wealth was not invested to spur on economic growth at home but was reinvested in the colonies. When he died in 1970 after a reign of 35 years and a stroke two years earlier that had left him comatose, he left the country one of the poorest and least developed in Europe. Caetano, his successor, continued the same policies without the charisma. By 1974, fifty per cent of the national budget was being spent on upholding the status quo in the colonies. Eighty per cent of the armed forces were deployed in Africa, national service was unpopular, the rate of inflation high. Between the death of Salazar and the Revolution almost half a million people emigrated.

With devolution of the colonies, the government was left with the problem of what to do with 800,000 Portuguese returning from the colonies. Norberto was in charge of the former sanatorium at Guardão, where he was looking after the *retornados* from Angola and Mozambique, trying to get them started on a new life. He said it was difficult for them to find a place and adapt to post-colonial Portugal, adding sarcastically that in 1976 Soares had said that the word *retornado* would disappear from the language by 1981. It hadn't.

Their kitchen and dining room were in the converted prison cell of the old sanatorium. I made the mistake of telling them at some point that I needed a minimum of 4000 calories a day for the energy to walk. As good hosts they piled so much food onto my plate that I was hardly able to stand afterwards, and had to take the whole afternoon off for a digestive siesta in my room, a brief period of sunshine allowing me to dry off my sodden sleeping bag on the balcony railing. I had been invited back for supper, which was a more light-hearted affair at which they teased Padre Antonio mercilessly over his vows of chastity. The Padre later excused himself from taking coffee in their flat upstairs, saying that he had pastoral business to attend to. The flat was really their bedroom, hung with pictures of innocent children with huge dewy eyes, similar to those sold to tourists in the square at Montmartre. The bed took up most of the room, a large crucifix hanging on the wall above the headboard. The small balcony served as the recreation ground for a wiggly, fawning Labrador pup that ruled their lives. It was sad to see him stuck up there all day with nowhere to run or gambol, but they said he received a regular shampoo. I drank my coffee and left, reluctantly, to prepare for my departure the next morning.

In the middle of the night I was forced awake by a tremendous spasm of cramp in the left calf which left me feeling half crippled, dreaming the sort of dream that Freud would have loved to interpret. In the morning Padre Antonio took me to Arca, dropping me beside the ancient dolmen covered in moss. From there a track would lead north towards Oliveira de Frades. He got out of the car to shake hands, shyly presenting me with a bottle of Ruby Port.

'That's to keep up your spirits. Good luck. May God look after you.'

'Thank you, Padre.'

I was lost for words to express my feelings, and took my leave in a complete daze, bowled over by their generosity and kindness, already laden with a bottle of wine that Norberto had given me as well as some sandwiches that Maria had carefully prepared and wrapped in a linen napkin. When I opened it later, I found it had the letter 'N' embroidered in red in one corner.

It was 22nd March. Nothing much happened that morning but I was perfectly content to observe the countryside dotted with hay-cocks and maize driers

Espigueiro

called *espigueiros* raised above the ground on stone piles to keep them out of reach of rats and mice. Two old women stood and stared, one of them toothless, the other combing her long grey-black hair. A mute in a cafe babbled at me for a while before I retreated to the road. Outside Campia a driver stopped to ask if I should like a lift, but I refused, much to his surprise. In the village itself the priest was compensating for his small, female congregation by broadcasting the service over loudspeakers that could be heard all over the surrounding area. On the way down to cross the river Vouga at Sejães two men pruning vines called out, asking where I was going, chatting as they worked.

'How is it that you speak Portuguese with a Brazilian accent?'

'I was born in São Paulo.'

'Ah, I see. Look, if you'd like a glass of wine just wait for us by the fountain. We'll be down directly. We've almost finished for the morning.'

It had begun to drizzle again. I waited for them under cover in a doorway from which they invited me into their house for a drink and

41

then lunch.

The head of the family was a small, tough man with a shock of white hair, a bristly unshaven chin and bright blue eyes that twinkled as he talked. He could easily have been Welsh. He told me that much of the emigration was caused by the fragmentation of farms through inheritance over the generations, until the plots became too small to be economically viable. It was a system introduced to the north by the Swabians, a Celtic tribe, in the fourth century. He had been forced to emigrate, working for some years in Santos, Brazil, before inheriting the property from a childless uncle. The younger sons usually preferred to leave the country rather than remain landless, though most now went to France, Germany or Switzerland if they could get in. It was 4.30 before we'd finished our meal of chicken, roast potatoes and mixed vegetables. The heavy consumption of sweet white port was making me droop and outside the rain was getting steadily worse. My thoughts must have been written clearly on my face.

'You won't get far today, you know. You may as well stay here, don't you think? We'll prepare you a room and bed so you can have a good siesta.'

I dozed off over a comic book, woken later to be told there was hot water for a bath if I wanted one. I sat down to supper feeling warm, scrubbed and fresh. One of the sons of the house came in; his little boy ran up to him, grabbing him round the legs.

'*Pai*, Daddy, there's a man here who's taller than you are!'

Great hams hung in the chimney absorbing the woodsmoke, blackened cauldrons stood on tripods over the fire. We sat around it after supper while I described the Cambridgeshire countryside to them. They were amazed to hear that the farm where I lived had four tractors and that it only took two or three men and the farmer to look after 450 acres.

'There can't be much life in the countryside if there are so few people. Here we have many people, all with smallholdings, the majority scratching out their living with little hope of any financial reward. We don't starve, but we don't save money either; you have to go abroad if you want to do that. Sometimes you can sell some wine, a calf or a chicken or two. I can see that you are drawn towards it as if it were some kind of ideal life, but you only have to look around to see that it takes its toll.'

The mother, thin, careworn, with stockings unashamedly tattered and faded blue slippers, expressed her concern that I hadn't seen my parents for so long. To her it was unimaginable that her sons and daughters should leave home if it was not necessary. She quoted a short, popular poem:

'Eu não quero mais afetos
Que o calor de uma brasa
E o sorriso dos meus netos
A volta da minha casa.'

(I want nothing more/than the warmth of a fire/and the smile of my grandchildren/around my house).

She stretched out on the bench with a sigh, a smile lit up her face and eyes. She must have been very beautiful when she was young.

The wine on which they depended for their income was stored in the cellars below the house, which the elder son showed me by candlelight. The most impressive thing was an enormous stone amphora containing olive oil, about one metre high and almost as wide.

A good half metre of solid granite separated my room from the chatter of neighbours beneath the window early next morning. A cock crowed. Senhor Soares Vieira was outside in the yard chopping wood, even though he was seventy-seven years old. His wife had just come in from feeding the chickens. She heated up a bowl of milk, cut a slice of cheese and handed me a chunk of delicious, home-baked bread made from maize flour, which they call *broa*. The taste was similar to Mexican tortillas and brought memories flooding back. I thanked them as best I could before setting off, the old man showing me a short cut down to the river. It was still drizzling: he looked up at the sky and frowned.

'Never mind, João, it's what makes the world so green.'

The man in the mist ahead was carrying an umbrella against the rain, but it was full of holes like his clothes. He kept looking anxiously over his shoulder at the strange figure following him up onto the Serra de Arada, where the shepherds and cowmen, hunched by the low walls under wide umbrellas, seemed to have a penchant for bright yellow P.V.C. waterproof trousers.

The owner of the cafe in Manhouce had also been in Brazil, working in the docks at Santos for twenty years, saving enough money to open up business in his birthplace. He was very knowledgeable about local history and told me many things of interest. The earliest inhabitants of the area were the Lusitanians, a rather quarrelsome federation of tribes. Their most famous chief was Viriato, a popular folk hero, who put up a stiff resistance to the Romans, using hit-and-run tactics ideally suited to the terrain. The Romans neatly solved the problem by having him murdered in his bed and four hundred years of relative imperial peace ensued. It was the Romans who changed the name of the peninsular from Iberia to Hispania. When they withdrew at the end of the fifth century the

43

way was left open for successive invasions of Vandals, Swabians and Visigoths, but the only people to settle were the Swabians, who found the damp, cool climate similar to their homelands. It was they who fought the Moors when they invaded. He pointed to the stream below.

'You see that road and the little bridge? They're both Roman, part of the Hispanic network. The road came from Merida through Idanha to Porto, *Portus Cale* in those days. It was the main road until the Middle Ages, too.'

I followed the road over the bridge, walking thoughtfully on the large paving stones laid so long ago by some Roman engineer, the stream swollen from the recent rains, the tramp of the legions whispering in my ear.

A 'simply thatched' house

An unaccustomed fear gripped me when I lost my way on the short cut that he had recommended. My experiences on the Caramulo ridge had left their mark, teaching me an important lesson in caution. Fortunately a surly young shepherd put me on the right track to Albergaria das Cabras.

The *serra* was wild and desolate, with little vegetation and no trees. The stone houses of the isolated hamlet were mostly tiled, but some had huge, thick, irregular slates while others were simply thatched. The alleys were awash with muck. A man stopped me. He had lost one eye, the yellow orb that remained pointing giddily upwards at the overcast sky. A shiver ran up my spine, I could feel the hair rising on the nape of my neck. Clench your fist and protrude the thumb: he exuded an evilness that was positively physical.

'You had better be careful up there on the moors, young man, wherever you come from. Do you have a gun?'

'No, I do not.'

'Well, I wouldn't go up there if I were you. There are wolves. They killed a young girl only the other day. Tore her throat out, they did.'

Two old hags standing nearby wrung their withered hands together and rolled their eyes, setting up a low, mournful wail, gnashing the few yellow stubs left to them in their rotting gums. I left them quickly, unnerved, imagining glinting, evil eyes in the swirling mist, hearing the pant of hungry wolves with lolling tongues. The words of 'Through the Valley of the Shadow of Death' came spontaneously to comfort me. For some reason my right foot began to hurt badly. I limped on till Arouca appeared in the valley below.

It looked deceptively close. My foot had begin to swell painfully by the time I had made my way down to hobble past the convent into the centre of town. Three young girls helped me to a room in a *pensão*. John Hillaby says that a good walker is a biped, not a tripod, but I know I would still have been crawling through the undergrowth on the slopes above Arouca if I hadn't had my stave to support me.

In the privacy of the room I investigated the damage: the middle toe was broken or badly cracked. I might have to see a doctor; certainly there was no way I could continue until the swelling had eased off. I had no desire at all to stay in Arouca to convalesce, so I would take a bus to Porto, some three days' walk away. My friend Rob was teaching English somewhere there and he might be able to put me up if I was lucky. In any case it would be more interesting than a small provincial town like Arouca. It would involve a little detective work finding out where he worked, but that would be fun. I arranged the bed so that I could sleep with my foot as high in the air as possible, propped on an open drawer of the chest, and slept fitfully till morning.

Porto was less noisy and polluted than I had expected since no city buses were running. The drivers had gone on strike because their wages weren't keeping up with inflation. They wanted an increase of 2000 escudos a month, which would take their basic pay to 14,000, about £135. In one of the churches, among the gilt and bleeding Christs, was a chapel hung with wax arms, legs, heads, even entire bodies of the faithful, like the spares department at Madame Tussaud's. Catholicism often seems merely a veneer for much more pagan, primitive superstitions. The faithful believe the saint to whom the chapel is dedicated will intercede with the Almighty, helping them to overcome the diseased part of their body. In a nearby shop window a portrait of the Saviour exposing his heart stood next to one of a fair-haired lady posing provocatively in a bikini. After the silent wilderness, the noise, bustle and ceaseless human activity had my mind whirling. I found a clean, inexpensive room with a view out over the mottled red roofs of the city and unpacked, opening my pack, turning the room into total chaos.

My fifth telephone call found Rob working at the British Institute. We met that afternoon. Just to see a face that I knew was as good as returning home; I had been on my own now for a week. There was room in his flat, a bed, music to listen to, books, time to rest and put my feet up. One of the first things I did was borrow a pair of trousers and get all my clothes washed. It was acceptable to stink like a mediaeval peasant on the *serra* but not in the city.

Rob introduced me to the Port Houses of Calem and Ferrara one drunken afternoon and we were out to dinner most nights, celebrating birthdays and generally moving in the company of his friends. It was all a far cry from the hooting of owls in the stillness of a moonlit night. The international news washed over me: Ronald Biggs was about to be recaptured, the unions in Poland were getting restless, the situation looking grim for their hopes of solidarity. The days flashed by, my toe was healed but the insidious chains of comfort made it progressively more difficult to leave. On the evening of my last day I did full justice to a sumptuous meal prepared by his girlfriend's mother. We washed up afterwards, to show how enlightened we were.

'Never marry a Portuguese man, Paula,' commented her mother.

I said a heartfelt good-bye in the early hours of Monday, 30th March, Rob standing sleepily in his dressing gown at the door waiting to go back to bed. I put little pressure on my feet by taking the train to Santo Tirso to avoid the suburbs, whence I followed the river Ave to Guimarães, formerly the capital of Portugal before Lisbon was taken from the Moors. This was industrial Portugal, with its building sites, factory chimneys, piles of smoking rubbish and traffic blasting its way uphill. I got off the main roads as soon as possible, making for the hilltop shrine of Nossa Senhora do Monte, an outcrop strewn with boulders with fine views in every direction. The shrubs, oaks and plane trees were all budding madly among the vineyards and well-cultivated gardens. Rob had given me the address of some friends in Guimarães, so I made my way through the after-work bustle in squares and cafes and down the narrow streets that were dominated by four-storey buildings that had elegant wooden balconies, fine arched gateways and over-hanging roofs to protect them from the elements. Maggie and Roland found me waiting on their doorstep, gave me a bed for the night, fed me and provided a plentiful supply of Lapsang Souchong while we watched television. Reagan had been shot, but was recovering in hospital.

It was the last day of March. I set off early. The countryside began to open out once more. A tall peasant with a mattock over his shoulder was keen to impress on me the importance of planting things in the right place where they would receive the correct amount of sunlight, then talked morosely of the young flocking into the cities or going abroad to work. The vines in the area produce the light, acid

46

wine called *Vinho Verde*. They train them up trees and telegraph poles and have to use long ladders to prune them.

The mist cleared that afternoon and I finally caught sight of the snow-capped mountain peaks of the Gerez in the barren, poverty-stricken province of Trás-os-Montes. After re-crossing the Ave by a seven-arched Roman bridge and drinking a glass of wine in an old coaching inn on the far bank, I detoured to inspect the remains of the Celtic village strong-hold of Briteiros. The ruins were well cared for, the concentric defence system of walls, ditches and banks that had protected their circular huts and paved streets still visible. The blurb I picked up at the empty guard-house was an interesting read, with a French and awkward English transla-tion of the original for tourists:

'. . . Rectangular, circular and elyptical houses, some simple some complex, streets and little squares perfectly, pipes, almost intact, for taking the water to the public foun-tains, the funeral monument, artistically, designed and with beaut-iful motives . . . all this, and every-thing else we can admire as simple tourists or as students or as scholars, will help us to meditate on this very ancient civilization which belongs, no doubt, to the history of origin of the lusitanians.'

I camped out that night for the first time in more than a week, on a comfortable bed of pine needles in a wood the other side of Amares. Clouds were obscuring the stars as I drifted off to sleep, only to be woken an hour later by the patter of rain

47

Ponte da Barca

drops. Would it never stop? It was April Fools' Day. I curled up mournfully, not stirring till a local church clock struck eight. Taking shelter from the heavy rain and bitter wind in the doorway of a locked chapel, I collected water from the dripping corrugated iron roof and made a bowl of porridge. Morale was low; the knowledge that I was going to get wet was far more demoralising than the fact of being wet.

I was thus happily soaked by the time I arrived in the thermal resort of Caldelas which was full of closed and shuttered grand hotels, like an out of season Yorkshire seaside town on a wet and windy winter's day. In the one open cafe I fortified myself with a snack, coffee and spirits, deciding to follow the road to Ponte da Barca.

It continued raining hard until mid afternoon, when I stopped to refuel on a wet stone seat overlooking the Minho province. A watery sun was trying to come through the clouds that hung low over the bright green terraces and vineyards; the oaks were just beginning to put out their first tender leaves, the hedges were in flower. I trucked along down the road, the mad rush to the frontier on, listening to the birds, a cuckoo calling, the river running quietly below, my clothes drying out. I was tempted to rest in a bar at Ponte da Barca, but decided against it as my feet were sore and it would be more painful to stop than soldier on.

At Arcos de Valdevez I checked into a *pensão* and cooked my supper furtively in the room, a thing I hadn't done since South America. Memories of sleazy, cockroach-infested rooms came back to haunt me. In the cafe where I went for a night-cap they were showing a 1940s American film on the television. The sexy peroxide blonde pecked the brilcreemed hero lightly on the cheek.

'Good night, my darling.'

A draught from the door was beginning to freeze my kidneys.

'Could I have a glass of hot milk?'

A discussion ensued on how easy it was to say there wasn't any milk when in fact there was, but there wasn't anyway. It was definitely time for bed.

I had walked some ten miles and just passed a sign saying 56 kilometres to Valença when a lorry carrying a heavy load of gravel stopped and the driver asked if I should like a lift. I jumped at the opportunity of knocking a chunk off the distance to the frontier. We shuddered and groaned up the serpentine road to Extremo, where we ground to a halt outside the bar. He bought me a drink and a sandwich while trying to persuade me to come as far as Monção, but I turned him down.

'It's dangerous out on the mountains by yourself. There are wolves . . .'

'Yes, I know, but I have a gun.' It was a lie but it saved going through a now familiar conversation.

The track which followed the contours of the mountain to Abedim could easily have been mistaken for a stream as it was often six inches under water, the mud squelching much as the rural lanes of Old England must once have done. A girl carrying washing up through the village with practised step greeted me with a charming laugh, two men stopped to chat, joking about the 'crop sprayer' I carried on my back. I was happy to be off the road and did not regret turning down the lift. In the surrounding enclosures were pointed stooks of hay and granaries, the houses themselves were tiled in mottled red, built of a mossy, grey-green granite still shiny from the recent rain.

I lunched on *broa* and sardines before climbing up to Gandrachão, then crossing the high, gorse-covered slopes to Taião, above Valença. The sun came out for a brief moment. Below lay the snaking waters of the river Minho glistening in the evening haze beneath the purple mountain shadows of Galicia. One last haul and I would be in Spain.

The next morning I walked out of Valença past the cars lining up to cross the frontier, had my passport stamped at the border post and walked wonderingly along the catwalk of the long, grey, iron bridge over the Minho. The whole of Portugal lay behind. I had crossed it on foot in thirty-five days. As the crow flies, I had covered some 540 kilometres in 26 walking days, and I was no bird. The figures were unimportant, however. It was enough simply to have done it, to have seen so much and met so many people. It had proved to be a friendly, sympathetic, hospitable but backward and rather lonely country. The good times had undoubtedly made up for the slog, fatigue, blisters, broken toes, mist, rain and occasional bouts of misery—all of which were felt more acutely as a result of the effort involved. The Spanish authorities greeted me with a grin: I was definitely one of the few long-distance walkers they had through that day.

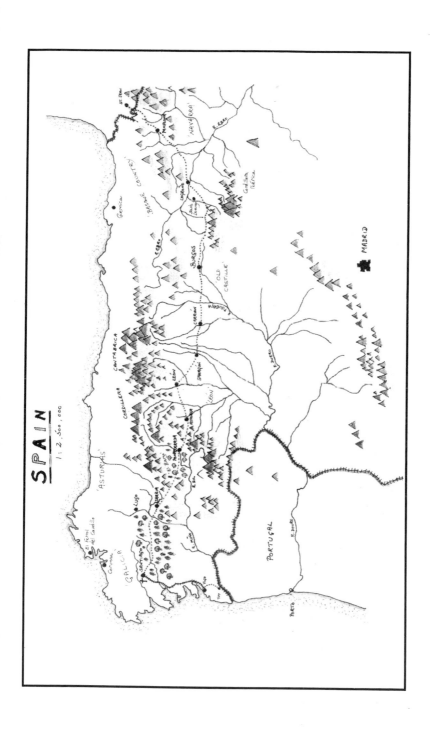

Spain

Santiago de Compostela is the city of Saint James, son of Zebedee, brother of John, known as the Boanerges, the impetuous 'Sons of Thunder'. According to legend he was martyred in Jerusalem in AD 44, on his return from preaching the gospel in Iberia. His decapitated body was smuggled away to a waiting ship and borne across the sea by a miraculous wind to north-west Spain, the land of the Callaeci, hence Galicia, where his body was buried somewhere a few miles inland from Padrón.

The exact site of the tomb was lost during the persecutions, but one day a humble shepherd saw a bright star hovering over a wood and found three ancient marble tombs there. Word of the vision reached Bishop Teodomiro, who intelligently recognised the remains of St. James and his two disciples, persuading Alfonso II, 'the chaste', King of León, to become the first pilgrim to the 'Field of the Star' in AD 899.

To the crusaders he was *Santiago Matamoros*, 'Moorkiller', epitome of the fanatical Christian knight riding over the heads of his enemies, sword in hand, white banner with a red cross flying, appearing for the first time at the Battle of Clavijo in AD 844 to lead the Christian army against the Moors. It was to cries of *Santiago y cierra España!* that they were driven out of the peninsular, despite the fact that most of the agriculture and commerce was dependent on their more advanced level of civilisation. Both Christian and Moslem had learnt to live quite peacefully together; Alfonso VI (1065–1109) was known as 'Emperor of the Two Religions'. Sadly much of the heartland of Spain was laid waste in the religious wars and never fully recovered.

During the Middle Ages his tomb grew to be a rival to Rome and Jerusalem, pilgrims flocking to Santiago from places as far away as Paris, the German mediaeval maps referring to the area as 'Jacobsland'. With the pilgrims came artisans and adventurers, so the Order of the Knights of Santiago was formed to look after them;

hotels and hospitals were built to accommodate them and the Christian hold on the north of Spain was thus cleverly reinforced. Even guide books were produced: the *Codex Calixtinus* gave helpful hints about the Kingdoms the pilgrim would have to pass through, warning of poisonous rivers, stating, among other things, that the fish and meat in Spain and Galicia would make the traveller sick, describing the Galicians as 'irascible' and 'quarrelsome'.

The remains of the Saint were lost once again when hidden away from the threat of a marauding Sir Francis Drake, who called the place 'The principal emporium of Papal Superstition', its people the enemies of 'Godes true Gospell', but they were rediscovered in 1879.

I had held to a romantic vision of myself entering the great city on foot as so many thousands had done before. My Spanish maps, from the Instituto Geográfico Militar in Madrid, only began at Santiago, but I had thought it possible to use my compass to follow minor roads from the border to the city. The road I took to Vigo became a dual carriageway, heavy international traffic crashed by, filling the air with fumes. Then it began to rain. I gritted my teeth, covering the 30 kilometres to Vigo at a cracking pace, but the elation I had felt on crossing the frontier evaporated, leaving me unwillingly trapped in an urban sprawl, the way out as horrible as the way in. The road maps on offer in the shops were of little use unless I was prepared to take a very circuitous coastal route. I was having to control an ever-increasing sense of claustrophobia. In the end I went to the station and, after some hesitation, bought a ticket direct to Santiago, a distance of 100 kilometres. I was not prepared to ignore heavy traffic as Sebastian Snow had done on his epic walk up the Pan-American Highway, neither was I bound by any rule that said I must walk every inch of the way. Clearly it was the simplest, most sensible thing to do, but I still felt ashamed at my weakness, as if I were cheating. It was a salutary lesson, at any rate, in twentieth-century reality. I never dreamt I would arrive by train.

The 'Casa de Huéspedes Cuba', a guesthouse in one of the streets that led down from the main square, had a room on the third floor up the worn wooden steps of a crooked staircase. After cooking supper, I went down to the bar and drowned my sorrows with a gin and tonic. Alcohol is amazingly cheap in Spain, the tots more than generous, a single measure equivalent to a British triple. Everyone was watching the Eurovision Song Contest on the television: France was leading with 26 points, until Ireland was suddenly found to have 326, but this mistake by the host country was quickly rectified. The one score of ten for Spain's contribution was greeted by cheers and cries of *'Arriba!'*, but there wasn't a smiling face in the bar when the United Kingdom won with a jolly ditty entitled 'Making your mind

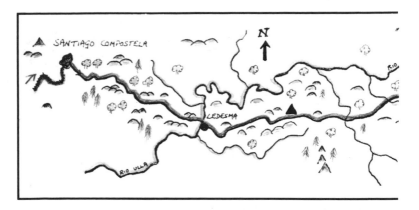

up', sung by four plastic flowers called Bucks Fizz. After another gin and tonic I headed unsteadily upstairs to bed.

The only sound in the early hours of the morning was that of footsteps as an austere, black-coated figure walked hurriedly across the empty street into the shadowy portico on his way to mass. High above the city, between the elegant bell towers of the cathedral, stands the statue of a solitary pilgrim, looking calmly down onto the square. Broad steps led me up to the intricately sculpted portals where Christ holds out his wounded palms, flanked by Maestro Mateo's players with their viols, lutes, pipes, harps and hurdy-gurdy. As the pilgrim enters, he touches the base of the Tree of Jesse in token of safe arrival. Countless others have worn narrow grooves into the soft stone with their fingers. The nave is magnificently solid, severe, simple Romanesque, in stark contrast to the chancel where the high altar stands in lavish, baroque, golden splendour above the tomb of the Patron Saint of All the Spains.

Happily, Santiago is not just a religious centre. The streets came alive as the sun rose higher, dispelling the long, chill shadows. It was good to sit outside a cafe at midday sipping Soberano brandy, observing the university students at the tables around. There seemed to be a greater freedom and liveliness in the people than I had seen in Portugal, more passion in the hot discussions and light laughter. The women, particularly, struck me as being very different, attractive and fiery by nature with flashing black eyes, independent and emancipated. I made no friends, though. It is more difficult in cities anyway, where there are so many strangers. I resolved to leave the next day.

I started east under the pilgrim gate in the early morning with a mist still hanging in the valleys, but the day promised well and a

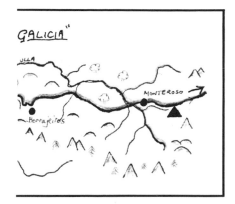

warbler sang cheerfully from an oak tree. I walked all day over gently undulating hills south of the river Ulla, the earth very red, the lower slopes checked with tiny fields of maize, potatoes or cabbage and stands of pine, oak, chestnut, even eucalyptus. Wild flowers grew in profusion on the banks either side of the lane, their blues, pinks and whites contrasting with the purple and yellow of the heather and broom on the upper, unproductive slopes.

The only incident of note happened after lunch. A car stopped, a young man wound down the window, leant out and asked if I would like a cup of coffee. He lived with his parents a few hundred yards away, who had also just finished eating. I chewed on a spare rib at the table in the smoky kitchen, trying to follow what they said as they spoke *Gallego*, the Galician language, a mixture of Spanish and Portuguese.

'We have a friend who likes adventures and travelling just like you. He crossed the Sahara in a jeep once. We wouldn't have invited you in, otherwise. People around here are not open or hospitable by nature. When someone knocks at their door, it has to be because they want something from them.'

The father talked of Galicia, his wife pitching in the occasional remark in a very loud voice. It was one of the five kingdoms of old Spain, the remotest and most backward corner of the peninsular, about the size of Wales. The 'Garden of Spain', linguistically, geographically and culturally has more in common with the north of Portugal than the rest of Spain. The climate is cool and temperate, rainfall abundant, more than 600 millimetres a year minimum. The region produces a quarter of Spain's timber, a third of her cows and a lot of apples. Traditions are fundamentally Celtic, their system of land inheritance ensuring that three quarters of the plots are under one hectare. It was the last part of the peninsular to come under the Roman Empire and its influence was only superficial as was that of the Moors. Asturias was the one area they never subdued and it was from there that the Reconquest was begun. Galicia is densely populated, although emigration to foreign countries is almost as great as in Portugal and the women are normally left behind to look

55

after the smallholdings. Efforts have been made by the government to form co-operatives and make production more economically viable, but most of rural Galicia remains contentedly untouched by the central bureaucracy in Madrid.

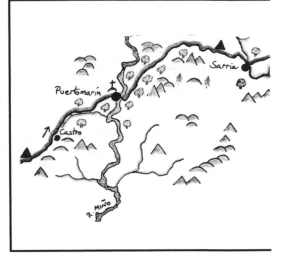

The air was hot and heavy during the night as if a storm were brewing, but it only rained heavily and I was well protected by my plastic sheet. The morning broke cool and fresh. I strode along with a tune in my head, humming, thinking of approaching breakfast, listening to the lowing of cows and the rumbles from my stomach. A group of labourers loading a trailer with hay hailed me jovially, offering me a sandwich and a swig of wine. The woman in the shop where I stopped to buy provisions happened to have worked for eight years in the kitchens of a preparatory school called Lichfield. She chatted away in guttural English while her customers looked on in admiration. The local cheese she sold came in a pear-shaped skin, tied at the neck with string. It was quite delicious, soft and juicy with a slightly bitter taste. As I was leaving she produced four eggs and gave them to me with a smile.

About a mile from Borrajeiros a blue van stopped and the driver gave me a lift to the village. He was carrying vegetables for the local shop, where we had a drink of wine together. He spoke English well, telling me he had first worked as a waiter in Reigate, before getting a job as a mechanic during the day, working at night as a porter in the hospital where his wife did the cleaning. They were there for seven years until the immigration laws changed, making it almost impossible for them to return any more.

I asked if he had enjoyed his time in England.

'It was all right. I worked like a slave and earned plenty of money, so I managed to set up in business here, but I didn't make any friends, really. They are not quick to give, the English, and I got tired of being called a "dago".'

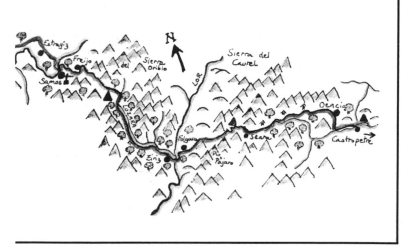

The subject changed to education, which started the shop-woman on a long complaint. He winked and left.

'It's so difficult, so expensive, to educate your children. Then, just a year before they have finished their studies they have to go and do their military service, wasting time playing soldiers, and when they do eventually come out with a degree there's no work for them . . .'

I took my leave as soon as tact permitted. The rest of the day was peacefully uneventful.

The sun had just risen over the trees on the horizon when I stopped to ask for water in the hamlet of Castro. A group of men were already at work in the old walled lane which they were widening with pick axes and shovels so that a tractor could pass through.

'Where are you going?'

'I'm trying to get to Puertomarín.'

'Well, you don't want to come this way. There's a good road up there.'

'No, really, I'm trying to follow the footpath.'

'The *camino?*'

'That's right.'

'Would you like a drink?'

'That would be very nice.'

The foreman went off. He was a very large man with massive shoulders and a stomach to match. He came back carrying a jug of wine and a basket covered with a cloth which he placed carefully on the wall.

'There you are, tuck in, I'm sure you must be hungry.'

The basket contained a clean glass, bread, cheese and home-smoked bacon. It was the most delicious bacon that I have ever tasted, with almost no meat in it, but the raw, salty fat melted like butter on the bread. I washed the meal down with wine while they worked. At the side of the lane they had almost completed building a bread oven. A thin, frail old man was crouched inside rendering the brickwork.

'The houses were made of granite schist'

They insisted that I finish all the wine before leaving, even though it was so early. I whistled merrily as I continued down the lanes, checking the way with another group of people at a crossroads.

'Would you like some breakfast?'

I sadly turned the offer down. A wizened old man took me by the arm and showed me the path, which later became overgrown and difficult to follow, forcing me back onto the tarmac, though not before I got completely soaked in an attempt to jump a stream.

I had lunch on the eastern side of the river Miño, looking over to Puertomarín. The drowned ruins of the old town were still visible on the banks of the lake that formed when they dammed the river for hydro-electricity. They had pulled down the pilgrim church and rebuilt it on the hill above the new town.

It rained later, but an enormous oak gave shelter from which to watch a rainbow spread over the sky. I followed the lanes on through the beautiful, rolling countryside, the air sweet with the smell of wet earth and leaf mould.

Two uncomplaining oxen were coming up the hill, drawing a creaking, squeaking cart piled high with broom, which is used as fodder and bedding for the animals. They call this nerve jangling racket the *chirrido*. It is said to frighten away wolves and bears, even the Devil himself. The cart had solid wooden wheels without spokes or axles, the same as those used two thousand years ago by the Romans and the Egyptians before them.

Spring was just arriving. The trees were still in bud, bees buzzed from blossom to blossom in the orchards while cuckoos called incessantly; a woodpecker hammered away diligently somewhere in the woods and a magpie swooped across the road, followed by its mate. The tiny fields were divided by walls of upright slabs of slate, some with little heaps of manured broom ready to be forked out, some with oxen ploughing and harrowing. Cows grazed contentedly around Romanesque chapels, stone crosses stood at the side of the road. The houses were made of granite schist, with irregular slate roofs, the peasants living above their animals for warmth and convenience. A church bell sounded the evening Angelus. Light was fading from the range of mountains to the east, the Sierra del Oribio, which I would tackle the next day.

Black slugs a good four inches long were crawling all over the road that led down into Sarria, chasing a convoy of black and orange caterpillars. The town was full of banks and modern buildings. I wandered around hunting in vain for a shop that sold porridge oats, contenting myself in the end with a packet of baby cereal from the chemist called *Cinco Cereales*. My mother wrote to me later to tell me it was the same stuff that I had been fed on as a child. It was a palatable alternative, though rather too smoothly processed for my adult tastes. It was past eleven when I settled down by the side of the road to cook a large, substantial breakfast. The sun was hot, a woman stopped gardening on the other side of the wall to lean over and talk.

'I see a lot of people like you go past, especially in the summer, but they always travel in groups. I remember one group of Frenchmen particularly who were all travelling on horseback, about twenty of them. They . . .'

She was old and kept forgetting her train of thought, breaking off in a perplexed fashion to ask what she had been saying. A shepherd passed by and waved.

'Why do you travel alone?' she asked.

'I prefer to. I do get lonely sometimes, but this means I have to talk to someone if I don't want to go crazy and that way I learn more about your people and your country. If you're with a friend, people tend to think you've got all the company you need or want and leave you alone.'

'It's a sacrifice though.'

'Yes, in a way it is, but it's worth it. Would you have been talking to me if I hadn't been alone?'

'Perhaps not. Anyway, with the kind of pilgrimage you've undertaken St. Peter will fling open the doors of heaven for you!'

The other side of Estragiz I stripped off and plunged into the freezing water of a stream beneath some landlord's large, whitewashed house with Greek statues in the formal, walled gardens. Most of the productive land in the region is owned by the nobility or middle classes, who let the property to peasants and do nothing for it except collect the rent once a month. After washing some clothes, hanging them on the line (a length of string running from one side of my pack to another, where they could dry off as I walked along) and scrubbing out the pots, I set off for Samos.

The octagonal dome of the monastery dominates the town, which lies unmolested in a valley beneath the Sierra del Oribio. The petrol pump attendant wandered up as I was sitting outside a cafe drinking wine and tucking into bread and cheese; he pulled up a crate and sat down. He was a kindly old man. I asked him if he'd fought in the Civil War.

'I did, yes, but I certainly didn't enjoy it. I fought for Franco, like most people in Galicia. He was born here too, at El Ferrol on the coast near Coruña. Things were over pretty quickly. Any resistance was in the mountains, where we had the odd skirmish. The shepherds were the ones who suffered most for they were constantly taken for questioning as spies. I was glad when it was all over.'

When he found out I was English, he spoke with approval of the Queen, saying the system was similar to the one they had now with their King Juan Carlos, adding that Tejero might well have succeeded in his February coup if it hadn't been for the intervention of the King, who upheld the people's democratic rights.

An ancient monk was weeding the steps of the monastery church, a bespectacled man with misty blue eyes and white stubble on his cheeks, dressed in the thick black habit of the Benedictines. He looked up as I approached, asking if I would like to see round the monastery. On the tour he insisted on practising his English, although I understood little of what he had to say. It appeared there was room for one hundred monks, but there were only ten, including two young priests studying for their vows. There seemed to be enough money coming in to pay for new stained glass windows to be commissioned, as well as a long mural in the cloisters depicting the life of Saint Benedict. He pointed to the final scene in which the saint was surrounded by his disciples in the last moments of his life.

'You see that disciple on the right? That's the Abbot's face, though he's dead now. That man on his left is the present Bishop of Lugo. They didn't include my portrait, though.'

He grinned. He had been there since the age of nine. The monastery was founded at the time of the Visigoths, but all traces of the original buildings had been destroyed by a fire in 1951. All that remained was a stone fountain in the centre of the cloisters, the bowl

60

supported by four frolicking, naked mermaids, a reminder, no doubt, of the temptations of the flesh. The cooking and washing was all done by nuns of the same order, which left the monks with time to meditate, pray, garden and brew liqueur. I bought two miniature bottles before I left, called 'Liqueur Pax'.

The rest of the day was spent climbing to the crest of the Oribio, where a woman in an isolated house gave me water from a rusty, converted oil can. The view was magnificent: I could see right back to Santiago over the blue hills and woods. It was one of my greatest pleasures to sit looking back and say to myself 'I came all that way on foot', trying to remember the incidents along the way. I camped on a grassy track a little way down from the house on the only flat piece of land that I could find, stripping off to rub myself down.

'Hey, look at the madman!'

I hadn't thought that I would be observed. I grinned and shouted something rude back.

Planning my route over the Sierra del Caurel to Ponferrada was a tricky business, involving the corners of three maps. I checked my proposed route with a man driving his donkey uphill from Lózara. He was most helpful: I should follow the river to Eiríz, cross to Folgoso, where I could take a path up over the mountain beside Pía Pájaro, its highest peak at 1600 metres. Once over, I should head for Seara and a track from there would take me through various villages to Ponferrada.

The sun was not yet high enough to reach into the Lózara gorge. My breath steamed in the chilly air. A couple off to work were coming towards me leading a team of oxen with bits of old rubber tyre over their heads. They said it was to protect the leather of the yoke from the sun and rain. An hour or so later another pair of oxen passed, but this time the yoke was covered with the skin of an animal I did not recognise: yellow with small black splotches.

'Excuse me, *Señor*, could you tell me what kind of animal that skin comes from?'

'That? It's the skin of a dog, of course.'

I noticed the same phenomenon throughout the morning, catching sight of dog skins stretched out to cure on frames in the sun in front of the houses.

I have seldom walked in surroundings of such great beauty. The sides of the gorge levelled off beside the shallow, fast running river, forming narrow strips of pasture and fields. Springs trickled down the banks, the dewy chestnut woods were carpeted in a mass of bright primroses. The boles of these trees were enormously old, hollow, mossy, full of holes and breaches. A landslide had buried the track at one point, but there was evidence that a cow had been able to pass over the slippery schist, so I balanced carefully on the edge of the steep drop down to the river and sidled my way gingerly across to safety on the path the other side, grateful once again for the stave that helped me to keep my balance.

'... built of a reddish-brown stone'

The path wound on over an old bridge of logs covered with earth, away from the noisy, rushing river to Cortes. There was no one in sight in the alleyway that ran through the centre of the uncannily quiet, seemingly deserted village that was built of a reddish-brown stone. I felt as though I was deep in the bowels of the earth, close to the slow heartbeat of a different age, the primitive, instinctive life of survival that underlies all civilisations. Even the granite was marked, centuries of carts having cut deep ruts into the rocky track that led out. 'You come sometimes upon the clustered houses of a hamlet untouched by men's restlessness, untouched by their need, by their thought, as if forgotten by time itself' (Conrad). A shepherd looked at me, but we did not speak and break the silence.

Smoke wafted out of the doorway of a house in Eiríz and I could hear women's voices inside. I had traversed the gorge by late afternoon, reprovisioned in Folgoso and started on the climb up to the Pía Pájaro. It began to rain steadily, my boots were soon awash, but the climbing kept me warm enough. The path, little more than a goat track, suddenly petered out, leaving me with the choice of either going back or cutting directly up to the pass, where I could just make out the line of another track. I chose to attack the slope, pulling out all my reserves of energy, lunging and fighting through the thick, waist-deep cover of gorse and heather, gasping for breath and sweating profusely, gaining the path and pass in about half an hour. Here, I stopped briefly to pour the water from my boots and change my socks. Looking up, I saw the whole of Galicia spread out beneath me. My eyes were on a line with the grey clouds, hazy rays of sun breaking through and playing on the distant, inky-blue ridges.

The clouds that had so recently looked beautiful and majestic suddenly swept in low over the mountains, wrapping the world in mist. To my astonishment I found drifts of snow over the path. I had to scrunch my way through them to a depth of more than a foot at times; I was still in my shorts.

My luck then deserted me almost completely. The path, which had been so good, disappeared and I couldn't see far enough through the mist to make out where it started again. It was no time or place to get lost. I pushed eastwards, heading down on a compass bearing in the hope of finding some form of shelter for the night. I found nothing but slopes of fire-blackened broom, strewn with loose rocks and boulders. It was still raining sporadically and the ground promised a lumpy night. I caught sight of an outcrop near a stream in the rapidly fading light and resigned myself to sleeping there. I could go no further. I would have to wait for morning to bring a new day and fresh hope. At least the rock gave some protection against the wind and rain. I set up my plastic in the lee of the wind, got the stove working, and after a pleasantly hot meal of rice and tuna, crawled into an uncomfortable foetus position beneath the plastic. Sleep came easily, though, as I was incredibly tired and insensible to discomfort.

At some time during the night I became aware that rain was beating on the plastic and the wind was getting stronger, but I was too sleepy for it to disturb my rest. Was that a roll of thunder in the distance? I drifted off again. For a split second the rocky slopes were lit up vividly. Instantly I was wide awake, fully conscious of my extremely vulnerable position: alone, high up on an exposed mountain with absolutely nowhere to shelter. Thunder rolled menacingly in the black skies above. Another flash of lightning turned the world blue and my heart to ice. Automatically I counted the intervals between lightning and thunder. They were getting progressively shorter. My thoughts turned to the primroses in the gorge that morning. Nature is a fickle friend. Here she was again, just as beautiful but savage now and very angry. Another flash, another clap of thunder, very close this time. Of course I would know nothing about it if I were struck, but logic was no good. The prospect of an imminent death was very frightening. I had never been so close to crashing clouds before. I think all men staring death in the face turn to their maker and pray 'Please God, do not take me now'. A blinding bolt of electric blue light hammered down on a boulder twenty yards away as a deafening thunderclap burst overhead, shaking the ground. I was rigid with fear, unable to shut my eyes, blessing those I loved in turn, a comfortingly long list. I resolved to die bravely.

It was the closest it came. The storm rolled away as quickly as it had arrived, leaving the mountain very dark and silent for a while until the rain and wind returned. I fumbled around in my pack until my hand closed around a miniature bottle of Benedictine; I sat back

63

against the rock, lit a cigarette, sipped at the liqueur and tried to relax. In vain, since the wind veered round bringing squalls of rain rushing in from the unprotected side. I spent the soggy hours till morning grimly holding on to the plastic to prevent it from being blown away.

A more welcome dawn there never was. With a rush of hope I saw a clear blue streak appear between the clouds and daylight revealed a village below, no more than an hour's walk away. The villagers would tell me where I was. I packed up and made my way down, light-headed with exhaustion and relief that I was still alive to tell the tale.

'Excuse me. Can you tell me how to get to Seara?'

'This *is* Seara, *hombre*. Where have you come from?'

'I've come from the mountains.'

'You can't possibly have spent the night up there in that storm ...'

'Well, I didn't intend to, but I got lost in the mist.'

'You must be mad.'

'I think you're probably right.'

I was too exhausted to go far that morning, so instead I took advantage of a break in the clouds to dry everything out in a quarry and stretch out on the ground for a nap. In the afternoon I took the track on to Oencia. It was easy to follow, so I could let my mind wander, dreaming for no good reason of a tin of frankfurters. At the shop in the village it was a choice of sardines or tuna. I bought another tin of tuna, talking with the shopkeeper while the shadows filled with curious villagers who stood quietly listening to the conversation. Many of them wore painted clogs very like Dutch clogs, except that they were raised off the ground on three stubby blocks like Japanese slippers. They call them *madreñas*, which are apparently essential for walking the muddy streets. I passed neat rows of them by the steps of the terraced houses as I walked down to the river. An old woman was singing in the valley, tidying the graves in the cemetery.

I was pondering whether to investigate an abandoned building above Castropetre when a man appeared carrying four heavy planks of wood on his shoulder.

'Do you think anyone would mind if I spent the night up there?' I asked.

'I don't see why. It's the old school.'

'Why's it empty?'

'Not enough children. The few we have are taken down the road to Friera every morning in a truck, if they aren't playing truant.'

Illiteracy is much lower in Spain than in Portugal. Only 5.7 per cent of the population could neither read nor write in 1966.

Education is officially free from the age of six to fourteen. The classrooms, when I got there, were locked, the desks gathering dust, but I swept out the landing on the second floor with a switch of broom and made myself at home, fetched water from a nearby spring, and after a decent supper, lay down to listen to the rain. It was a wonderful feeling to have a roof for the night.

I woke feeling well rested and refreshed as dawn was breaking, and stopped at a cafe a few miles down the road at Cabarcos. The proprietress thought I was French, so I played along. A group of workmen entered for their morning shot of spirits. Some of them had worked in France and Holland. They were not very complimentary.

'The French just used to laze around chatting together and skiving when the boss wasn't there. Then when they saw him coming they would all start working frantically. We had to work all the time and if anything went wrong it was always us who got the blame.'

I passed a working water mill on the way down to the river Sil, and watched the stones grinding the grain to flour in the dusty, scented gloom. The miller waved.

'Where are you going?'

'Ponferrada.'

It felt very strange to emerge from the mountains into the flat fields and vineyards of a valley, meeting cars and lorries and other symbols of progress. It had surprised me quite enough the night before to see two street lamps in the village of Castropetre. A woman drawing water from a well beside an old stone house with a roof of rough, heavy slates was the only reminder of the backward, silent world that I had left behind. The well was oddly out of place amongst the smart, whitewashed bungalows that were surrounded by tall fences and iron gates to keep out intruders. The orchards of apple trees were in bloom, the poplars just breaking into leaf, colouring the valley with translucent brown, gold and green.

The young driver of a Citroën 2CV gave me a lift into Ponferrada, bought me a drink and arranged to meet me later when I had found lodgings for the night. When I did meet him again he was in the company of two young women, their eyes glazed and distant from smoking hashish, which is much more common in Spain now that Franco is no longer there.

'You've walked all the way from Portugal? *Demasiado!* (Far out!), that's really too much!'

I wanted company badly, but not theirs. They seemed vacuous and corrupt and I wanted nothing to do with them, so I returned sadly to my room and bed.

I wrote a few letters and did various chores before leaving my room the next morning. As I walked out into the street, I found myself in the middle of a religious procession. A statue of Christ on a donkey was being paraded through the streets on the shoulders of short, burly men in tight black suits. The rest of the people were carrying bunches of bay leaves and crosses made from rushes. I realised with a shock that it was Palm Sunday and that it was therefore a week since I had left Santiago. The church was packed and mass already under way when I went in. Anything more different from an Anglican service is hard to imagine: a steady flow of worshippers came in and out the few minutes I was there, strolling down the aisle, chatting together, waving to their friends, seemingly oblivious to the priests at the high altar. I retreated to the castle of the Knights Templar.

Ponferrada Castle

The name has a certain ring about it and the Knights were, indeed, a very powerful force, owning thirty-eight lordships in Aragón alone. When they renounced their right to rule these, they were given six castles, an income of one thousand shillings a year and a fifth part of any land that was conquered from the Moors. In addition, they were exempt from many taxes and received a tenth of all Royal revenues. What started as a religious order became primarily a Merchant Bank. The Spanish branch were more farmers and business men than romantic warriors, while the majority of the lower Orders were illiterate craftsmen or shepherds, devoted to prayer and work, though avid players of knuckle-bones and hopscotch in their free time. Simple but shrewd, their duty was to raise funds for the knights fighting in the Crusades. The castle had been well restored, an impressive monument to the Order. The sluggish, badly polluted waters of the Sil slid by in the gully below.

In the evening I went to a film called 'Supercop'. The youth of the town were there in force, chewing gum and spitting from the balcony onto the heads of their friends below. I was looking forward to leaving the place. There was something rotten about it that made me uneasy.

A woman with bright auburn hair hailed me from her garden on the outskirts of Ponferrada, inviting me to a drink of wine and a sandwich on the terrace of her large, modern bungalow. I sat back in a deck chair, sipping light-coloured, potent wine, entertaining her with tales of great adventures.

'I have often dreamed of travelling,' she said, 'but I can't. You are so lucky, you have no ties, you can travel the world at leisure.'

She was a doctor's wife and obviously bored with the restrictions imposed on her by children and marriage. I carried her dreams with me to Molinaseca, which was a lovely village that retained much of its medieval charm.

The owner of the bar at Riego delayed his lunch to open up and serve a glass of wine. As I drank, he drew my attention to a triangular, wooden contraption that hung from the ceiling in the middle of the room. Eleven bells hung on three horizontal slats. They were graded by size and controlled by a cord attached to one of the corners. Seeing that he had my complete attention, he reached over for the end of the cord and pulled gently. The smallest bells rang. He pulled a little harder and the centre row chimed in unison. For a while he dexterously handled the cord to produce variations with the different bells, until he gave the cord a sudden jerk and all the bells rang out together.

'*Y bailan los gitanos!*' (Let the gypsies dance!) he cried with a great laugh.

He was very proud of his invention and went on to show me some carvings he had made from old church beams, talking the while.

'We had an old American lady through here once. She was very rich, travelling on a mule with a footman to look after her. I fed them on trout, which she said was the best she had ever tasted. Another time we had an English aristocrat through, travelling with his wife, three children and two donkeys. They were in a terrible state; they had got into trouble in the mountains south of here.'

We said good-bye, as his lunch would be getting cold.

'Alla, adiós.'

I set off at a fair pace to Acebo, where I was confronted by an imposing coat of arms above the doorway of one of the many deserted houses. I had the sneaking suspicion that eyes were following me from behind the shutters and did not stop. A hiker was coming towards me, the first fellow walker that I had seen on the journey. He was English, from Portsmouth, spending a two-week holiday following the route of Sir John Moore on his retreat to Corunna.

Moore had advanced into Spain from Portugal with the intention of luring Napoleon and his Generals from the South and Madrid, which he thought besieged, but not fallen. It was a stratagem that worked perfectly. Napoleon heard of his advance, left Madrid guarded and set off in pursuit over the Guadarrama mountains with

50,000 men, whom he led personally through the snow on a forced march, ordering Soult to attack from the east with the same number of men. Moore had about 25,000. The moment he heard that his plan had worked, he ordered the retreat, hoping to reach Vigo or

Corunna where ships would take his army round to strike at the south of Spain with Napoleon stuck up in the mountainous north. It was an ambitious plan. It was Christmas time, 1808, the roads crackling with ice. August Schaumann was there to witness the march:

> 'No pen can describe the horrors that followed in the wake of the retreat . . . every minute a horse would collapse beneath its rider and be shot dead. The road was strewn with the dead horses, blood-stained snow, broken carts, scrapped ammunition, spiked guns, dead mules, donkeys and dogs, starved and frozen soldiers, women and children, wading through snow and mud over dead bodies. The howling of the wind sounded like the groaning of the damned.'

Drunkenness, looting, plunder and rape were commonplace and there was little Moore could do about it. The starving troops, forced to suck leather to keep alive, at one point found a supply of raw salt fish and rum in a monastery. The combination of the two drove many of them insane. One stood swaying in the middle of the road shouting that he was General Moore, ordering the troops to turn and give battle, saying he would kill the first man to pass. The troopers simply rode over him.

Six thousand men were lost on the retreat. By 11th January they were in sight of Corunna, but no ships were waiting for them. The wind had not been propitious. At the Battle of Corunna, Moore was fatally wounded, struck on the left breast by a cannon shot, dying in great pain some hours later, but not before he heard the French had been defeated. 'I hope the people of England will be satisfied,' he said.

The wind that greeted me as I came over the crest of the Montes

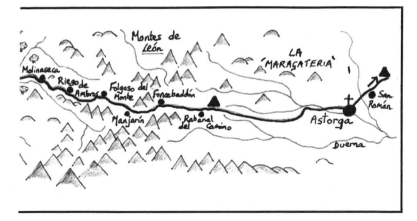

de León was keen and bitter. The tablelands of Central Spain stretched out to the horizon, dominated by the sky. White, fluffy cumulus glowed in the sun above heavy, dark grey clouds from which sheets of driving rain were falling as they moved rapidly over the plain. Wispy clouds above these broke to reveal a patch of pale blue, another, bigger break revealed a darker blue, a ray of sunlight piercing through, running over the empty, burnt wasteland below. The villages of Manjarín and Foncebadón were even more deserted than Acebo, the thatched roofs of the houses green with moss, their walls slowly crumbling into ruin.

I reached Rabanal del Camino just before nightfall and camped the other side. I would have had a good night's sleep had I not kicked over the pack at some point, whereupon the whole construction collapsed on top of me. It was raining, so I waited some time before leaping nude into the cold moonlight, drinking water from a puddle that had formed on the new length of plastic that I had bought in Ponferrada, and setting things to rights.

It seemed common practice for women not to dress in the morning. The young woman in her dressing gown and slippers who served me a drink at a roadside inn shrugged her shoulders sleepily when asked why the countryside was so deserted.

'Quién sabe?' (who knows?) (And who cares? she seemed to say.)

The twin steeples of the cathedral at Astorga stood out clearly on the flat horizon. It was further than it looked and lunch time when I arrived, the heavenly smell of freshly baked bread wafting through the streets in the outskirts. I followed my nose through a dark passageway that was white with flour, into the bakery, where the owner brought out a large, round, crusty kilo loaf straight from the oven for me. Turning a corner past a lorry being loaded with waste paper, I came face to face with Gaudí's Palace, a remarkably eccentric building of well-masoned, regular blocks of light grey granite. It looked like a toy palace where it stood next to the old cathedral. Antonio Gaudí was a Catalan architect, famous for his 'tender doors of calf's liver', as Dalí characteristically put it. Gaudí was commissioned by the bishop to replace the palace burnt down in 1893, but the building was left unfinished at his death, remaining a skeleton until it was converted into the Museo del Camino with an interesting exhibition about the Pilgrim Way. It was lovely inside: Gaudí, the architect, had an unusual gift for the unexpected, combining pillars and arches in such a way as to create sudden openings, shifts of focus and perspective.

Gaudí's Palace

A party of German tourists were climbing into their air-conditioned bus in the square outside and rolled off in comfort to their next destination. The cathedral was shut, but I admired the gargoyles: pagan beasts with lions' manes, faces a cross between camels and monkeys.

The other side of Astorga was completely different, well cultivated, a mass of poles, crossbars and wire, up which men were working on ladders preparing the frames for hops. A mule clopped down the earth road from San Román. A farmer had got his tractor stuck in a ditch the other side; the wheels were still spinning. I asked if he needed any help.

'No thanks. I'll have to go and get my oxen to pull it out. What are you doing here, anyway?'

I explained. He looked me up and down with curiosity. He wore the typical blue overalls and beret of a labourer, and had two gold teeth.

'Are you a hippy?'

'Not really. I'm a teacher.'

'You're lucky, you young people. Things have changed a great deal since I was a boy. There was real poverty then, people living from hand to mouth, but now everyone's quite well off, even if they

70

don't like to show it or admit it. You see those houses down there? They don't look up to much from the outside, but you can be sure that inside they've got a television, washing machine and all mod cons. Trouble is the young don't appreciate it, go about drinking and drugging themselves silly. It's terrible for a father to see it happening to his sons right in front of his eyes. There's a lot of it in the cities now, but I'm lucky. My five children have all got their heads screwed on the right way.'

I mentioned Ponferrada and the glazed eyes of the girls. He said it was just as bad in Astorga.

'Did you fight in the Civil War?'

'Oh, yes. Everybody was involved in one way or the other, even if they didn't want to be. Most of us were just trying to keep out of the way. It was brother shooting brother, after all.'

He paused, looking around, thinking, making his mind up whether to go on, then pointed to a spot on the northern horizon.

'You see that ridge up there? The Nationalists came into the town one day, rounded up anyone suspected of Republican sympathies, bundled them into lorries, took them up there and gunned them down. The clergy worked hand in hand with Franco's men. Thank God I'm an atheist! If you didn't toe the line, wear a hat and go to church regularly that was enough to get you branded a Commie. People took to wearing crosses so there could be no mistake, even when they hated the priests. They have changed a lot since then, they're more liberal now. They were not all bad either. There was one priest I remember who stood up to them when they came the second time, said they should shoot him as well if they were going to take away all those innocent people. The squad backed off and let the men they had collected go back to their homes and families. He was a brave man, but an exception.'

We had been talking for more than an hour and it had begun to rain lightly. He said I should watch out, that it sometimes snowed in May up on the *meseta*. Then he remembered he had a tractor to get out of the ditch. Before he left, I asked him why the countryside on the other side of Astorga was so deserted.

'This is the 'Maragatería.' San Román there was where the *Maragatos* had their headquarters.'

'Something to do with cats?'

He smiled.

'No, nothing to do with cats at all. The *Maragatos* were a strange people, kept themselves to themselves, only marrying their own kind and that sort of thing, a bit like gypsies except that they were honest and hard working. I've heard it said they were descended from the Moors, but no one really knows. They used to carry the gold between

71

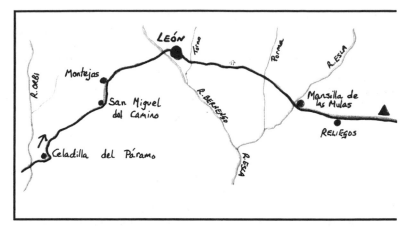

between Castile and Galicia among other things. There are hardly any of them around now. They all went off to work in Madrid. Most of the fisheries there are owned by them. They do come back for holidays, but they don't stay long. Adiós.'

'Hey!' he shouted from down the road. 'Be careful of the wolves!'

He went off chuckling to himself. The rest of the day was spent walking over the plain, or *páramo*. For a few miles bands of scrubby oak protected the crops from the wind, but these soon disappeared, leaving nothing but an endless expanse of flat wheatland. At last I sighted Antoñán del Valle, left my pack on a wooded knoll above the village and went looking for water.

A woman had been washing clothes in the basins beside the communal well, which had deep grooves where centuries of ropes had cut into the stone. She had laid the clothes out on the grass to dry. A curious man wandered up and asked why I was travelling.

'Es una promesa.' (It's a vow I've made.) It is common practice among Catholics to make a solemn promise to a saint, pledging oneself to some difficult task in return for the saint's intervention with God on one's behalf. There was a grain of truth in the statement, an element of purification, but more than that it was something that was readily acceptable. I was tired of the burden of frequently raised eyebrows and incomprehension. With three simple words I solved the problem. They both nodded their heads and asked no further questions. After that I resorted to this excuse quite frequently, for simplicity's sake. 'No Spaniard ever walks for pleasure, and none except trampers and beggars—it is not supposed that anyone should do so except from compulsion' (Richard Ford).

I returned to my wood for supper. The sun filled the shallow valley with soft evening light. Darkness fell to the sound of sheep bells and

the shouts of shepherds returning from the day's pasture. The growing moon bathed the settlement in an eerie light: it could have been a cultivated crater on some unknown planet.

The sun was rising as I made my way through the sleeping village. A great white stork glided by, landing awkwardly on its nest beside the cross on the church tower, which had a wooden balcony from which the local priest could keep an eye on his erring flock. The walls of the older houses were made of earth, strengthened with straw, the garden walls protected from erosion by lumps of turf on top.

Most of the day was spent avoiding the major roads that lead in to León, the track winding over the unchanging countryside. It could have been Cambridgeshire, expect that this was flatter, with even fewer trees, and to the north were the white caps of the mountains of the Cordillera Cantábrica, the Peña Ubiña like a vast plum pudding with cream poured over the top. There were strange knolls around the villages with low doors set into the sides, like air raid shelters or hobbit dwellings. They were, in fact, cellars for the fizzy local wines. I talked with a shepherd wearing a beret and a coarse white blanket with wide checks slung over his shoulder to protect him from the wind. He was munching bread and sausage, washing it down with wine. He had once worked in a factory in the north, but three months was enough. The sulphuric acid fumes had been too much for his lungs.

'I decided it was better to be poor and healthy and came home. Many of us had to leave Spain in the first place only because we were denied the right to work. That old goat Franco (he used the word *cabrón* which is rather stronger) called it a great adventure, but then what did he know about it? He certainly didn't care. People didn't want to leave, they had to. Then when we got to the other countries they treated us like dirt, not human beings at all. We got work all right, so we couldn't complain, but they'd sell you for a glass of beer, some of them.'

He threw a stone at some adventurous sheep. They ran back into the flock.

'I knew men who did nothing but work and sleep, work and sleep, day in day out, eating cheap food, giving up smoking, even women, all just to save up as much money as possible so they could get out and go home. But they were caught up in the same old system when they got back. Juan Carlos hasn't changed anything. The bosses are still the bosses, the people just as afraid now as they were at the time of the Inquisition.'

He was the only person I had seen or talked to for hours. These areas of Spain often have a population density as low as twenty people to the square kilometre. It must be a life of great solitude for such a man. We were both very grateful for each other's company.

León. I thought the name had something to do with 'lion', but in fact it is a corruption of the Latin *Legio,* the city founded by the Seventh Roman Legion who built their camp in a strategic position at the confluence of the rivers Bernesga and Torío. It became the capital of the expanding Christian Kingdom of Asturias and León, needing strong castles to protect its eastern borders, hence the name 'Castile'.

I made straight for the cathedral, guided through the suburbs by the steeples, the dusty streets busy with people. Bright sunlight picked out the details on the fine gothic façade, in front of which some children were playing a vaguely familiar game. A handkerchief was placed equidistant between two teams, the umpire allotting each child a number so there were two ones, two twos, two threes etc. If your number was called, you had to rush forward and beat your opponent to the hanky. *'Mandarín...Mandarín...número...trés.'*

The inevitable scuffle ensued between two young lads. Nannies rushed forward to quell the riot. It was the call of *'Mandarín ...'* that struck a chord somewhere at the back of my mind. As I was admiring the rich colours of the rose windows from the dark, gloomy interior, I remembered hearing that cry under the lemon trees in the Palace gardens in Seville.

The town itself I liked. It was unpretentiously attractive, with wooden colonnades around the squares, market places bustling with activity, fine palaces and a maze of narrow streets in which to wander freely. It amused me to see signs on every bar door proclaiming *'Hay Limonada',* as if it were a town of teetotalers.

I slept between clean white sheets in a tidy hostel off one of the back streets near the fish market.

The next morning I headed south across the river Torío. New blocks of flats were mushrooming everywhere, dwarfing older, crumbling houses. I had twelve kilometres to walk down the main road to Mansilla de las Mulas, where I could turn east again on a dirt road to Sahagún. It is about one hundred miles as the crow flies from León to Burgos, where the De Suso Mata family were expecting me, though I had let them know no specific time of arrival. Such things were simply not possible. I was looking forward to seeing Manuel.

Easter holiday traffic crashed by, shaking the graceful, painted wooden pillars of the old store house where I had lunch. Mansilla was a small, fortified town ringed with high mud walls, very pretty in a dusty sort of way. The Bar España was a smoky gambling den. I stopped to drink a glass or two of wine before setting out on the roads across the plain. I got a good rest that night in a wood, the only shelter for miles around. The moon was almost full, shining on the white bones of the skeleton of a dog.

The 17th April was an uneventful, tiring day. Sahagún was full of monuments to its glorious past. A bold notice announced that the visitor should visit the museum in the Cluniac monastery, so I dutifully rang the bell and waited. Footsteps sounded hollowly behind the thick, studded oak door, the grille opened, the gold teeth of a smiling nun glinted in the shadow.

'I'm sorry, but we're not open today. If you would like to come back on Monday ...'

The plain stretched on, with not a spot of cover for a camp. Outside Moratinos there were more hillocks with doors set into the sides, perhaps the cave dwellings of some ancient Iberian tribe, but more likely cellars. With relief, I spotted a stand of trees in the distance over to the north. To get there, I had to crunch over fields of lentils and young corn dotted with wild grape hyacinths. The stand turned out to be a garden, an oasis in the desert, fenced off from the wind. Frogs hopped madly back to the pool, a young cherry tree was in blossom. There was just enough room between the plots of vegetables to stretch out and sleep. A nightingale sang in the night.

A tree on the meseta —
a rare sight

The towers of the church at Bustillo appeared on the horizon. The dirt road made for easy walking, but this was outweighed by the mental effect of the landscape. The towers seemed to hang there indefinitely, coming no closer however hard and fast I walked, the circular dovecots and houses of adobe merging into the landscape, blotting out all sense of time. There was nothing to look at except the sky. *'Si el cielo de Castilla es alto, es porque lo habrán levantado los campesinos de tanto mirarlo'* (If the sky in Castile is

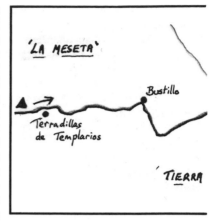

high, it is because the peasants have lifted it by looking at it so much). The wind was relentless, tiring, fraying the nerve ends. It became perfectly understandable that Don Quixote should mistake a flock of sheep for a great army.

If you fly over England on a clear day it is a patchwork of fields and woods, every inch carefully cultivated, well husbanded, man making his mark on nature. But here the elements and nature conspire against him, moulding him, working on *him*. The land is described variously as austere, harsh, arid, bleak, barren, the Spanish talk of *'Cainismo'*, the curse of Cain that has fallen on the poverty-stricken, ignorant, tenacious, isolated inhabitants who farm the land on the dry farming methods introduced by the Moors. They have their sayings: *'Más caga un buey que cien golondrinas'* (the ox is always bigger than the frog), or *'lo mío es mío pero lo de todos no es de nadie'* (What's mine is mine but what's everybody's is nobody's) —they are not communists by nature.

In some places where the wind and storms have stripped the top soil from the ridges, population density falls to eight or nine per square kilometre. Irrigation has helped but only in a few areas, because the rivers that drain the old lake basin to the Duero have cut deeply into the surface, making it very expensive to raise the water to the right level. Yet this area is luckier than those further south, for here at least, the melting winter snows allow the wheat a better start.

Historically, I was walking the northern edge of the Tierra de Campos, the *Campi Gothici* settled by the Visigoths in return for their services to the Roman Empire. They were an elite minority of warriors, electing their King according to his 'worthiness', which led to bitter feuds and rivalries that weakened their resistance to the Moorish invasions. The Leonese Monarchy claimed to be their

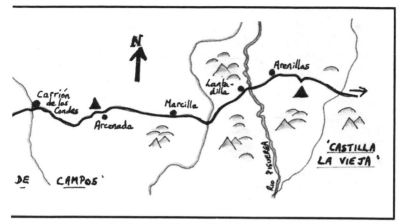

descendants, while the Christian Knights inherited their warrior blood. To the man who wanted to get anywhere in the system it was very important firstly to prove that one came of a pure-bred line without a hint of Moorish blood and secondly, to guard your honour as your life. The word *Hidalgo,* the equivalent of the British 'Gentleman' is a corruption of *Hijo del Godo,* 'Son of the Goth'.

Fears of not finding any food were dispelled in Carrión de los Condes, which was not as impressive a place as the name implied. A shepherd was herding his flock along the road on the other side of the town. He complained bitterly that the farmers were ploughing up every available inch of land, forcing him to graze his sheep in the gullies and along the verges of the road.

'You need to have a hundred eyes when you're on the road, because nobody bothers to slow down.'

I asked if he knew of any place where I could spend the night. He suggested a hermitage just off the road an hour or so away.

I camped in the portico of the hermitage. Roses were growing up the whitewashed, solid stone pillars, there were seats and old millstones on the closely cropped grass around, vineyards too, the vines themselves like lumpy, deflated footballs, each in its own hollow. Evening was drawing in, I was moved by the beauty and simplicity of the place, content to watch the sun set and the full moon rise, blotting out the stars with its cold white light as it did so. It was Easter.

I slept well, though the stone slabs of the porch were rather hard and cold. The only company I had all morning was that of a beady-eyed green frog who watched me as I made breakfast in his ditch out of the wind. The high point of the day came when walking through

Lantadilla in the company of a young student from Valladolid who had been in Guatemala at the same time as I had. We were waylaid by a tipsy teacher from Madrid, back in his native village for the holiday, who brought us a glass of chilled red wine and then lectured us for half an hour on how good life had been under Franco and how people now had too much liberty and abused it.

Paco came with me as far as the Roman bridge that crosses the river Pisuerga, the old border between the Kingdom of León and that of Castilla la Vieja, the traditional heart of Spain. The Spanish language is, in fact, the Castilian dialect spoken by the people of this region. I went on alone over the bridge, walking until nightfall, when I built my shelter in an eroded ravine that gave a measure of protection from the biting wind. The temperature dropped very quickly when the sun had set. *'En Castilla, ya se sabe, nueve meses de invierno, y trés de infierno'* (In Castile, as everyone knows, there are nine months of winter and three of hell).

The moon fooled the birds, who started singing much too early, though quite where they had spent the night I will never know. The plastic sheet was stiff with beautifully patterned frost. The landscape was changing, becoming more hilly, the soil grey. Foamy white rocks were piled by the side of the fields in mounds, the houses were once again built of stone. A combination of lack of food, sleet and a viciously cold wind kept me on the move through the little villages on the old pilgrim road. I was approaching a station in the outskirts of Burgos when the level crossing barriers came down. I ran, the pack bumping up and down on my back awkwardly, just making it onto the platform as the train pulled in. The station master held up the train while he got me a ticket, accepting 15 pesetas instead of 27 as he didn't have any change. A few magic minutes later I was in Burgos. It was Monday, 20th April.

I went the rounds of hostels until I found a bed in the 'Pensión General Mola'. Emilio Mola Vidal was the nationalist commander of the Army of the North

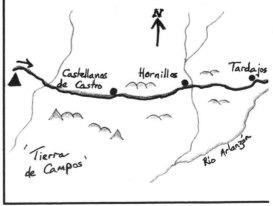

78

during the Civil War. Antony Beevor described him as playing the Cid to Franco's Alfonso. He it was who said such things as 'Those who are not with us are against us' and 'It is necessary to spread an atmosphere of terror. Anyone who is overtly or secretly a supporter of the Popular Front must be shot'. He was killed on 3rd June, 1937 when his plane crashed on take-off from Burgos airport.

The *pensión* was run by Señor Navarro, a thin, sad, grey-haired man who was having to do all the cooking and cleaning as his wife was in hospital. Frank Sinatra was crooning sweetly on television when I arrived. I shared a room with two old men, Gregorio and 'El Ciego'. Gregorio was in bed already with a towel wrapped around his head as he felt ill. 'El Ciego' was middle-aged, blind and completely drunk. The night was spent shaking Gregorio's bed to stop him snoring like an old pig, and being woken by 'El Ciego' singing at four o'clock in the morning, groping around the room looking for something that he couldn't see. According to Gregorio, who was once a shepherd and now on a state pension, he got his money once a week and then blew it all on alcohol. They were kind to me though, and the hostel was cheap, the bed comfortable enough.

I visited the old part of the town in the early hours of that first morning before there were too many people around, admiring the soft ash-grey colour of the walls and the sharp, jagged spires of the cathedral, which Gautier described as a 'whirlpool of sculpture'. I found it too ornamental, all sense of line lost in the mass of heavy detail. The town itself grew down from the castle towards the banks of the river Arlanzón. It had its heyday in the sixteenth century, when the population was 21,900, but this fell to 3000 in the eighteenth century. During the Civil War it became the headquarters

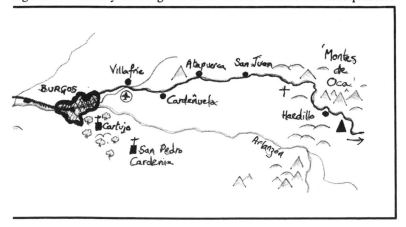

for the Nationalist Government and has now become one of the areas of industrial development sponsored by the government.

I was wandering the uninspiring streets on the other side of the river, eating an orange, when to my surprise, I distinctly heard someone call my name. I turned round to find a small woman with kind brown eyes looking up at me quizzically.

'Are you John Waite?'

'Yes, I am. Who are you?'

'I'm Ana, the sister of Manuel. We've been expecting you to arrive for a while now. I thought it must be you. I'm on my way to my father's office. Do you want to come?'

She introduced me to her father who made walking signs with two fingers of his right hand and then pointed to his temple.

'*Está chiflado.*' (You're bonkers.)

Despite my insanity, I was invited to lunch at their flat. The tent I had sent from Portugal was waiting for me, but I sent it back to England the next day. Señor de Suso Mata was a large man with somewhat melancholic eyes. He quizzed me about my journey, keeping my glass well filled with deliciously fruity wine while his wife, a fine cook, served a heavenly meal. Manuel, my former student, was in Madrid but his brother Juan and two sisters Ana and Beatriz were there. After lunch we retired to the sitting room, where Señor de Suso opened a bottle of whisky in my honour. I lunched there every day during my stay.

The afternoon passed quickly as more and more friends arrived. In the evening we went out on the town, moving from bar to bar with a drink and a smoke in each. By one o'clock in the morning I was asleep on my feet. They did their best to persuade me that the night was young, but I retired to the hostel across the river through the cold, deserted, lamplit streets. It seemed to take an incredibly long time to get there.

The weather got worse, attempting to snow, the temperature dropping below freezing point. I was not going to continue in such conditions. The days merged one into the other. Juan lent me his bicycle for a tour of the surrounding countryside. I visited the Trappist monastery of San Pedro de la Cardeña, where the Cid lies buried beside his wife. It was here that he said good-bye before going into exile, swearing never again to cut his beard. He became known as *Barba Velluda* or 'Hairy Face'. Before a battle he had to plait his beard, then tuck it inside his helmet so that his enemies would not take unfair advantage. He died in 1099, at the age of 56.

I also went to see La Cartuja, a 'closed' monastery where they never come out or speak and Las Huelgas, a convent for nuns of aristocratic birth where the Nationalist Cabinet took an oath of allegiance to Franco and Spain.

Manuel arrived on Saturday and took me out for a meal, then on to a discotheque where I danced the night away in my boots. In the week that I was there I came to know more people that I would normally meet in a year. I would be sad to leave the city and the De Suso family who had made me feel so much at home.

I had got to bed at three o'clock that morning and my recollections of the rest of the day are hazy. Ana and Mirasol accompanied me as far as the outskirts of town before saying good-bye and turning back along the busy road. I took a track past the airport from which three squadrons of bombers of the Condor Legion had taken off on 26th April 1937 to carpet bomb Guernica. It was still chilly, the wind returning now that I was back out in the open countryside. It began to snow lightly as I crossed newly set plantations of pines and some old scrub woods along a waterlogged path. My boots soon got soaked through and my feet were sore. I took shelter from the filthy weather in the doorway of an old watermill. The owner saw me crouching there and kindly came to open the door so that I could get out of the wind. His dog barked furiously until it smelt sausage, then turned very friendly, wagging his tail and rubbing up against my legs. I gave him nothing for his pains. When they had left, I set up kitchen among the cobwebs, dust and mouse droppings, watching the river rush by underneath the rotting floorboards.

The temperature rose slightly and the snow turned to rain, which stopped in the afternoon. Occasionally the sky would clear briefly to expose the massive, rounded dome of the peak of San Millán in the Sierra de la Demanda to the south.

I camped on soggy pasture-land outside a village, sleeping in longjohns and a sweater as a precaution, waking to find with a shock that the world had turned white, the plastic weighed down with six inches of fluffy snow. I was perfectly warm in my sleeping bag, however, and went back to sleep. An hour or so later I packed up quickly, shaking the snow off the plastic, and followed the padmarks of a dog down to the village of Rábanos. There was no cafe, no one in sight in the still, white alleys. The owner of the cafe in the next village, Valmala, welcomed me with a glass of sweet muscatel. I asked if I could use one of the tables to cook my breakfast. He watched with interest as I set up the stove and set about making porridge.

'Would you like some eggs?' he asked.

News travelled fast. It wasn't long before a group of villagers had gathered round to watch the eccentric Englishman eat his porridge and fry eggs and bacon, wondering at his ability to stay out on such a night and not freeze to death. I explained how my tent worked, feeling pleased that the system was now nearing perfection. It sounded as if it was raining, but it was only the noisy fountain in the square outside and the melting snow dripping from the roof. I set off warm and happy to Pradoluengo.

It was a town of no particular interest, although the people in the covered market where I bought a generous portion of liver for supper were kind and friendly. It's principal industry was the manufacture of socks, so I bought a couple of pairs and threw two older pairs away. The ash, plane, oak and chestnut trees were just beginning to come into leaf. I took a short cut across the mountains, passing villages that were mostly abandoned or already in ruins. It was hard going and I would have done better to keep to the road. A week's rest had been sufficient to soften the skin on my feet so I had to stop and

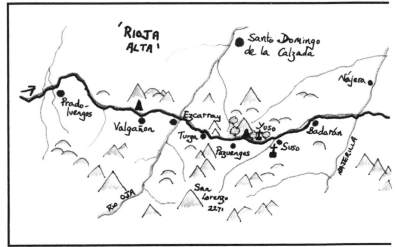

wash the blisters that had formed. It was a mundane task, quickly accomplished, quite routine. 'No hay atajo sin trabajo' as they say (there is no short cut without hard work).

The path led into a lush green valley, where the hedged fields were rich with dandelions and buttercups. Primroses brightened the banks of the river and in the distance I could hear the dull clinking of cow bells. The Iberian Peninsular slopes slightly west, so all the main rivers run into the Atlantic except the one after which it is named. I camped by the 'Church of the Three Fountains', whose waters run down to the Ebro, which in turn flows into the Mediterranean Sea.

Next morning I followed the stream down to Ezcaray, on the banks of the Río Oja, which gives the province and wine its name.

82

The young leaves of willow, alder and poplar rustled lightly in a warm breeze, a tourist passed, camera in hand, out to catch the sharp clarity of the morning light in the pretty streets of the village. I bought provisions for the day at the Co-operative and fresh, crusty rolls from the bakery before following two cows up the path to Turza, which lay at the top of a steep, overgrown valley filled with the scent of wild flowers and blossom, the peaks of San Lorenzo stark white against the deep blue sky. A shepherd boy took fright, running off among the crumbling walls of the long-abandoned village. I found water for breakfast at the fountain beside the church. The roof had fallen in, the bells were gone from the cracked tower where the remains of a human skeleton lay among the rubble, the skull crushed.

Thick snow covered the pass above the village. I took one last, long look at the mountains before pushing down cross-country to

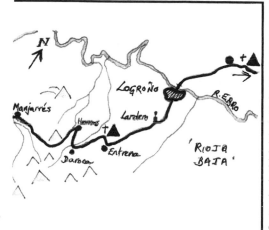

Pazuengos, yet another deserted village, though three men and an old woman were cutting poles for fences on a shelf overlooking the fertile, irrigated trough of the Ebro valley, partly hidden by a purple film of industrial pollution. I asked them why the villages were so deserted. The answer was simple, one I had heard many times before.

'The young ones watch television and it shows them a completely different world with different values, they get restless, unhappy, bored with the hard life up here, start dreaming of the easy money waiting for them in the cities. In the end they always leave, coming back once or twice a year for a holiday sometimes, but that's it. Twenty years ago there were seventy families living in this village. Now there are three and none of those left are young. When we die, the village will die with us.'

This is happening in all the remoter areas of Spain, an exodus of almost half a million people every year. First they move to a neighbouring town, then to a provincial capital and finally to one of the big industrial centres like Barcelona or Madrid, where the population increased by 78% between 1960 and 1975. The government provides no incentives for working the land, rather encouraging the mass migration, for a figure of 20–25% of the labour force in agriculture is much too high for a modern, industrial nation that has designs on joining the European Economic Community.

Grazing horses lifted their heads in surprise as I hopped down from the mountain to San Millán de la Cogolla where I left my staff and pack in the corner of a dark cafe, downed a glass of rich red wine, grinned at the apparition in the mirror and walked down the street towards the imposing monastery of Yuso. A relatively young Benedictine monk was beginning to show me round when the bell rang. He hurried off to answer it, coming back with four very English tourists. We greeted each other guardedly.

'Good afternoon.'

'Good afternoon. Lovely day, isn't it?'

'Yes, it has been, hasn't it?'

The prize possession of the monastery is an old Latin Codex called the *Glosas Emilianenses*. In the margin on page 72 of the manuscript some anonymous monk had jotted a translation of the Latin into his native Castilian dialect, the earliest recorded words of Spanish, a humble start to a language now spoken by over 300 million people. The monks are also proud to have the first extant writing of Basque, a strange language indeed, ancient but not Indo-European. The grammar is positively neolithic: 'I give the book to the boy' rendered as 'Book-the boy-the-to in the act of giving I have-it-him'. No one really knows its origins, though many have been tempted to speculate. Abbé Dominique Lahetjuzan, who died in 1818, was convinced that 'Euskara' was the language spoken by Adam and Eve in the Garden of Eden. Abbé Diharce de Bidassouet countered with the statement that it was quite clearly the language spoken by the Creator himself.

After the tour I sat on a bench in the courtyard with the monk, who was very friendly and recounted the story of San Millán with great enthusiasm. It seems he was a humble shepherd of the area until the day that he had a vision and went to sit at the feet of Felix, a hermit who lived on Mount Bilibio. He then went to live alone in a cave on the slopes of the mountain above the monastery. His reputation for saintliness and miracles grew so much that Bishop Didimus offered him a post as parish priest, despite the fact that he had not been formally trained. He accepted, but when the bishop heard that he was distributing the church's wealth among the poor, he immediately got the sack. He went back to his cave, where a group of disciples started a primitive monastic community. Forewarned by God, he died in AD 574 at the age of a hundred.

I was puzzled by the existence of two monasteries, Yuso and Suso.

The monk explained that the smaller one, Suso, hidden in the trees in a cleft of the mountain above, was the original building, whereas Yuso had been built later, in the middle of the eleventh century when King García decided to have San Millán's body transferred to the cathedral at Nájera. All went well until the cart arrived in the valley below Suso, at which point the oxen refused to budge any further. This was taken as yet another sign from God and the younger, more magnificent monastery was founded there, by the river. His remains are kept in the crypt in an ivory casket beautifully sculpted, the hand of God announcing the miracle. It was looted by Napoleon's soldiers in 1809, but luckily a resourceful monk thought to transfer the remains to a plain wooden box before they arrived.

'Do you think anyone would mind if I spent the night up there?'

'No, not at all. There's a spring just behind the church so you don't need to carry any water with you. *Vaya con Dios.*' (Go with God.)

The sun was now close to the horizon so I cut straight up the side of the mountain to the chapel, built around the caves where Millán had spent his life. The building itself was a wonderful mixture of architectural styles, solid visigothic, heavy romanesque and elegant mozarabic combining to give it a unique atmosphere. In a recess was the original tomb of black alabaster. The water from the nearby spring was incredibly sweet and thirst quenching. The saint had chosen his spot well.

I kept away from the more densely populated areas and main roads the next day by following tracks that ran parallel to the Ebro over the rolling foothills of the Cordillera Ibérica. Fine fields of strong, dark green wheat alternated with vineyards, the earth a reddy-brown, stone outcrops left for rough pasture and scrub woods, the houses built of red brick or mud between beams set on solid stone foundations. Peasants hoed their rows of potatoes and vegetables, while some roadworkers cleaned up their tar lorry in preparation for the May Day Parade. A lift from the driver of a mule cart took me into Medrano, a small town at the head of the valley that led to Logroño. A subtle change was occurring, the atmosphere was different, the houses much taller, plastered and painted. A cross by the roadside carried a photograph of the deceased man in his Sunday suit; the avenue was lined with flaky plane trees. I had crossed into the Mediterranean region.

I rose early from an uncomfortable night to cross the Ebro at Logroño. Outside Lardero was a large, square monument with statues of a group of civilians, respectable, besuited men, proud women and one small child. Families were laying wreaths and saying prayers at the base, where an inscription read: *'PARA QUE ESTAS LOCURAS NO SE REPITEN'* (May such madness never happen again). Something nasty had happened but they didn't say what.

Everything was closed in Logroño, where the houses had balconies enclosed in glass as they did in Madrid. An elderly woman went by, speaking unintelligible Basque to her companion. The *'Codex Calixtinus'* says they 'talk like a barking dog', Voltaire speaks of 'a little people who dance at the foot of the Pyrenees'. A young boy asked if he could try my pack on as I stood and watched a game of Pelota off the central square. He stood there proudly showing off to his friends, without moving.

'Is that *Pelota Vasca* they're playing?'

'*Riojana, viejo,*' they scolded.

I thought I might get a good view of the way on from the fortified heights of Viana, perched above the Ebro trough ten kilometres away. From its walls, I could see it, a track meandering past clumps of rock covered with gorse and heather, a yellow line against the soft green, well-watered land. A group of bereted men came up to inspect the map as I looked out. I asked if they knew anything about the monument at Lardero. There was silence for a moment, then one of them spoke.

'It's the monument to thirty-one civilians killed at La Barranca by the Nationalists. One of them was a child aged four.'

Thirty-one out of seven thousand killed by local purge committees, despite the fact that they had put up little resistance. The same thing happened all over Spain, adding another 200,000 dead to the half million or so killed during the Civil War and the 400,000 that fled to camps in France and other countries. With Franco in absolute control of the army, strikes were made illegal, agrarian reforms made under the Republic were abolished, and women were even liberated from having to work outside the home. He worked hand in glove with the Church expropriating the land of Republicans and giving it to loyal subjects in much the same way as the land conquered from the Moors was handed over to the Christian Knights at the Reconquest. The role played by the church was sickening. In the Basque Country the Carlists were offered a year less in purgatory for every 'Red' that they killed, the same kind of promise Ayatollah Khomeini makes to his boy soldiers. The Bishop of Burgos justified the killings and cruelty by saying that it would mean a shorter war. Talking of mass executions, a certain Father Martin Torrent was able to say 'Can any greater mercy be granted to a soul which has gone through life separated from God?' How Hilaire Belloc could possibly come to the

86

conclusion that it was 'a trial of strength between Jewish Communism and our traditional Christian Civilisation' will never be known.

> *'Tienen, por eso no lloran*
> *de plomo las calaveras*
> *... ordenan*
> *silencios de goma oscura*
> *y miedos de fina arena.'*

(Federico García Lorca, *Romance de la Guardia Civil Española,* 'they have skulls of lead, which is why they do not cry ... they impose a silence like dark rubber, a fear like fine sand.')

I was tired of the weight on my shoulders and my right ankle was causing me some pain. I needed to camp as soon as possible. A stone shelter hidden behind a hillock with a stream running by and surrounded by wild mint seemed exactly right. Four swallows came flying out in panic as I ducked through the doorway to inspect: an earth floor, a few stones and a tiny window to let in the air was all I could see. It would be warm and cosy, another home for the night.

I was woken by the sun streaming through the doorway onto my face. Outside, on two almond trees, the fruit was already the size of a prune stone. I packed up and set off happily, my ankle better for the rest. In the fields that rolled down towards the Ebro two men were rhythmically scything alfalfa, swishing methodically down two neat rows. The village of Lazagurría was silent, the wide streets empty except for a woman sweeping the pavement outside her house.

'Could I have some water?'

'Of course, young man. Where are you going?'

'Pamplona.'

'On foot?'

'Yes.'

'*Ai, pobrecito!*' (you poor thing). Do you not have enough money to take the bus?

My right ankle began to cause problems again, making me wince from time to time, but I thought the pain might disappear if I ignored it. A notice in large black letters on the side of the church in the spacious square in Sesma announced:

'Home for the night'

NO PELOTA PLAYING. This was unusual, since many churches had lines and numbers painted on their walls for precisely this purpose. It was obviously where the game had originated, like Fives between the buttresses of Eton College Chapel.

A beckoning cry came from a nearby

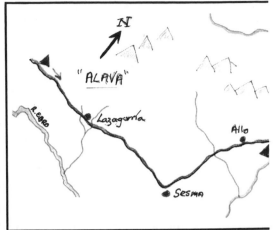

cafe. A blast of loud rock music hit me between the eyes. A group of tiddly youths who were lounging around in the semi-darkness offered me a beer, which I accepted gratefully. They said they were meant to be out in the fields picking asparagus that afternoon, but had thought it better to wait for the heat to die down a little before going out. I limped out of town. The pain was not going to go away after all. I resorted to howling into the wind and singing to take my mind off it, but progress to Allo got slower and slower. I went into a shop there to buy provisions for the weekend and ask if they had a bandage.

'Hey, Luisa, there's a foreigner just come in. You'd better look after him, see if you can understand what he wants.'

'Oh, all right, Fernando. Yes?'

'Good evening, Señora. I wondered if you would be so kind as to cut me a medium-sized slice of that delicious looking cheese you have under the glass there, next to the cartons of strawberry yoghurt?'

She looked at me with raised eyebrows. Her husband glanced at her from the other side of the shop, the atmosphere became instantly more friendly.

'You speak Spanish very well.'

'Well, I try, but I'm a bit rusty at the moment.'

'Where are you from?'

'England. Ickleton, Cambridgeshire.'

'You say Cambridge? Well, there's a coincidence! There's a great university there, is there not? One of the village girls went off to learn English at one of those special schools they have there for foreigners. Blow me if a month later she didn't marry one of the teachers and now she travels all over the world with him.'

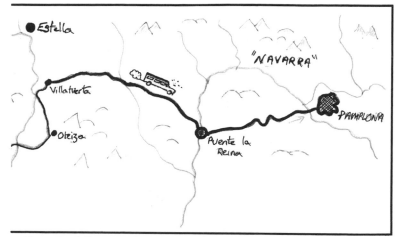

'Amazing! Do you know anywhere I can get a bandage for my ankle?'

'Try the chemist down the road. If it's not open just ring the bell.'

It was not open and no one answered the bell. I hobbled on, camping in a pleasant, leafy spot by a large, collapsing watermill on the banks of the River Ega. I didn't get up till past eleven. It was Sunday, after all, and I had no desire at all to walk anywhere. I made my way gingerly to Oteiza where everyone was dressed in their Sunday best and looked straight through me. I thought with a certain horror that I too would be buried in the clothes that I was wearing that day. It was still more than twenty miles to Pamplona, the city of Pompey, across hills and mountains that would put the finishing touches to the sprain. It was senseless to struggle on; it was time to swallow my pride and take a bus. The situation was not as bad as it could have been since I had made friends with a man called Alberto in Burgos. A student at the University of Pamplona, studying Medicine, he had given me his address and told me to call in when I arrived.

It took more than three hours to walk the six kilometres to Villatuerta, an appropriate name, 'Twistedville', on the main road to Pamplona. A young soldier was waiting at the bus stop, on his way back to barracks to complete his fourteen months service. Local friends quipped and joked as they passed by.

'Hah! It'll be their turn soon enough, then I'll be the one who's laughing.'

The bus arrived, packed and old. I found a seat next to a young woman who offered me a cigarette, but all attempts at conversation were drowned out by the noise of the engine and a general rattling

89

of loose metal. We ground through Puente la Reina, catching a brief glimpse of the old pilgrim bridge arching high over the river. It was not long before the apartment blocks of the city came into view. On the eleventh floor of one of these Alberto greeted me warmly and showed me in.

He lived with three other medical students. They gave me a special spray and bandaged the offending ankle, which mended quite quickly. I took the opportunity to have my boots resoled by the local cobbler, who had great difficulty finding soles that were big enough. There was time to tour the town, eat well, drink, read and watch television. The news was as depressing and bloody as ever: a general had been killed instantly by a terrorist bomb as he got into his car outside his home in central Madrid. They showed everything in graphic detail, saying an organisation of the extreme left claimed responsibility, though it was just as likely they were funded by the extreme right in an attempt to destabilise the country and prompt another coup. Bobby Sands had died in the H Block at Belfast after a hunger strike that had started on 1st March. It was a strange thought that as I had been walking he had been getting progressively weaker. The average man can expect to last eighty days without food as long as he takes water. The Spanish press accused Mrs. Thatcher of harsh inflexibility.

I met up with my friends Ana and Javier, who took me around Soria, the land of Antonio Machado. We also visited Santo Domingo de la Calzada. In the cathedral, a white cock was strutting around in a coop above one of the side altars, interrupting mass with sonorous crowing. It would seem that a family travelling to Santiago stopped at the local inn, where the innkeeper's daughter took a fancy to the son. When her advances were rejected, she took revenge by putting two silver cups in his baggage, denouncing him as the family left. She had obviously been reading her Bible. The unfortunate man protested his innocence but was hanged for theft. The parents continued sadly on their way, but found on their return from the shrine that Saint James had supported him and kept him alive. They rushed into town, demanding that he be released and pardoned, but the mayor just laughed at them.

'You don't really expect me to believe your fantasy do you? It's as likely your son is still alive as it is likely this roasted cock on the dish before me will stand up and crow three times!'

The cock promptly did so, the boy was cut down from the scaffold, and the family left, rejoicing in the miracle. The people of Santo Domingo vie with each other to provide a new white cockerel for the cathedral coop once a year.

Nine days passed before I was ready to tackle the Pyrenees and the border with France.

* * *

It was 13th May before I set off once more, with a small guitar fixed to the pack with a length of string and rubber bands made from strips of old tyre tubes. I hoped the joys of music would make up for the extra weight. I was soon sweating up the mountainsides where there was no visible path to follow, getting lost and slashed by the thick under-growth. I camped below the village of Erro in the soft grass of a meadow beside the river, watching the colours of the wild flowers slowly fading in the evening light, listening to the shallow waters burble, the birds twittering in the woods of pine and beech, and the happy hiss of the stove cooking tripe '*a la Madrileña*', a special treat to celebrate my arrival at the foot of the Pyrenees.

The story runs that Hercules, on his way to lift the castle of Geryon, a three-bodied monster who reigned over Western Iberia, was hospitably received by a petty ruler called Bebryx. Unfortunately the hero got extremely drunk over dinner with his host and ravished his daughter, who then died of grief. He realised what he'd done when he sobered up the next morning and wandered remorsefully into the mountains calling her name 'Pyrene ... Pyrene ... Pyrene ...'

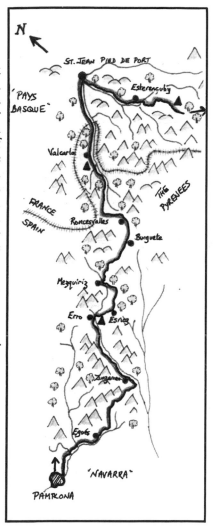

There was little traffic on the road from Burguete to Roncesvalles. I wandered round, watched closely by suspicious soldiers in the barracks above, once the old hospital that served some 30,000 meals

'The hayloft'

a year to passing pilgrims. From here the road wound up to a tiny chapel at the pass, dedicated to Charlemagne. The *Chanson de Roland* tells of how a detachment of his army under Roland was ambushed and slain to the last man by a group of Saracen Spaniards. The spring that rose just behind the chapel was perhaps the one from which the warlike Archbishop Turpin had brought water to the fainting Roland in the Oliphant. The battle took place in AD 779; the Saracens were, in fact, Basques who were angry with the Emperor for pulling down the walls of Pamplona after he had driven out the Moors.

I was fondly imagining scenes from the battle from the cross of St. James on a knoll above the chapel, when an army jeep appeared and took a track off into the woods. A minute later another drove up, followed by two army troop-carriers. Soldiers in battledress jumped out and moved off quickly, fanning out over the hillside, taking up strategic positions at the edge of the forest. An army sergeant and a dapper policeman in a light blue uniform came up and saluted, asking for my passport. He checked the pack as well, but only as far as the dirty socks on top.

'Are you after the E.T.A.?,' I asked.

'Yes, we are.'

'Is it dangerous to continue?'

The guns had made me nervous. The sergeant roared with laughter and slapped me on the back.

'Of course not, *hombre*. You have nothing to fear.'

I took the road down towards Valcarlos, on the border with France, where the young leaves of the beautiful beech forest floated above the russet floor like bright green clouds. Cuckoos were calling, crickets chirping, as the tinkling of cow bells rose from the lush meadows in the valley below. A hawk hovered in the sky above, streams flowed and cascaded down the soft slopes covered in broom and wild flowers, some new and strange, others old friends.

I was very tired. My back, shoulders and legs all ached together, my feet were sore from covering some twenty miles that day. The open door of a hayloft called me to a comfortable rest. There, above grunting pigs, I spent my last night in Spain.

PART TWO

From the Pyrenees to Grenoble

'Les vrais voyageurs sont ceux-la seuls qui partent
Pour partir . . .'

(The only real travellers are those who leave for the sake
of leaving . . .)
(Charles Baudelaire, *Les Fleurs du Mal*).

'The old style peasant, sozzled, semi-illiterate, living
little better than his animals, does still exist in some
areas, but he is a dying species.'
(John Ardagh, *France in the 1980s*).

'I allow nobody to run France down in my presence. I
consider it a very fine country indeed. On a clear day you
can see England from it.'
(John Gibbons, O.E. *'Afoot in Italy'*).

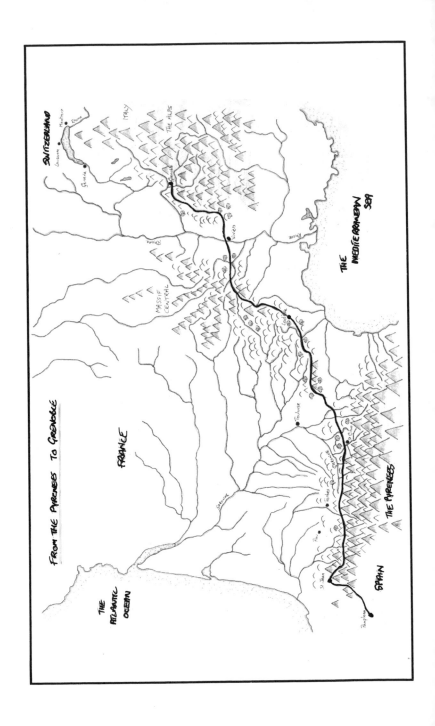

FROM THE PYRENEES TO GRENOBLE

France

The immaculately dressed border guards politely detained me while they checked my credentials with Central Records at Hendaye. All was in order. They stamped my passport and I followed the river valley down towards St. Jean-Pied-de-Port. It was 15th May. Two foals lay basking in the bright sunlight in one of the meadows, while their contented mothers stood gazing idly into the distance. Two policemen stopped me to check my passport.

'What do you do for food?' asked one.

My French was painfully rusty and awkward.

'I don't die of hunger yet.'

I walked into St. Jean across the river Nive, through the pilgrim gate in the old town walls, struck by the orderliness of life this side of the border where the streets were tidy, the houses neat and well painted. On the outskirts a bulldozer was levelling top soil for the lawn of a newly-built villa. My mind instantly returned to the mist-wrapped slopes of the Caramulo, in Portugal. It was an indication of the wealth of this new country that they could even consider the use of a bulldozer for such a domestic purpose. The frontier that I had crossed was not so much cultural, for this was still the Basque Country, but economic. Since the end of the Second World War the economy of France has boomed, leaving its southern neighbours way behind. Eighty-five per cent of its land is productive and in 1971 France supplied the EEC with between 40 and 47% of its milk, sugar and grain and between 24 and 29% of its eggs, potatoes and meat.

At a stationer's in the centre an elderly couple were picking through the postcards. I bought a map of the area that would be quite sufficient for my purposes, a *Carte Touristique* issued by the National Geographic Institute, to a scale of 1:100,000. It was good not to have to travel to Paris for my maps. In Spain and Portugal you could only get detailed maps from military or official sources. People often asked if the maps were not top secret, as if they were still living in an age when satellite pictures and high

St. Jean-Pied-de-Port

altitude reconnaissance aircraft did not exist. Unlike Iberia, again, walking in the countryside is an accepted practice, so I would no longer have to resort to tales of a religious vow to gain credibility and understanding. As early as 1943 a special committee was set up to organise a network of long-distance footpaths, and there are now some 30,000 kilometres of marked trails criss-crossing the whole of France, particularly the mountain areas. As in England, the French have a country code, rule 12 being to 'think of others as you think of yourselves'. There is even a mountain code which warns you not to go into the mountains alone and to leave word of your route and proposed time of return. Walks have been graded 1 to 8, the latter being the most difficult, requiring the skills of a real mountaineer. Walkers themselves have been defined: a 'Backpacker' being 'a walker who camps, carries all the necessary equipment to sustain life and progresses without outside help or shelter for up to a week'; a 'Long-Distance Walker' someone who 'will cover up to twenty miles a day or more, staying in hotels, *gîtes* and hostels'. I thought I should thus be defined as a 'Long-Distance Backpacker'.

I opened out the crisp, crackling new map and perused it fondly over a glass of red wine, sitting at a red metal table in a comfortably elastic chair, shaded from the midday sun by a budding plane tree. It would be no Sunday picnic excursion. The path wound for 700 kilometres (435 miles) over the High Pyrenees to the Mediterranean coast. I would follow it as far as Andorra, then head down to St. Girons, where Michael and Sandra would put me up, giving me time to rest before continuing on to the Languedoc, old haunts and more familiar territory.

My boots had been well soled at the cobbler's in Pamplona, but the restitching had tightened them substantially. A large blister had developed as a consequence and hindered progress towards Estérençuby until it was bathed in the river and carefully bound. Cows, horses and sheep with long, shaggy coats and curling horns were grazing in the pastures, the grass a rare, bright green. A school bus pulled into the square, children poured out, chattering, singing, playing ball. I hesitated to start the ascent into the mountains, as there was thunder in the air, which was now thick and heavy. I hung around for a few minutes watching the sky, the clouds sailing in. Sure enough it poured with rain. I took shelter on the terrace of an empty restaurant, where a woman was busy repainting the walls a brilliant white in preparation for the summer months of the tourist season. Her daughter had spent a month with a family in Salisbury the year before and enjoyed it so much she was off again that year. It was my conversation for the day. The people were rather more surly than they had been, and spoke French with a very heavy accent.

The storm passed over rapidly, driven away by the wind, so I set off up the track into the low mountains of the western chain of the Pyrenees, the soft slopes a model of painstaking husbandry.

'*Bon courage!*' the woman called out after me.

I was going to need it. A rainbow arched in the sky over the mountains.

I had a sorry breakfast the next morning, after a hard climb to the summit of Mount Iraukotuturu, for I found that I had left behind the bag containing my bread and most of the provisions that I had bought in St. Jean, a stupid, careless thing to do, especially in the mountains, since I had no intention of going back for the stuff, even if it meant going hungry for a while. I could smell rain on the way but a chilly wind blew up and drove away the clouds as I continued through the ancient forest of Iraty, the sun filtering through the thick tops of the trees in bright shafts. A shepherd stopped to chat. He had come up a few days before to graze his flock on the high mountain pasture until 1st November, the traditional day for a return to the valley, before the snows set in. I asked if he had trouble with the border, which is very irregular and takes little account of a shepherd's needs, but he said there were various agreements between the two countries which allowed him to take his flock over the border at certain points in the same way that the Spanish could. It must make it very difficult for the border guards to stop terrorist movements and contraband in cheap alcohol. He also told me of a *Centre Commercial* a little further on, which was heartening news.

The footpath was emblazoned with red and white stripes which were helpful, but I felt very weak from lack of fuel. My heart sank into my boots when I found the shop closed and deserted. It was obviously the sort of place that was open only in high summer. A group of walkers must have noticed the gloomy cloud that hung over me.

'Is everything all right?'

I explained the situation.

'Well, we're here for the weekend, staying in one of those chalets up there. Why don't you come and have a bite to eat with us?'

I accepted gratefully. It was tea time. They produced hot chocolate, bread and jam.

'Would you like a shower? How about staying the night? There's plenty of room, but I'm afraid we can't offer you a bed. There are plenty of cushions, though, if you don't mind sleeping on the floor.'

Roget, Nicole, Annie and the little Jean were from Hendaye, on the coast. They had come for the weekend, to get away, well stocked with provisions for feasting and drinking. The French are justly proud of their reputation as connoisseurs of the good life, and are very choosy about the food they eat: nothing but the best. This attitude to life can make them very materialistic at times, taking the form of a perpetual grumbling about the price they have to pay for what in the majority of countries would be a life of absolute luxury. The conversation changed from a long list of complaints to the subject of the E.T.A., *Euzkadi ta Azkatasuna,* 'Basque Nation and Liberty'. It seems they have an office in Hendaye and the French government leaves them in peace. Mud in the eye of Spain.

'Are you Basques yourselves?'

'Oh, yes, very much so, but we think of ourselves as French before anything else. Personally I have no truck with the terrorists. They are fanatics, ideologists. They kill innocent people to provoke a

98

reaction in the government so that they have something to fight, but it won't work. Their movement is built around the language that

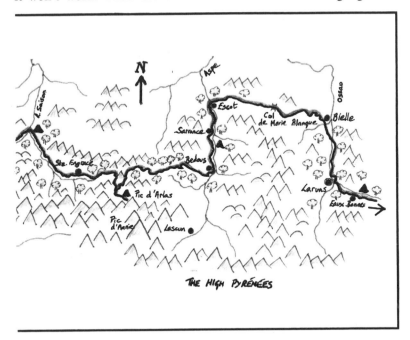

they speak, but there are too many people in the Basque Countries who no longer practise it or have never known how to speak it or had the desire to learn it, particularly in the cities where the money is made. Of course *Euzkara* is still alive, but it is not growing, it has become fossilised. If it dies or simply becomes a local curiosity, which I think likely, the terrorists will have to find another reason for their existence.'

I slept on cushions downstairs, waking to a breakfast of black coffee and warm croissants with butter and strawberry jam, then went to play in the woods with little Jean. After an hour of hide-and-seek we sat on the veranda drawing helicopters and bombs.

'Hey, Jean,' cried Annie, 'why don't you keep quiet and leave John in peace?'

I took to the road after another coffee. They passed on their way back to Hendaye, stopping to give me a lift, surprised that I preferred to walk and turned their offer down. There was no magic in sitting shut inside a well-suspended capsule of steel: the noisy engine would drown the song of the river and birds, the croak of frogs. The smell of petrol and plastic seats would cover that of flowers, fresh air, wet grass and animals, the windows would shut out the wind, the roof block the sun and sky and most important of all, we should go too fast. They would soon be home, but what adventures would befall them if they were to walk to the coast instead! Then they would know that they had been away. I was perfectly happy to walk, to feel the earth beneath my feet. I had been independent of the combustion engine for long enough now to stand back and look at it for what it was, a convenient vehicle for getting from one point to another at good speed without travelling in any other sense.

I stopped outside Larrau to rest my aching back and shoulders while washing my blistered feet. Two pigeons sat on the grey wall opposite outlined against the snow capped Pic d'Orhy, which marked the beginning of the High Pyrenees. Cattle grazed in the fields around, sharing their pasture with a plain chocolate baby donkey and a tan pony with a swishing blond mane and tail. After shopping for much needed food, I followed the noisy, rushing, boulder-strewn river until evening set in; time to camp and sleep. Moonlight slowly lit the valley as the mosquitoes began to dive and zing.

The lane wound up to Sainte Engrâce, where I stopped to visit the eleventh-century church. The clock struck twelve as I pushed open the iron gate and passed through into the well-kept graveyard. The headstones had names like Arouexeko, Astainhandy, Chutako. Inside, beneath the bell tower, was a wooden balcony with chairs and rows of hat pegs on the wall. For some reason the pews all faced this balcony rather than the altar. Almost fifty names graced the monument to those who had fallen in the First World War. France lost a million men at Verdun alone.

'The pointed stooks of hay'

The sun was shining brightly but the wind was very strong, doing its best to catch me off balance and knock me over. A hawk curved in the currents above, two cows watched myopically as I ate my lunch: sardines again. There were echoes of Galicia in the pointed stooks of hay and the use of bracken as bedding for the animals.

It was a good day, the path twisting up towards the Pic d'Arlas, taking me above the snow line, where I frequently got lost because it was covered by drifts. The climbing itself was not pleasant from then on, for I kept grazing my shins on rocks hidden beneath the snow, slipping down between them, cursing. The one advantage was that the snow muffled the sound of my footsteps that usually frightened away any animals before I had a chance to see them. On a drift in one of the gullies two fox cubs were playing together, running happily in circles, chasing their tails, wrestling together, nipping each other's ears.

At 1800 metres I found shelter at the base of a ski lift and settled down for an early night. I would need all my strength and energy to cross the pass to Lescun the next morning, a shallow trough between the peaks of Arlas and Annie, the snow and ice glinting in the light of the full moon. The wind sang all night in the wires overhead.

I ventured on next morning. No path was visible, but I thought that I would be all right if I followed a compass bearing and walked with due caution. The wind hammered down from the heights, knocking me over as I slid and slithered on the slippery ice. Suddenly the innocent looking snow gave way beneath me. I dropped, startled, into a hole some four feet deep. The snow had formed a roof over the gap between two rocks, melting away to leave nothing but a thin crust through which I had plunged. I hauled myself out, shaken and unnerved, wondering what I would have done if the hole had been thirty feet deep. The same thing happened again. I sat back against the top of a pine that protruded from the snow to take stock of my situation. In an hour I had covered about half a mile. It was perfectly clear that I would have to abandon my plan: I was not equipped for such conditions and it was foolish to continue alone.

So I slid gracefully down the ice to the idle ski resort I had passed the evening before. One of the cafes was open, thankfully, the owner a large man with a splendid double chin and a vast expanse of stomach covered with a faded blue apron. I told him of my escapade on the slopes.

'You must be crazy to even think of trying to get over the pass at this time of year. I know it well, but at the moment I'd have difficulty getting over it with skis on, particularly with the wind that's blown up these last few days.'

His rather more elegant wife added:

'You really should know the path is impassable for another month —until mid June at the earliest!'

I hung my head in shame, pensively dunking a croissant that I could ill afford in hot, milky coffee. A look at the map showed the path frequently crossing passes well above the snow line, often over 2000 metres. I would have to keep to small roads and lanes in the foothills when a path was not possible. It was a great disappointment. An hour or so later I stopped to build a fire and cook breakfast. My sense of despondency only increased when I made a complete mess of the *maizena*, a kind of corn flour that I had unwillingly bought as a substitute for porridge. I threw it away in disgust and was singing a slow blues when a hiker appeared on the road above. We continued together. It was the first time that I had had company on my walk since Piers left. My bad mood and memories of the morning faded as we trucked along at a good pace, talking the while. He was called Beat, a Swiss Railway Station Master, or at least that was his ambition, for he had only just finished his apprenticeship. He was very proud of the Swiss train service, particularly of its reputation for cleanliness and punctuality. It was his last day's walking—he had come from the coast in a week—and he was on his way to catch a train to Pau, where he would catch another home to put his feet up for a few days before embarking on his career. We sat eating lunch together on the banks of the Gave d'Aspe. He produced cheese and a delicious fruit bread that he had brought all the way from Switzerland, saying he wasn't very fond of French bread and nothing could compare with Swiss chocolate or cheese. We slaked our thirst later in Bedous with a cold Kronenburg and then shook hands.

'By the way, would you like the rest of the bacon I brought with me?'

'That would be very kind of you, if you don't think you'll need it.'

'No, I won't need it again. I'll have supper in a restaurant in Pau this evening and I'll be home for breakfast.'

I woke from a deep, restful sleep in a ravine among buttercups, cow parsley and nettles and took the road to Escot, passing the sleepy village of Sarrance at a time when the world is still fresh and there is little traffic. I crested the Col de Marie Blanque in the midday heat, the sweat drying in a gentle breeze. A man was coming up the road wheeling a bicycle past an old *bergerie* with a slate roof and walls of stone with a beautifully solid arched doorway. He was off to artificially inseminate his cows.

'Ah, it was a sad day for the bull when they introduced A.I! They'll do it to us soon enough if the Women's Liberation Movement has anything to do with the matter. It's always been the woman who wears the trousers around here, anyway!'

He made a gesture with his right hand to show a man being led by the ring in his nose and laughed heartily. His nose was as red as a strawberry, mine white from a dollop of cream I had applied to protect it from sunburn.

'We had an earthquake here a couple of years back, in February of all times. You should have felt the earth shake, it's a strange feeling, you are so helpless. It makes you realise we are all living on a great monster that we have absolutely no power to control.'

The date above the door of his house was 1680, a common practice in places where the inhabitants take a pride in their work and local traditions. He pointed out a short cut that took me down a grassy, twisting path to Bielle. A woman was watering her garden, a remarkably tall man with twinkling blue eyes under his beret stopped me in the street between the black and white houses. He was a farmer, as well.

'It's no wonder people leave the isolated farms, you know. The life is much too hard, they see too many people living off tourism. After all, why spend the year scratching the earth for long hours when in four months, if you put up your prices enough, you can suck enough out of the tourists to sit back and relax for the rest of the year?'

'The black and white houses'

A group of schoolchildren were returning from a hiking trip, carrying little packs that had contained their picnics. Their eyes grew wide as saucers when they saw the green monster on my back.

'You are well equipped, Monsieur.'

'I have to be.'

The road bypassed Laruns, sheltering in the pastoral valley below, where the pointed pyramids of the church towers were dwarfed by the mountains that rose up into the clouds above. Eaux Bonnes is a thermal resort but it was quiet, out of season. The one cafe that was open stung me 4.50 francs, about fifty pence, for the privilege of a small bottle of Pepsi and a straw. The words of the farmer in Bielle came back to me in force. I felt deeply resentful that I should be paying not just for the Pepsi, but also for the smart BMW parked outside. I would have to be more careful in future and ask the price before ordering a drink. I spent the night in the open garage of a holiday home, tossing restlessly, disturbed by the roaring of the nearby waterfall, dreaming of marriage to Annie at the chalet, a nightmare confounded by my inability to find a suit for the occasion.

103

The morning was misty, chilly and humid, the mist growing steadily thicker, the village of La Gourette a ghostly line of buildings and closed shops. The highest part of the road on was the Col d'Aubisque at 1700 metres. I thought that there would be no problems, although a sign warned that the road was blocked. It must surely apply to cars and buses. I headed up the road in a determined way.

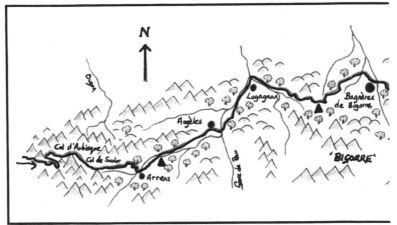

It was drizzling lightly now. Drifts of snow appeared which almost covered the road, but I clambered round or over them with no great difficulty. The road began to climb more steeply, becoming narrow, hugging the contours of the mountain as it climbed. An avalanche from the peak had completely blocked the road, sloping at an angle of 35 degrees to the side, where it dropped away out of sight into the mist. I was not prepared to turn back. If I were very careful, I could pass the twenty metres of slithery ice on foot. There was no hurry, the drop was too close to take any risks.

I began to pick my way slowly over the slippery surface, kicking out footholds in the ice, leaning slightly into the slope, jabbing my stave into the crust as a precaution. I did not wish to disappear over the side if I slipped. About half way across it began to pour with rain, gusts of wind making me sway sickeningly, the water running down over my already misted glasses, blinding me. I gritted my teeth, kicked out another foothold, then another. Time moved very slowly indeed. 'Hold on, John. Don't go too fast. Be patient, you're almost there.' With one foot back on the solid surface of the road I could breathe more comfortably, but I soon found another obstacle in my path: the blocked mouth of a tunnel. I had to hack and kick my way through, but I made it. I had come over the pass.

104

I was soaked to the skin and very cold. There was no cover or shelter of any kind in sight, so there was nothing for it but to keep moving. A two-hour forced march kept me warm enough. Eventually the *refuge* at the Col de Soulor emerged from the mist. Shelter at last, perhaps a cup of something hot, even a fire.

Monsieur Louis Poulot was the owner of the remarkable shop-cum-cafe.

'Where the hell have you been?'

'I've just come over the Col d'Aubisque.'

'Isn't it blocked?'

'Not completely, but I wouldn't try it on a motor-cycle.'

He smiled.

'You're crazy, you know that? Are you English?'

Under the overhanging roof of corrugated iron was kept anything that was remotely saleable: bric-a-brac, torn postcards, walking sticks with horn handles which he made himself, food, coffee, drink, knick-knacks, gewgaws, bits and pieces. I was the only person there.

'You'd better get over by the fire, take off some of those wet clothes and dry out a bit or you'll catch your death of cold. I'll make you a cup of coffee.'

He primed the fire with a few branches and I sat down by the flames in the alcove where there was a rough bench, taking off my boots and socks, steaming gently. A cat came and settled on my lap, two Pyrenean dogs wandered up to be stroked, their tails wagging. I fell asleep after the strong, sweet coffee had warmed me from the inside, only waking when the place was invaded by a bus-load of tourists who had been visiting the sacred shrine of the Madonna at Lourdes. The sun had come out but the mist had not lifted from the surrounding peaks, which remained sadly invisible. The pilgrims swarmed all over the shop, sending M. Poulot hither and thither. An elderly lady approached.

'How much is this stick, young man?'

'The price is marked on it, Madame. It is very cheap considering it is made by a local craftsman from the horns of a rare Pyrenean antelope. A very fine souvenir of your visit, do you not think? You have to pay M. Poulot, who is over there.'

She wandered off in his direction with the stick. It was very quiet when they had gone. M. Poulot poured two glasses of wine and mopped his brow, then came over to join me at the fire, bringing a large slice of ham for me to eat with my bread and cheese. He talked as I ate. He had two children of whom he was very proud, a son studying to be a chef and a younger daughter who was still at school, very bright, the apple of her father's eye.

'I noticed you are wearing a wedding ring,' I said.

'Yes. I was married, but my wife died when giving birth to my daughter. She was only twenty-seven. I have lived here since then alone, looking after the children. It was our twenty-third anniversary last month.'

'Her death must have been a terrible shock.'

'It still is. My daughter becomes more and more like her mother every day. Sometimes she uses gestures that I have only seen her mother use. It is strange, as if she were still here.'

His eyes clouded over with sorrow and he looked away. We sat in silence for a while, listening to the fire crackle. An elegant, self-confident policeman strode in. He wore shiny, calf-length leather boots, long white socks neatly turned over at the top, smart blue trousers with a red flash and a light blue jersey with the badge of his local constabulary sewn on the breast. M. Poulot got up to serve him a beer and turned on the television. François Mitterand appeared on the screen in the middle of a flowery and mostly empty inaugural speech. After more than thirty years of solid conservative government the people of France had voted for a change. The social structure of the country had not made the same progress as the economy, reform was needed. Mitterand was sixty-four. I remember thinking that he could do with a visit to the dentist.

'Where are you going?'

I started from my reverie. The policeman was talking to me.

'Arrens, Officer.'

'On foot?'

'Yes.'

'Where are you going to spend the night?'

'I'm not sure. I dare say I'll find somewhere.'

'Do you sleep out?'

'Most of the time. It's officially illegal in this country, isn't it?'

'Yes. Have you come far?'

'Portugal.'

'Hah! An uncivilised lot, those Portuguese, don't you think?'

'I like them. They are a kind and very hospitable people.'

The time had come to leave. I said goodbye to M. Poulot with regret. I didn't wish to leave and felt that he didn't want me to go, but neither of us said anything.

'Here. Take this as a souvenir. It's one of the cards I make to while away the winter evenings. It's a pressed Edelweiss. You have to know the mountains well before you can find them.'

I shouldered my load and clumped off down the road to Arrens, where there was no mist and the shops were still open. The grocer had Quaker Oats and knew M. Poulot well.

Edelweiss

'He's a good man, but what a tragedy, really. He told you did he? Did he tell you that his wife's brother died in an accident on the way to the funeral?'

I was sitting on the pavement outside munching through a bar of chocolate to give me the energy for the last lap of the day when a young boy cycled towards me. We swapped chocolate for chewing gum and got talking. He was called Frederick and his voice was breaking. Quite how the conversation drifted onto the subject of the effect of chick peas on his father's digestive system I can't remember, but afterwards he pedalled off to catch up a friend. I found a copse of pine trees further on along the valley, startling a rabbit that bolted off into the long grass. I slept solidly, for it had been a long and tiring day.

The river ran to Argelès, where it joined the Gave de Pau, flowing on to Lugagnan which was only a few miles from Lourdes, but I turned east towards a different Mecca, up into the mountains again, away from the traffic and asphalt. It was real tourist trap country, the boarding houses displaying signs advertising *Chambres, Tout Confort* and *Zimmer*.

I camped on soft grass beside a stone barn set in pasture full of wild flowers and slugs. The clouds that had threatened more rain during the day had been whisked away to leave the mellow lines of the worn mountains exposed, the sky a clean washed blue. The valley was suffused with pink evening light, the sharp silhouette of the farmhouse I had passed earlier stood out to the west. I wondered if the old man sitting out on the wooden terrace was still leaning on his stick watching the sun set. The chill rose as the light faded. An owl screeched, the frogs croaked, the crickets began to tune up for the night and the cuckoos finally went to sleep. Was it a week, then, that I had been in France?

107

In Bagnères-de-Bigorre there were signs of rugby fever everywhere. Their team was in the final against Béziers that afternoon. The cafes were crowded, madly excited sports cars screeched around, with black and white flags fluttering. A public holiday had been promised with no school for the children if the team won. No school ... the shops were shut until mid afternoon, so I rested on a bench in the shady central square, waiting to buy food for the weekend, which meant a heavier pack than at any other time of the week. The result of the match came out just as I was leaving. They had lost 13:22. The town went into mourning.

The view from the Pic des Palombiers above the town was impressive, the rich plains of Tarbes and Pau rolling north into the haze, the old Roman province of Aquitania. In 1152, Eleanor, Duchess of Aquitaine, was married to a young Frenchman, Henry Plantagenet of Anjou. Her marriage to Louis VII of France had been annulled a few weeks before. Two years later, at the age of twenty-one, Henry was crowned King of England. The Angevin Empire stretched from the border with Scotland to the Pyrenees, but by the middle of the thirteenth century, King John had lost all but England and Gascony, or Aquitaine, to the Kings of France. It remained in English hands until 1453, mainly due to its economic dependence on England for the export of wine. The population of Bordeaux at the time was greater than that of London.

A Citroën 2CV stopped behind me, driven by a young woman with enormous Dior spectacles.

'Would you like a lift?'

'It's all right, I'm quite happy walking, but thank you for the thought.'

'I only live round the corner. Come and have a cup of tea. Tell us some stories to brighten our lives a bit. We have some friends coming round for supper. You could join us.'

I accepted the invitation without hesitation. Françoise and Chris lived in a ramshackle house hidden in a glade of oak and chestnut trees in the fold of a hill beneath the village of Banios. The house was rented to them by the local farmer, though the State paid as they were both on the dole. They had a small son called Vincent, who had a cleft palate and couldn't pronounce his 'c's'.

'*Etoute, étoute,*' he would say. His mother looked harassed.

'*T'as fini de m'emmerder, donc?*' (Have you finished fooling around?)

We sat outside while I entertained them with the guitar and stories of wild adventures in the mountains, bears, wolves and snakes in profusion. When their two friends arrived, we tucked into spaghetti, and drank a toast to the new socialist government. They wanted to talk about Ireland, unable to understand what they saw as the complete indifference of the English towards its fate. Over generous portions of ice-cream, I tried to produce a coherent argument in defence with little success and steered the conversation instead to the adventures of a Canadian they had met in Afghanistan, who was going round the world on a penny farthing, attracting huge crowds in the process. We talked of grape picking with the Portuguese, whom they disliked, and shoplifting, which they did with no feeling of conscience.

'How do you think we got the ice cream?'

Their friends left, but not before they had invited me to stay at their house which lay a convenient day's walk east. I slept on the tiles of the kitchen floor on a carpet rescued from the dustbin. During the night it rained heavily. I smiled contentedly in a half sleep. Such a good feeling to have a solid roof over my head.

It was drizzling monotonously in the morning, the dripping woods were blanketed in mist. Françoise and Chris sat reading the paper while I played with Vincent, who seemed happy to have a companion. I had no desire at all to take off into the soggy countryside, but I didn't want to hang around either. The atmosphere was sad, their lives seemed empty and boring, bumping along from day to day with no glimmer of light at the end of the tunnel; they appeared to have lost all hope for the future. Perhaps it was just the weather. I got ready to leave.

'Why don't you wait for the weather to clear up?' asked Françoise.

'I would love to, but I might still be in Portugal if I did that.'

I set off into the mist with a destination: the house of their friends. It was a rare, comforting feeling to know where I would be that night: in a house by the railway line near Lortet. Their friends had given me an exact address in case I couldn't find it and had to ask. It added a new dimension of security, although I had got used to being homeless and never knowing exactly where I would be at night.

Francis and Martine were newly married and lived in a two up two down cottage beside the disused railway line to Tarbes, once the house of the local station master. I arrived at eight, after a good march, stopping once for a little warmth in a cafe. No greater contrast from the morning could be imagined. They were giving the kitchen a coat of pale blue paint and welcomed me with a smile, downing tools, putting on the kettle for a cup of tea, which I drank by the fire as I listened to their happy chatter over the soft choral music on the radio.

Martine prepared supper and showed me to my room after we had eaten. There was a mattress on the floor with clean sheets and an eiderdown. I drifted off that night dreaming of the world turning slowly in space, myself a contented, unimportant speck on the surface of the planet.

I stayed three nights in all, leading a peaceful, domestic life, doing the shopping, taking the dog for walks or making myself useful in the garden with a little horticultural wisdom and digging. The dog was called Rasta after Bob Marley, who had died a few days before. On the second day we collected a brand new fridge and cooker which we installed in the spotless kitchen. Martine celebrated by using the oven to cook *Pommes Dauphinoises* as a special treat. The weather had been dreary, their hospitality made it difficult to leave, but I had resolved to head on the next day come rain or shine. It would only take about three days to reach St. Girons. I had expected to come crashing out of the mountains like a wild boar, but this would have to do.

I did not stop to look around St. Bertrand, the ancient capital of the Comminges. Charging along like a horse heading for home, excited at the thought of seeing Michel and Sandra again, I camped the other side of the Garonne, slept and took to the road once more as soon as it was light. The countryside was hilly, the ridges covered in forest that looked like green wool from a distance. The roses were beginning to bloom, some early cherries were already ripe, tiny green apples, pears and walnuts were beginning to form on the trees. Calves, foals and lambs gambolled in the fields, a red squirrel 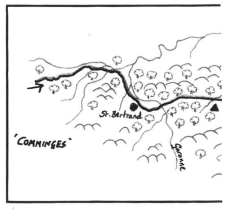 paused motionless on the branch of an oak, directly above a woodpecker that was knocking a hole in the trunk of a dead tree.

Then I was in countryside that I knew, with views of the distant snowy crags that I recognised. A beer at St. Lizier saw me over the last hill, the fortified tower of the church at Montjoie rising to welcome me to familiar territory. It was not long before I was crunching down the drive to the farmhouse, having covered a good eighty kilometres in two days. I turned the corner.

They were sitting by the front door digesting supper, happy to see me. I shook hands with Michel, kissed Sandra and soon had a drink

110

in my hand. Sandra heated up some soup and made a salad. I left my boots and socks outside. I was warm and happy, it was a pleasure to talk English after such a long time. Piers was the greatest topic of conversation. He was like a son to Michel and had spent a few weeks with them on his way back from Portugal, sleeping in the loft, giving the impression that the journey had been, more than anything else, too slow, though he said that he had never felt fitter than when he had stopped walking.

At mealtimes Michel would tell stories of his chequered career and adventures as a harsh schoolmaster in Australia or cattle rancher in Argentina, of his son who was drowned in a whirlpool while trying to save the life of another man, of the time he went round France on horseback with a friend, at the age of eighteen. One day they arrived at a magnificent château. They were called up to be inspected by the lord of the manor, passed the interview and were taken in and looked after. Another time they were fed in a rude peasant farmhouse where they ate from bowls that were hollowed out of the table itself and wiped clean after use with a piece of bread. At one point they were caught scrumping cherries by a rough farmer who threatened them

with his pitchfork, saying he would use it on their nether regions unless they paid up instantly. Only then did he let them down from the tree.

I always felt ignorant in his presence. He would spark off desires to read, learn and grow more knowledgeable, particularly about history. A history teacher himself, he could argue with facts, which soon put paid to any wishy-washy argument based on feeling and vague speculation. He was a monarchist, thought little of the Republic and even less of the new socialist government. He would test you at every turn with provocative statements: 'When hitching, you compromise your liberty' or 'Protestant countries produce no art'.

One of the first things I did was wash all my clothes, which badly needed it. I did some gardening for them, planting soya beans in the hard clay soil, but mostly I rested, ate and drank or listened and talked with Sandra while she cooked for us. The maize was sprouting, chickens ran squawking round the yard while Emily, the misnamed gander, plotted his next attack on the intruder. I wrote letters, read books, watched the sun climb and slide gently behind the familiar silhouette of the Pyrenees in the evening. The month of May bowed out. It was tempting to stay on and on, but my feet were itching. I could perhaps find work at Mas Bas if I arrived in time. The plan was to head north-east across the Ariège to Castelnaudary, on the Canal du Midi, up into the Parc Naturel du Haut Languedoc where I could join a footpath along the Montagne Noire and the ridges of the Espinouse to Bédarieux, where Piers' little house, or was waiting. Mas Bas was only a day's walk from there. I thought it would take about ten days or a fortnight.

I set off at four in the afternoon on 2nd June, after a sad farewell, loaded with bread, cheese, ham, butter, eggs and jam. With the Pyrenees shrouded in mist, I felt lonely and sad, especially when I camped in the grounds of a private zoo that was deserted, the cages empty. The water from the stream was murky and had to be boiled carefully, the night was hot, the dawn brought thunder and rain. I missed the conversation and love, the woods were oddly silent, breathing heavily. I was definitely on the road again.

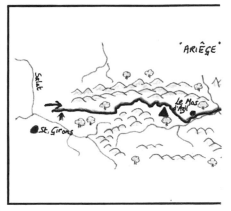

The Grotte du Mas-d'Azil was formed as the river wore its way through the soft limestone, leaving a low, wide tunnel beneath thousands of tons of rock that seemed to be just waiting to collapse and crush me like an ant beneath the foot of an elephant. It smelt of caves and was damp like a catacomb.

It began to rain heavily late that morning but I plodded on until lunchtime, when I took shelter in a slatted wooden barn in the middle of a run-down village. The population of the Ariège has dropped by

112

40% since the beginning of the century, most of the people having left for Toulouse or the more fertile agricultural belt along the river. In 1939 the population of Toulouse was 180,000, whereas now it is over half a million. The government was worried by the concentration of industry around Paris, where seventeen per cent of the 53 million people in France were living, so they promoted Toulouse as an industrial zone to counterbalance the pull of Paris. It is now the centre of the Aerospace Industry with other important chemical works. They call it 'L'Anti-Paris'.

A man walked by, the first I had seen for hours.

'Do you think it's all right if I take some water from that tap?'

It was a poor opening gambit, but it worked. He stopped and we struck up conversation. He had incredibly sparkly blue eyes hidden beneath his wide, floppy beret. Berets are out of fashion these days and only the old men wear them.

'Are you from Paris?'

My French must be improving, I thought.

'No, I'm from Cambridge.'

'*Où ça?*' (Where's that?)

'*En Angleterre.*'

' He caught sight of the guitar.

'I used to play the mandolin, you know. Sang beneath the balcony of my fiancée, I did, until I was told to belt up and stop disturbing the peace. She married me anyway,' he added with a chortle.

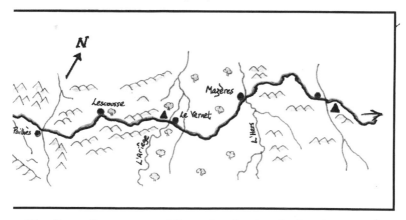

The first mile or so on a blister that has just had an hour's rest is always the worst. The pain eases off after a while as long as you don't stop, which makes for good progress and fewer rests, but the big toe on my right foot was worrying me. At about eight that evening I passed a deserted farmhouse with a spacious open barn where sheep must have been wintered. It was a good spot to camp for it was out of the wind and had a tap nearby where I could have a thorough wash in peace. The hair on the back of my neck rose when I saw a man standing by my things in the half light, swaying drunkenly. I hurriedly wrapped a towel around my nakedness and approached. It was only my ground sheet waving from the post where I had hung it. I had taken my glasses off to wash.

I walked out of the hills, across the river Ariège at Le Vernet, the fields a patchwork of tall, strong wheat, barley and oats, with a fair amount of pasture for horses. It was 4th June. The elder, dog rose and blackberry were in flower, the gardens around the houses neatly tended. There was even a rainbow. Lizards skittered away into the cracks in walls, and insects were becoming daily more numerous. I picked my way through the debris of the market at Mazères before taking to the hills on the other side, a land of châteaux with slate roofs, turrets and battlements glimpsed through the great wrought iron gates in the walls that surrounded their parks. The Languedoc has been a part of France since 1226, formerly ruled by the House of Toulouse. It is the land of the troubadours, who wrote their lyric poetry in the *langue d'oc,* the 'language of yes', spoken in the southern half of France until it gave way to the Frankish language spoken north of the Loire, the *langue d'oïl,* the mediaeval mother of modern French. *Hoc ille (fecit)* became *oïl* which became *oui.*

It was a tiring day. I was fed up with the hot asphalt lanes, which were giving me more blisters, but at least I found a pleasant spot to camp, on a knoll above the village of Salles beside a bush of wild honeysuckle that spread its heady perfume on the still, evening air.

I reached Castelnaudary by late morning, one of the major ports on the Canal du Midi. In France there are still 7000 kilometres of navigable waterways and 6500 barges plying them, transporting 95

A farmhouse near Castelnaudary

114

million tons a year compared to 5 million in England. The canal stretches from Sète, on the Mediterranean coast, to Toulouse, a distance of about 150 miles. From there the Garonne is navigable to the Atlantic coast. It was thus known as the 'Canal of the Two Seas', the brainchild of Paul Riquet de Bonrepos, a native of Béziers. Its main purpose was to avoid the sea passage round Gibraltar, thus cutting the revenues of the King of Spain. Riquet died a year before its completion, in 1681.

It was tempting to follow the shady tow-path down to Carcassone, but I chose instead to head for St Papoul and visit the old abbey there. The cloisters were beautifully cool, the Romanesque pillars carved with heads that each had two bodies, the church itself dilapidated, the air heavy with the scent of lilies. The eyes in the face of an apostle with features finely traced in the stained glass came alive with the sun behind them, while primitive lions and eagles played on the older stone columns. One had the figure of a man with an axe by his side, his arms outstretched, possibly nailed. For some reason the sculptor had got the thumbs the wrong way round.

The air had cooled and the sun was low in the sky when I reached Verdun-en-Lauragais. The pump wasn't working, so I asked a woman in the village if she would kindly fill my water bottle. We stood chatting over the half door. I asked her what she thought of Mitterand. Her husband appeared. It was amazing how their originally open, friendly faces set hard at the mention of politics and presidents. The complaints against Giscard d'Estaing rolled out. Their daughter was studying law, they had to meet the expenses of her education from their own pocket, the pension wasn't big enough, prices were going up and, oh, it was a hard life. Their daughter was summoned to prove it, but I thanked them hurriedly and beat a retreat before she arrived.

From a soft, dry field of long grass I scanned the rolling hills and the plain that I had crossed. In the morning the whole chain of the Pyrenees had been visible, peaks pink in the first rays of the sun, soaring up above the rising mist, but now they were obscured by a thin, purple-brown film of industrial smog drifting down the valley from Toulouse. I would not see them again.

I woke once to see the black sky a mass of stars, the Milky Way so bright and close I felt I should be able to touch it, but drifted off into other galaxies before I could.

The Montagne Noire is the most southerly ridge of the Massif Central and marks the beginning of the Parc Naturel du Haut Languedoc. It was with a feeling of unmitigated happiness that I left the asphalt lanes that I had been following since turning back from the High Pyrenees and took a soft, springy path through sun-dappled forests of beech and pine. I found a sunny creek at the Lac de Lampy, swam in the shallow water and then had breakfast. It is one of the lakes Riquet had built to make sure of an adequate supply of water for his canal in the hot summer months. I dried off in the sun, changed the bandage that was protecting my big toe and headed off to Arfons singing happily. Here I shopped for the weekend, overloading as usual. I stopped for supper and bed when I found a little hunter's lodge, but there were so many mosquitoes I moved on to higher ground, camping in a dark, gloomy, Tolkienish pine wood. It was a terrible night. The lakes were a perfect breeding ground for mosquitoes, but it was the tiny, invisible airborne midges that made sleep impossible, attacking in swarms, setting fire to my face. I itched, swore and sweated away the hours of darkness. At the very first hint of light I packed up feverishly and ran for the open air, wearing my cagoule as some form of protection from the insatiable little bloodsuckers.

The lake at Les Montagnés was ringed with grand holiday homes, all with mosquito netting in the windows. I climbed out of the valley to breakfast by the walls of a silent church. I was busy cooking, with my stuff laid out all over the grass to dry, when the first car arrived. I had forgotten that it was Sunday, Whit Sunday in fact, which meant Monday would be a bank holiday and the shops would be shut. I would have to open my emergency rations. More cars rolled up, out of which stepped people in their Sunday best accompanying young girls in frothy white dresses for their first communion. They

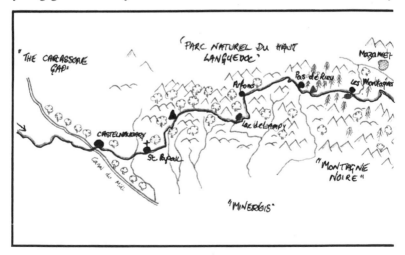

116

were polite enough not to notice me. I finished hurriedly and disappeared on the serpentine path to the Pic de Nore, where I was hoping the *refuge* marked on the map might turn out to be a good place to rest and catch up on sleep.

In St Papoul there had been a monument to a doctor shot in the Resistance, the spot where he was executed marked with a double cross. Here in the mountains there were more crosses where men of the Maquis had lost their lives. The word *maquis* means undergrowth. Most of them had fled to the mountains to avoid being sent to do forced labour in Germany. It was at the end of July 1944 that the German airforce bombed those hiding in the Montagne Noire, causing 'serious losses', but the real danger came from within: the *Franc Garde,* or *Milice,* Frenchmen collaborating with the Nazis. The Maquis lost more men through betrayal before the great battles began, than they did in fighting.

The sun began to bake the countryside. I was dunking my head in a sheep trough to cool down when a French family arrived carrying picnic baskets and children. The afternoon passed in their pleasant company as we ate a leisurely lunch in the shade of the woods. Later, a young woman and her doddery father wearing a topi approached.

'We've been looking for ages for signs marking the G.R.7, but we can only find 68, 72 and 86.'

They had mistaken the numbers on trees for those of the path. I set them right and they moved off thankfully.

The *refuge* was set off from a small road in an open wood, with water piped in from a spring. The door was not locked. Inside were wooden bunks, a large table, benches and a fireplace, the mantlepiece choked with empty bottles. Here I would certainly get a good night's sleep. An elderly woman came hobbling by, wishing me a peaceful evening in an extraordinary regional accent I couldn't place. Perhaps she was Portuguese.

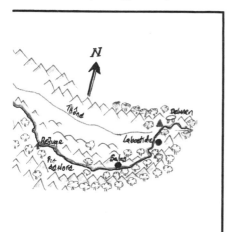

I had been alone for about a minute when I heard the sound of a car with the radio blaring. A well-fed bearded Frenchman poked his head round the corner of the hut. He asked me what I was doing and I told him. He disappeared back to his car to talk with a friend over the intercom of his 'Citizen Band' radio.

'There's an Englishman here at the *refuge*, George.'

The crackling voice of his friend carried distinctly through the still air:

'*Eh bien, on ne peut pas le foûtre dehors!*' (Well, we can't chuck him out, can we?)

The invasion began with the arrival of several flashy GTs with waving aerials. The party started with a few bottles of 'Ricard' and a game: an egg was placed behind the back wheel of a car on the gravelly slope down to the *refuge*. Each driver had to start off up the slope without slipping back and crushing the egg. Engines revved, tyres squealed, spectators cheered or jeered, stones flew everywhere. One of them hit a young boy on the temple and he was led off bleating to be molly-coddled by the busy wives and girlfriends, who were running around preparing Paella, barbecuing chops and laying out the table in the *refuge* with wine, pâté, cheese, bread and various salads. I was invited, of course, though they had little option.

They were good people at heart, carpenters, bricklayers, lorry drivers and even a former Légionnaire who entertained me with dirty stories in coarse gutter French while clipping the children over the ears if they came too close. What they all had in common was their love of the CB radio. They met two or three times a year to see each other and have a good fling. One fat little boy almost set fire to the hut with a jerry can of petrol, but he seemed unconcerned. When light faded we all packed into the hut—there must have been at least thirty of us—to continue feasting into the early hours; there was plenty of wine to loosen the tongue. We parted good friends. They dismantled the generator, the strings of electric light bulbs, let off the remaining fireworks and sped away into the night. I lay back on one of the bunks and sank into deep sleep.

It was late morning. I was bent over the spring dashing my face with cold water in an effort to get the brain cells back into action when three young girls came up.

'Are you the man who's on his way to Yugoslavia on foot?'

'Well, that direction, anyway.'

They giggled. Any ideas I had nurtured of a peaceful breakfast were shattered by the arrival of more cars soon after. Bank Holiday picnics began to take shape on all sides.

'Would you like to join us for a piece of cake and a glass of wine?'

A small boy was looking up at me inquiringly. Such an invitation was not to be turned down.

The cake turned out to be *Panettone*, an Italian delicacy usually eaten at Christmas time. A long-distance lorry driver friend had given it to them with a bottle of sweet white wine to wash it down. We sat in the shade talking. The husband was a prison officer and had lived in Djibouti, on the Gulf of Aden, where he had been in charge of the Prison Service.

'Always slept with a revolver under the pillow, just in case of trouble. Never had to use it, mind. Natives liked me. Saw I had no wish to impose my values on them, making them live like Europeans. That's the big mistake all the colonial powers have made, you know, trying to make the natives adapt to their ways when they should have been the ones trying to adapt. All they did in the end was build up resentment.'

His wife passed me a sandwich of charcoal-grilled sausage. It would be a crime to call it a hot dog. She topped up my glass with a smile. When I took my leave she gave me a further supply of sausage and a large slice of cake in case I got peckish. I needn't have worried about food for the day.

'Au revoir, Madame, Monsieur. Merci mille fois.'

'On dit pas "Merci", on dit "Merde".'

It was the kind of man he was. His last words rang in my ears: 'watch out for the snakes!'

He was right. Not long after I had set off I almost stepped on one. A small, silvery grey creature, it slid off into the rough scrub at the side of the track, leaving a distinctly snaky shape in the dust.

The view from the ridge of the Montagne Noire was magnificent, to the south were the vineyards of the Minervois, to the north the long, forested valley running east to St. Pons. I would cross over to the other side, the Espinouse, at Labastide-Rouairoux.

Once back in the forest it was a fantastic walk. I sped along on a cushion of crackling beech leaves, crashing through the undergrowth that was slowly reclaiming the mossy ruins of a forgotten hamlet, arriving soaked in sweat at a house on the edge of the town. A man was in his garden watering. I asked if I could have a little, half expecting a shower from his hose.

'My wife's in the kitchen. Ask her.'

I peered through the doorway into the clean, civilised kitchen.

'Wouldn't you prefer some wine?' she asked, filling my extended tin cup almost to the brim before adding a little water from a bottle in the fridge. The cup held a pint. I drank it down in one draught like a thirsty dog.

'Thank you very much, Madame. Just what the doctor ordered.'

The idiom did not translate very well.

'Allez, au revoir, jeune homme.'

The local bar was full of Algerians playing pool and chattering in loud Arabic. There are four million foreigners living in France. The Portuguese top the league with 866,000, but there is no real problem here as they are European and integrate quite well. The Algerians come second on the list with 780,000. Like the West Indians in Britain, many of them have lived and worked in France for a long time, arriving well before the Declaration of Independence in 1962, and their children have been educated at state schools and brought up in the country. Yet they have a different religion, a different skin colour, different customs and traditions, different food, an alien language. They normally live apart in their own areas, often in overcrowded housing, doing the most unpleasant, dirty, dangerous jobs, mostly in building and public works. The French call them the *'Pieds Noirs'* or 'Blackfeet', *'Bicots'* when they want to be particularly rude. According to the polls, the majority of Frenchmen disapprove of mixed marriages and an even greater number believe that the Algerians cannot integrate into society. Certainly it is not encouraged and their culture works against them. With 1.6 million unemployed they are the first to be accused of taking away jobs from 'real' Frenchmen, though I doubt if the average Frank would much like their jobs. They cannot feel very welcome.

A friend of theirs drew up in a plush American convertible and held an incomprehensible conversation over the noise of the car stereo cassette which was blaring Arabic wail music into the street.

I wanted to sleep by the dolmen marked on the map, but getting there involved a steep climb out. The sweat was pouring off me, my heart thumping because of the wine I had drunk earlier. I made it just before night fell. It was a magical place to sleep, like Avebury or Stonehenge.

I was covering ground quicker than I had imagined. In two days, if I pushed myself, I could be in Bédarieux. Summer had well and truly arrived and the sun beat down on the bare limestone ridge, so I was looking forward to a swim in the lake I had spotted on the map ten hard miles ahead. I stripped off, plunged in, thrashed out into the centre and lay floating on my back in the cold water for a while before heading back to sunbathe and pass away the heat of the day stretched out under a convenient bush. I was thus dozing pleasantly when I heard the sound of paddling and a dinghy hove into view, rowed by a skinny lad noticeably younger than his companion, a pretty woman in her twenties. They were both German, from a scout camp over the other side of the lake. She was doing the cooking for the ninety-odd scouts in return for which she got her keep, pocket money and a free holiday away from the office where she worked as a secretary. They paddled away. When the temperature cooled down

120

a little, I set off for an isolated hermitage called St. Martin du Froid. The path led over the ridge round eroded granite crags, following a track back into the woods once well-worn by muleteers, the stones carefully laid, built up onto the sides of giddy precipices. Four young deer crashed away through the trees.

The chapel lay at the head of a narrow valley with a clear stream running through. It had been abandoned long ago and was slowly crumbling back into the earth. The two arches and what remained of the roof were supported by stout poles. I slept between them, hoping the structure would not choose that night to collapse and pin me to the ground with no one within miles to hear my cries for help.

I survived, and scrambled down past a lake through uninhabited, overgrown countryside to Bardou the next morning. A long line of clean cars stood idly beneath the village (they couldn't get into the village) which had been turned into a cluster of holiday homes by Germans. I hurried on, taking another fine stone path into the Gorge d'Héric, where a young man with a thick black beard was hoeing a plot of vegetables beneath the tiny bridge at the base of the gorge. I waved. He returned my greeting with a cold stare. Héric village was half deserted, though there was a small community of young people living there judging by the traces of primitive habitation. John Ardagh, the author of *France In The 1980s,* reckons there are 10,000 settlers of this kind in the remote rural areas of France, an exodus from the city which started when the young became disillusioned with the events of May 1968. Then they had dropped out by the thousand, flocking to the country intent on a life of rural bliss, buying cheap in the areas where nobody wanted to live any more because life was too hard. Many of the communes split up when faced with the realities of this life, while very few of those left survived the first long winter.

A young woman with long fair hair was washing children's clothes

121

in a basin in the half-ruined village. I greeted her cordially as I passed, yet she didn't even look up or speak, she didn't even smile. It was very odd.

Late that afternoon I walked into the sleepy, leafy town of Lamalou-les-Bains in the company of a man staying at the sanatorium who had lost his thumb and forefinger in a chain saw. The terraces above the town were lined with cherry trees, the fruit ripe, irresistibly tempting. From Lamalou it was plain sailing down the south bank of the Orb to Bédarieux, where I celebrated my arrival on home ground with a litre of beer before staggering up the steep, stony path to Piers' *mas* overlooking the lights of the town. The clock tower in the centre struck ten. It was 10th June, which meant that I had been travelling for over three months now. I would take this opportunity to have a real break before walking on. The fact that I had come most of the way from the south of Portugal on foot seemed an abstract and remote achievement. My main task now was to digest the experience.

There was a note on the table from Piers beginning 'Hail John' and another from my old friend Rupert Hildyard who was staying up at Mas Bas with Ella who was awaiting her first child. Rupert's mother had bought one of the houses in the courtyard of Mas Bas some ten years before as a holiday home and I had stayed there at various times. I was greatly looking forward to seeing them again and renewing my friendship with Monsieur Auguste Balp and his wife who farmed the surrounding land. I had worked for him for three months the first time I went there and again a few years later, so I had got to know the people and the place well; as a simple farming community it must be typical of the many similar communities I had recently passed through. Perhaps I would be able to work for him again.

The tall plane trees on either side of the road from Bédarieux to Le Mas Blanc were planted for their shade, so that oxen pulling heavy loads should not suffer the midday heat. The Orb flows past below, a beautifully clean river with many pools, the fast running, shallow water ideal for trout, fat shadows flicking gently in the current beneath the surface.

At Le Mas Blanc you turn off past the church into the hills on an empty country road that winds with the stream through brittle, red lead soil and climbs gently from vineyards or scrubby pasture-land to woods of chestnut and dwarf oak. Sometimes the slopes 'accidentally' catch fire and then fresh, tender, bright green grass (excellent grazing) springs up from the blackened earth. At a crossroads one of those distinctive signs like dice set on squat pillars, courtesy of

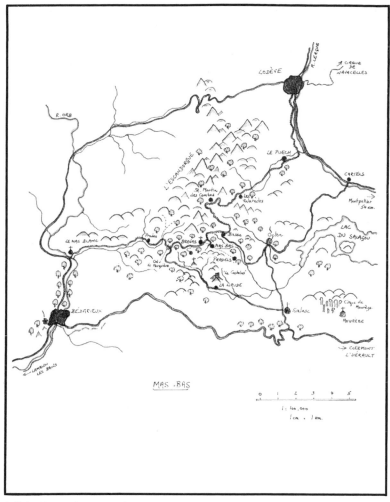

MAS, BAS

Michelin, points out the way to Brenas over a small stone bridge. The road twists past Prades, an abandoned farm now converted into a club and restaurant where the jet set of Bédarieux or the coast come to dance the night away. At the Col de Merquière, a new valley opens out below, running in a curve to Salasc, Octon and the Lake of Salagou, out of sight beyond the eastern hills. On a bluff in the middle of the valley stand the ruins of 'Le Castelas', one of the castles torn down by Cardinal Richelieu in the seventeenth century, brooding over the farmhouse of the Oliers at La Lieude.

The road forks right into the valley or left to Brenas village,

123

further up at the foot of the Escandorgue. From here you catch the first glimpse of a cluster of stone houses in a dip below, the roof tiles held in place by large stones so the Mistral will not blow them off. A path leads down between small fields and vineyards, past an old iron cross into an alleyway and the central courtyard of Mas Bas.

★ ★ ★

I first went to Mas Bas more than ten years ago, after Mrs. Hildyard had bought one of the houses as a holiday home. A Mme Crébassa had offered me work, which I accepted gladly. A widow, she was living by herself at the time in a house apart from the village. Her son had left to work as a postman in Bédarieux. All her husband's hard work seemed pointless now that her only child refused to follow in his father's footsteps. It made her very bitter. She had looked frail and thin, a small, birdlike woman with grey hair always done up neatly into a bun, but you only had to look at her face to see that she was tough as nails. It was pinched and weather worn, with thin lips, piercing, calculating eyes and a hawkish nose. She was certainly not as old as she looked.

Every day we would go down to her vineyards at the base of the Castelas where we pruned the vines, spending long hours bent double over the ground picking up the *sarments*, the vine shoots, and tying them into bundles which would serve as firewood for the winter.

'*Ça n'vaut pas la peine, cette saloperie de terre,*' she would mumble all day, cursing the land, lamenting the hardships she had to endure. (It's not worth the bother, this bloody land.) I thought at first she was saying that the land was very expensive, complaining of the *salaud prix*, the 'terrible price'.

One day we butchered two kids. First we tied all four of the poor creatures' legs together, Mme. Crébassa doing one, while I copied her with the other. Next we laid them on the seat of a chair, passed their legs through the back and held them there with a broken broom handle so they were unable to move or struggle. Then she searched for the jugular vein, jabbed in the knife and left them to bleed slowly to death, collecting the blood in a tray. I thought if I couldn't do it I shouldn't be eating meat. I like meat, so I did it. The worst part was the noise they made as they died. It could have been a human baby screaming. It is the traditional peasant way of slaughter. They believe, like the Moslems and Jews, that the meat will be tainted if the animal is not bled to death.

When the deed was done we skinned and gutted them. She sold one in Bédarieux when we went to visit her son. The other we had had for supper the same night. It was tasty, but tough. To the clotted

124

blood she had added onion and garlic, a touch of thyme and rosemary, then fried it in a large pan, laughing when I baulked at the idea of fresh blood pudding.

She had fed and promised to pay me for almost a month, but when no money passed hands I left her to work for M. Auguste Balp, who lived with his wife and family in one of the houses round the courtyard.

I liked Auguste Balp a lot. A *'brave homme'* he was, short, solid with slightly bandy legs and an enormously powerful back and shoulders. He had a grin that lit up his face, baring a row of small, stained teeth. He wore a beret at all times, which he would take off only to wipe the sweat from his forehead. Working for him was paradise after the skinflint Mme Crébassa. I would be woken at the crack of dawn by shouts from the courtyard below.

'Oh, Jeanot, au boulot!' (To work, Johnny Boy!)

We would have a quick coffee before setting off for the fields, cutting and baling hay. He had just bought his first tractor, a green Deutz of which he was extremely proud. It had a curved bar on one side over the mudguard where a passenger could sit. After an hour or so we would return to breakfast, a slice of home-cured ham and a raw egg topped with vinegar and olive oil, mopped up with bread, sunk with a glass of wine. Then back to work until it was too hot to continue, when we retired to the shade of the terrace to talk, smoke and drink. He had a special metal basket in which he would lower bottles of wine into the well. The wine came up nicely chilled.

He had been a labourer at St. Martin des Combes like his father, but came to Mas Bas and married the daughter of the farmer at Pradels. She was older than he was with an illegimate child by another man. He farmed the father-in-law's land as well as that at Mas Bas which he had under a bizarre arrangement from Courtès, the last survivor of an old local family like the Crébassas and Oliers. Courtès retained a part of the house for himself, leaving the rest to Balp and his family. In return Balp did all the work and fed him. Courtès boasted proudly that he had never had to work in his life. He was consequently a tedious old man with a warped, often childish sense of humour leading a boring, sadly pointless life.

At one point Rupert Hildyard had bought a vintage 1935 Terot 350cc side valve single cylinder motorcycle. Courtès looked a little surprised to see it, saying he had once had one of the same model and year. Soon after, it transpired he actually knew the owner and where it had come from. Finally all was revealed when Balp himself said that the former owner was the very same man who had run off with Courtès' wife some thirty years before.

Balp's father-in-law was a faith healer as well as a farmer. One day the car wouldn't start. He held his divining pendulum, a wooden bob hung on a light thread, over the engine, watching the oscillations attentively, head on one side, pronouncing the problem to be the spark plugs. It was the distributor. He even tried to cure the Hildyards' asthma from long distance, but with little success. He lived alone at Pradels. One Sunday the Balp family went out for the day without telling him beforehand. It was winter. He came to see them, found the house locked and no one around so went to sit in one of the old bangers in front of the house. When the family got back, they found that he had died of the cold. They were not sure what to do with the body so they put it in the boot of the car. I will always remember sitting on a wall near his house watching two naked children playing in the wild fields and brambles. The scene etched itself in my memory, a fantasy of natural innocence.

Lunch at twelve was always the biggest meal of the day. There used to be eight of us around the table: M. and Mme Balp, their two children who were coming up to their teens, called Daniel and Régine, Courtès, Cavalhier, Canot the shepherd and myself. They say Cavalhier was an orphan. The French government used to pay people to take them in. He was a keen hunter, sometimes bringing back a brace or two of wild wood pigeon and he often helped around the farm. In the summer he went combining on the plains around Béziers where he could earn good money.

Mme Balp would set a large pot of soup on the table, add a ladleful of olive oil and stir it in, after which we would help ourselves while she got one of the large loaves of bread off a shelf and blessed it by making the sign of the cross on it with her knife. Holding it against her stomach, she would cut off large hunks with practised dexterity without making a single crumb. These loaves were more than a foot long and almost as wide, weighing two kilos. The soup was followed by a mixed salad, meat, possibly an omelette, vegetables (all served separately) and home-made goat's cheese or fresh sheep cheese, which I loved with a little sugar sprinkled over the top. The feast was rounded off with a choice of fruit. Between us we would normally empty three or four bottles of wine at a sitting. I loved those meals; the conversations that we had. When we tired of talking we could always tease Canot, who ate like a pig at a trough and never paid the slightest attention to anybody.

Such a meal had to be well digested, so everyone retired for a siesta until the air cooled, waking to a cup of coffee before returning to the fields to work till the sun set. After supper we would talk a little more before heading for bed. I was friendly with the dogs until I caught their fleas, after which I kept my distance.

Canot would sometimes visit me in the evening. You could hear him shuffling across the yard, calling his sheep dog to her slops, on his way to milk the goats. The sheep had already been milked. He was a small, middle-aged man who seldom washed, almost always had a growth of black bristles over his face, wore boots that had holes in them and clothes that must have come from the French equivalent of Oxfam. He slept up the steps from the Hildyards' house in a dusty room the other side of a pile of oats. Sometimes he brought with him a rusty tin full of fresh goat's milk which he would hand over with admonitions to say nothing of the matter to the boss, placing the tip of his index finger beneath his right eye and pulling the skin down with a click of the tongue in a characteristic gesture. He came from a family of fifteen children and was at least half Spanish. His father had been one of the refugees from the Spanish Civil War, from Catalonia possibly. He had a sister in Montpellier and a friend in Lodève. He would sit on the bench opposite talking in a gruff voice while I listened, nodding wisely though I understood little of what he said. Even the Balps made fun of the way he talked. They spoke patois among themselves, a variation of *langue d'oc* by the sound of it. It wasn't too difficult to understand, so they were careful about what they said in front of me when they realised.

The Hildyard's courtyard

Canot was a simpleton, happy and grateful to have a friend who did not mock. It was agreed we would go off to the Fête at Lodève together and have a meal with his friend at the same time. The day arrived. He appeared transformed in shiny black shoes, a dark suit with white shirt and tie, topped with a soft felt hat and respectably shaved. We made a fine, Quixotic pair.

His friend lived up a dark, dirty flight of steps off one of the narrow streets of the old part of town, but the little flat was clean. We had a good meal before hitting the town, wandering among the crowds, shooting at ducks, ogling the ladies, getting steadily more and more drunk. In the early hours of the morning we staggered back the fifteen kilometres to Mas Bas, just in time for him to have a cup of coffee and take the flock out for the day. I went straight to bed, crying off work.

Balp never paid him, saying that when he first arrived he had, but Canot used to take his money, walk down to Bédarieux or Lodève after work, get completely drunk, return at four in the morning and then fall asleep on the job. So he stopped paying him, yet Canot had stayed. There was a simple peasant logic somewhere in this apparent slavery. I wondered if he was still there.

Harvest time came. We started combining. No one in the commune had enough land to warrant the personal ownership of a combine, so it was shared between the local farmers, who all worked together, even M. Castand, the mayor of Brenas. There were others, but I forget their names. The combine was an old Massey Ferguson which cut a strip about six foot wide. My job was to stand at the back of the machine filling sacks with corn as it was threshed, dropping the sacks off into the field as we went. In the evening we went round the field humping the sacks onto the trailer before returning to the yard for a well-earned drink.

We spent one entire day at the end of the harvest carrying the sacks up three flights of stairs to the bins in the granary, which was at the top of the house away from rats and mice. It was hard work, for the sacks weighed a good 50 kilos. It was no wonder Balp had such a broad back. They gave the smaller ones to me when they could.

Balp also had grazing rights on the slopes around the Castelas which allowed him to keep a sizeable flock of sheep, which they milked by hand in season. The milk was collected and taken away to Roquefort to make the famous cheese. It paid well, providing him with his main source of income. The sheep also provided wool. The shearer came one day, a real professional. He would pick up a sheep with one hand, swing it round effortlessly and sit it on its bottom, an undignified position, its legs sticking out awkwardly above the soft underbelly. It took him less than a day to shear the whole flock.

Balp kept goats for cheese and meat, rabbits, chickens, ducks, and pigs which they fattened on chestnuts before the ritual pre-Christmas slaughter, something I was glad that I never had to witness. It seemed they were tied to a ladder before having their throats cut and made a terrible noise. Cavalhier had explained the details with great glee.

The oats and hay kept the sheep through the winter, the wheat he sold. The vineyard provided enough wine for the year, something in the region of 3000 litres, which they made themselves with a wine press in the garage and stored in the cellars beneath the house. They had two vegetable gardens which provided all the greens and tomatoes they needed, so the only things that they had to buy in were bread, sugar, coffee, salt and oil. A baker and a grocery van called once a week so he didn't need to use his one beaten-up old car very much. He was paying off the farm, though, so he was not left with much money to play around with.

Balp was thus as near self-sufficient as seems practicable. To a romantic seventeen-year-old it appeared to be the perfect life, but I had not been there in winter to witness the storms, the icy winds and snow, the isolation when all communication with the outside world is cut off for long, tedious months. Neither had I been there long enough to perceive the undercurrents, scandals and petty jealousies, rivalry and feuds. They will tell you it is not worth scratching the surface of an ungrateful land for a living, but they are hooked to it, loving it obstinately, hoarding it possessively.

I had returned at various times in the intervening years. The first time Balp invited me to supper. I went with pleasure, thinking fondly of former happy evenings sitting around the table chatting, but came away sadly disappointed. They had bought a television and installed it on the shelf above the fridge where the bread had been. It was on all through the meal. The old atmosphere had gone.

M. Balp was getting in the last of the hay when I arrived this time. It meant there would be no paid work until the harvest, so I would have to look elsewhere. We sat talking on the steps near the empty pig sties as he brought me up to date with all the news. Canot was dead. This came as a shock. He had been left some money by an uncle and gone off to his sister in Montpellier to collect it. Then they heard that he was dead. It was all they knew.

Cavalhier the orphan had gone too. He got drunk once too often, forgot to turn left at the junction to Bédarieux, went straight on and crashed into the solid, unyielding trunk of a plane tree. He was dead when they found him.

Daniel the son, was doing well in his studies for accountancy and Régine was learning to programme computers. They came back at the weekends to help out but the rest of the time M. and Mme Balp had to do all the work themselves. The Roquefort collection was still running, but the truck arrived to collect the milk at six in the morning which meant getting up at three every day. Now the Roquefort people were saying that they lived too far away, that it was no longer economic. He was not sure how much longer they would be coming.

Down the road Mme Crébassa now had permanent help. A Spanish-looking family had moved in. The father was working the land for Mme Crébassa as a sharecropper, which is rare in France.

His wife was a faded, beaten old stick with a gammy leg who limped badly like her son Guy, the goat boy. You could see he hated his father by the way he looked at him, like a caged animal. Their other son, a little boy still, also suffered from a gammy leg, yet their daughter, an apprentice seamstress in Clermont L'Hérault, was stunningly attractive.

Mme Balp shuffled out into the courtyard in her slippers to feed the chickens. She smiled and began to call them.

'Vete, vete, vete, galline, vete...

They came running across the yard to peck up the corn. She had been suffering from a further bout of nervous depression, which Balp hoped would not lead to another breakdown. She looked terribly old, grey, worn and ill. Auguste was as jolly as ever or trying hard at least, but you could see that all hope had vanished. Mas Bas was dying a slow, weary death.

'What can we do?' he asked. 'Daniel won't be coming back when I get too old to run the place. He has an education. He sees no future for Mas Bas.'

I had supper with Ella and Rupert. It was good to be with old friends again. We talked of the trip, but I had great difficulty in the telling of the story. My memories were too vague, too many things had happened. I would have to consult my diary. Perhaps it would be worth writing a book, just to get things straight.

The next day I cycled down to Bédarieux to pick cherries on the terraces of Piers' *mas*. Armed with two buckets of the very best I went to the local grocer who took them at four francs a kilo. I spent the next few days happily commuting with more of the same, making forty francs which bought a new pair of shorts, black this time so that they would not look so dirty. I couldn't help noticing that the grocer was selling the cherries for nine francs a kilo, which undoubtedly covered overheads.

Saturday is market day in Lodève. The town was full. Travelling shops that had rolled in at dawn were now open in the High Street, their owners selling clothes, shoes, ironmongery and cloth from the lorries themselves. Other streets were filled with vans and stalls selling a vast range of vegetables, fruit, fresh meat, sausages and cheeses, while knots of people in from the surrounding countryside sold their poultry, rabbits, geese, porkers and eggs. Little old ladies in black hawked their trays of goat cheeses, 'zippies' (Hippies) sold country bread, cakes and biscuits or fragrant chestnut and clover mountain honey. The covered fish market had mussels, squid, whole tunny fish and live crabs amongst their elaborate displays. Under the trees in the square was all kinds of agricultural machinery: tractors, cultivators, rotovators, and pack sprayers for the vines. The cafes were crowded with people meeting, joking, drinking and reading copies of the *Midi Libre*. Algerian women swept through the crowds in long, ample cotton dresses while their menfolk clustered on street corners. With such markets it is no wonder the food in France is so good. It is a fine tradition, one that will certainly not disappear.

Rupert, Ella and the embryonic Luc left for Plymouth on Sunday, 21st June. I had been helping Tony Trepess to fix the terrace of the house which someone had put a curse on and he offered me work over at Le Puech where he lived. Tony was a tall, thin man with penetrating black eyes, a moustache, a prominent Cornish chin and a very good sense of humour. We spoke Irish most of the time, whiling away the day with anecdotes. For a fortnight I scraped walls, knocked holes, repointed, whitewashed, painted and generally made myself useful. Tony and Tamsin had one child, Francis, my *copain,* whom I remember most for his morning appearances, invariably coming sleepily downstairs yawning, before being rushed off to school to cries of 'Eat!'. Of Tamsin I remember best the delights of her excellent cooking, the treacle tart and custard in particular.

The longest day had passed, July was here. With the money that I had made I would have enough to keep going until September, by which time I should be in Italy. I had made tentative arrangements to meet my friend Anna in Padua at the end of August, which gave me just under two months. I consulted the maps: it was going to be mountains almost all the way. From the top of Brenas heights I looked north to the Cévennes, my next destination. After the Cévennes I would cross the Rhône valley to the Parc du Vercors, heading north-north-east to Grenoble and the French Alps. The next big town after that would be Montreux, in Switzerland. I was ready and raring to go.

I left on 5th July. The sun was just rising as I followed the river Lergue past the old cotton mill into the dim, sleepy streets of Lodève, crossing the Roman bridge before taking to the hills east of town. Young described it as 'dirty, ugly and ill built, with crooked close streets, but populous and very industrious'. That was in 1846 when it was a thriving mill town, well known for the quality of its cloth.

I broke a tooth at breakfast, which was not a good way to start since visits to the dentist were not included in the budget. It was only a small piece, though. I spat it out into the dust, where a black and orange beetle was busy scraping out a burrow in the ground, backing out every so often to roll another crumb of earth away with its hind legs. The broom was still in flower, filling the air with a heavy scent, attracting bees and butterflies that zigzagged around while horse-flies with green heads and dull grey bodies did their best to gorge on my flesh. A group of children went by, looking for flowers that retain their colour even when dried.

The pine woods gave way to an older landscape of scrub, wild lavender and thyme scattered with bleached white rocks, boulders and the thistly plants they stick to doors when a wild boar has been killed. La Vaquerie is on the southern edge of the Causse du Larzac, a desolate limestone plateau created by volcanic action millions of years ago in the Massif Central. It is a pretty village of tall, solid, plastered houses that are tucked into a final fold of hill away from the harsh winter winds; the village smelt of sheep and milk pails. I rested on a stone seat encircling the bole of a mature plane tree, watching huge fluffy cumuli fill the sky, before setting off across the Causse. There are no rivers here since the water all flows through the soft rock or cuts deep, invisible gorges into the plateau. The Causses are famous for their storms and strong winds. Towards the north the sky was black and gloomy, the clouds seeming almost pregnant, spawning smaller, round grey clouds like babies. Thunder rolled in the distance as I made my way over the plain to St. Maurice. A bolt of lightning suddenly joined heaven and earth, while the wind, whipping up from behind me, herded the clouds northwards. I watched the show with unconcerned fascination. Then quite unexpectedly the wind veered 180 degrees, blowing the storm straight towards me. What had been so pleasant a minute before now became a nasty threat. I took cover against a heap of stones and waited. A few drops fell and then just as suddenly as before the wind changed direction again and the storm moved away north. I had never experienced anything like it and stood in stunned amazement, watching the clouds swirl in the changing currents, before moving on.

I camped the other side of St. Maurice, where they kept sheep under the church. It had been a long first day, but I was very happy to be on my way once more. The rays of the setting sun fanned out from behind the black clouds on the horizon like the petals of an enormous flower, turning the sky a deep, glowing pink.

Nothing about the flocks of sheep grazing among the scrubby pastures and hedges of box prepares you for the roughly circular chasm that suddenly yawns at your feet; the Cirque de Navacelles is almost a mile across. Half a mile down the village of Navacelles nestles among trees and tiny fields of golden wheat by the river Vis that has cut its way slowly into the soft, chalky soil. In the Middle Ages there was a religious community there but all that remains today is some fifteen people and a good restaurant to keep the place

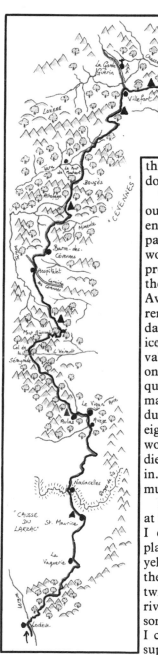

alive. I stopped for water by the church, listening to the birds and the cascade by the high, arching bridge that was built by English soldiers during the 100 Years War, then tackled the stiff climb back to the plateau and breakfast. It was easy to imagine Neanderthal man hunting mammoths over this bare, godforsaken land scattered with dolmens.

Two women woke me from a siesta outside the church at Mondardier as they entered the porch, neatly folding their parasols while they talked of how they would arrange the flowers. I was approaching the base of the National Park of the Cévennes now, the woods around Avèze hot and humid, the smell of the river reminiscent of the Thames on a summer's day. I threw myself in with joy, bought an ice cream in town and moved down the valley to Le Vigan, which, like Lodève, was once a prosperous place renowned for the quality of its clothing and hosiery. The main industry of the Cévennol towns during the sixteenth, seventeenth and eighteenth centuries was the rearing of silk worms and the spinning of the silk, but this died when cheaper imports were brought in. The factories have since closed and the mulberry trees have been rooted up.

I paid the price of buying too much food at the large supermarket on the outskirts as I climbed wearily to Aulas, a beautiful place, with a stone fountain quiet in the yellow light of the leafy square, flowers on the ironwork balconies and creepers twining up the glossy stone walls by the river. The local shopkeeper directed me to some communal ground just outside where I could camp. I washed, ate an enormous supper and lay down to sleep. I had entered

133

the Cévennes, in retrospect one of the loveliest areas through which I walked, so green and well-watered.

In the morning I followed a good track sometimes paved with large stone slabs that led up to the Espérou ridge. Inhabitants were few. The population of the area has dropped by almost a half since the turn of the century. The Lozère has only 14 people per square kilometre, making it the least populated *département* in France. The people traditionally resist any central authority, particularly Parisian. The separatist movement *Occitania* is not as strong as in Lower Languedoc, but a daubed *Tourists Out- Oc.* revealed the presence of at least one such idealist. The signs outside villages indicating the times of service at the local church are often blue, rather than the more common green, for the majority of Cévennols are Protestant. R.L.Stevenson describes them as 'intelligent after a countrified fashion, plain and dignified in manner'. They have their sayings too: 'He's as loaded with money as a toad with feathers' or 'A closed mouth gets no flies in it'.

A buzzard flapped off into the valley from a nearby tree, screeching a warning to the other animals. The song of birds and crickets filled the air, lupins, marigolds, buttercups, orchids, a hundred other wild flowers pricked the beech forest with colour, while hungry mosquitoes swarmed by the streams.

The Cévennes are the source of some of the great rivers in France. Within a few miles of each other are the sources of the Allier, flowing to the Loire, the Cèze and Ardèche flowing to the Rhône. The Col de la Séreyrède marks the watershed between those flowing to the Mediterranean like the Hérault, and those, like the Tarn, that wind their way west to the Atlantic. Inscribed at the base of the fountain of ice cold water on the Col is the following verse of Latin:

'Hanc gelidam fontem reservant tibi culmine montis
Accipe gratus aquam nec nimis hume vafram.'

Under that, in French, 'Our summits have guarded this travelling wave for you. Give thanks. Do not drink in haste. Beware of the water's coolness.' I have often been warned by the French to be careful with cold water. They believe it to be a potential killer, and certainly it can cause a chill in the stomach.

After lunch I rested in a shady pine wood down from the Col, protected from the insects by the mosquito netting that I had taken from Piers' *mas* where I had left the guitar. It made life much easier. I could read in peace the book I had brought for the long siestas, *Regain*, by Jean Giono.

* * *

The story is set in a remote mountain village called Aubignane, a little cluster of houses at the very edge of a plateau. The land is leprous, like an old, mangy dog. One house seems to have slid away from the others to the side of the stream below, the house of Panturle the hunter, an enormous, slow man like a tree trunk dressed in rags, with a hare lip like a red pepper. Since his mother died, he has talked to himself. There are only two other people in the village now, Mamèche and old Gaubert, once the cartwright and renowned for his ploughs, whose forge is at the top of the village. The forge is cold and dead, the chimney has fallen in, the rats have eaten away the leather on the bellows. When he gets bored, he goes to his anvil and taps at it with his hammer, just to hear the noise. The anvil is still shiny and alive.

Winter is on the way. Gaubert is leaving to go and live with his daughter in the valley below. Panturle takes his anvil down to the waiting cart, for he knows that it would be worse than death for Gaubert to leave it behind. Panturle and Mamèche are now the only souls left in the village. Mamèche is an old woman, 'La Piémontaise' they used to call her when the village was inhabited. As a young woman she had come from Italy with her husband, who specialised in digging wells. Aubignane was his last. It caved in just as he struck water, burying him alive. Nobody would drink the water, of course. She had a child by him, but that died, too.

Winter sets in, the hard, icy days drag by, indistinguishable one from another. Finally, the spring wind arrives, the stream thaws. Mamèche is in her house counting the last of her potatoes, enough for three or four days, she calculates. Somehow, she is going to find Panturle a woman. She sets off for the plateau. Panturle doesn't realise why she has left, having forgotten their conversation on the subject.

'Now I am alone', he says.

*   *   *

I looked up through the mosquito netting. A group of spastic children were coming by on the path, a tall, gangly, broad-shouldered lad hobbling in their wake, helping himself along with a staff crying 'Wait for me ... wait for me ...' It was time to get going again.

At 1565 metres, Mont Aigoual is the highest point in the Cévennes. Groups of tourists had come up the old drove road from Valleraugue to climb the observation tower and gaze out over the mountains. A dial at the summit named the distant peaks but the air was too thick and hazy to see much further than a thin trickle below

135

that marked the beginnings of the river Hérault. I walked on, camping in the middle of a forest, moonlight casting strange shadows as it filtered through the tree tops.

It took a while for the sun to gain the crest of the wooded valley and gather sufficient strength to disperse a lingering mist. A swallow swooped and twittered in the sky above. From a treeless ridge strewn with boulders, the ranges looked like a great herd of dinosaurs with woolly green backs petrified as they travelled north. The ridge led past weird rock formations caused by the whipping rain and wind of the bitter winters, to L'Hospitalet on the 'Corniche des Cévennes', a road built by troops of Louis XIV to suppress the Camisard Revolt of 1702. The Edict of Nantes had allowed the Huguenots freedom to practise their religion but Louis revoked it in 1685. Many Protestants emigrated while those who stayed resolved to fight. The revolt lasted for two years, though resistance in places went on for sixty or seventy years more without success.

The sun beat down remorselessly and there was little shade. The heat sapped my energy and weakened my will, making it difficult to keep going, the road burning through the soles of my boots, a toe hurting badly, my throat dry. The less I wished to continue, the more conscious I became of the weight of the pack, the aches and pains, the slow crawling of time. The wild strawberries by the wayside were sweet and refreshing but it had become too much of an effort to bend down and pick them. Even a song did not lift my growing melancholy. By the time I arrived in Barre des Cévennes my feet were swollen from the heat, the blister on one toe had turned painful and was full of pus and I felt like giving up. I found a quiet cafe in the long high street beneath overhanging cliffs, ordered a pastis from the proprietress and sat down gratefully in the cool, sipping the milky liquid leisurely as I escaped into Giono's world.

* * *

The scene had changed: two people were walking the desolate, treeless plateau above Aubignane: an old knife grinder caller Gédemus and a youngish woman by the name of Arsule, formerly 'Miss Irène of the Great Theatres of Paris and the Universe'. He had picked her up when she fell on hard times. She cooked for him and hauled the grinder when no one was there to see.

Suddenly she sees something sticking up in the grass to their right, something black with arms, like a scarecrow. Gédemus reassures her: it must be a dead tree. It happens again, though this time the tree moves. Gédemus goes off through the long grass with a knife at the ready. When he comes back, he says there was nothing, she must have been seeing things.

The wind is warm and strong, as if full of flowers. All day it caresses Arsule's body which responds to it like new wine. That evening, they camp in the ruins of La Trinité. The moon is out, a thick silver bar of light beneath the door of the tumbledown house they have occupied. They wake in the middle of the night at the sound of footsteps, a stone dislodged. They sit there terrified as a shadow blots out the bar of light. Someone tries the door gently, cautiously, but Gédemus has put a large stone against it. The shadow moves away, leaving just the wind.

They set off at dawn. The black scarecrow appears again. Now they are both frightened and Gédemus decides to turn off the path. They'll be all right, he says, there's a village nearby called Aubignane. They think it is deserted and rest on the grass outside Panturle's house. It is then that Arsule sees a pool of blood on the doorstep.

* * *

I closed the book, listening to the slow ticking of the clock in the cafe until it struck two. Woken from my reverie, I left to wind down into the Mimente valley, which R.L. Stevenson , on his travels with the donkey, described as 'a wild valley . . . looked upon in the clear air by many rocky peaks. The road . . . yet new.'

The same road was now a chaos of roadworks, for they were widening it with bulldozers. I climbed out and up to the Col de Bougès, near the woods of Altefage where I slept on a comfortable bed of heather, well protected from the wind among jagged outcrops of rock.

It was on a Sunday in July, 1702 that an assembly of angry Protestants had gathered on the Bougès to hear the preaching of Pierre 'Spirit' Séguier. Here was a true prophet of the wilderness, a 'tall, sinewy man with a thin, long, swarthy visage', his teeth missing, his hair long and unkempt, wild, about fifty years old. 'The Lord has commanded me to take up arms', he preached, 'to deliver our captive brethren and destroy the Arch-priest of Moloch'. Another prophet, Abraham Mazel, then told the crowd how he had dreamed he saw large, very fat oxen feeding on the choice plants of a garden. A voice had said 'Drive them away!'

The 'fat oxen' were led by Du Chayla, Catholic Arch-priest of the Cévennes, who had moved to nearby Pont de Montvert a little while before, his mission to continue the conversion of the Calvinists to the

137

True Religion. He had wasted no time converting the cellars of the house where he was staying into a dungeon where Protestants were kept in chains and tortured to deny their faith. After twenty years of repression and injustice, his harsh tactics had proved too much for the locals.

On the day after the sermon, fifty men met near the summit of the Bougès and marched on Pont de Montvert, singing psalms as they went. When they arrived at Du Chayla's residence, he ordered his guards to shoot. One of the band was killed. They angrily broke down the gates and rescued the prisoners before setting fire to the building. The Arch-priest fled to the top floor of the house but fell and broke his thigh bone in his attempt to escape from a window. When Séguier and his band discovered him, they knifed him to death mercilessly. The rest of the night they sat around his body chanting. At daybreak they returned to the mountains, destroying churches, crosses and all other signs of Catholicism on the way. The Camisard Revolt had begun.

Séguier was captured not long after and led in chains to Florac, where he was condemned to have his hands cut off before being burnt at the stake as a heretic.

As I made my way on through the woods next morning towards the barren southern plateau of the Lozère, I followed a shallow, winding river and wished the Romans had come to these mountains to straighten out the roads a bit. After passing several abandoned hamlets, I reached a pool of sunwarmed water a mile or so from the source of the Tarn where I stopped to bathe my feet. Refreshed, I felt better. After all, every step was taking me nearer the Alps. My heart lifted at the thought.

The desolate plateau was well populated with day trippers, as the French holiday season was now in full swing. I took the road down to Villefort. A family passing in their car stopped to give me a lift, which I accepted happily, piling in at the back with two children and a dog. We coasted gently downhill to the camping site where they were staying. The man offered me a beer, then a second, inviting me to stay for supper, which we ate at a table set under an awning beside the caravan, in *Tout Confort*. He was called Claude, an energetic man with eyes that flashed as he spoke.

'One must be positive, that's my philosophy.'

He was a social worker, but he didn't elaborate. He was on holiday and, as he said, more interested in finding out about my travels than talking about his work. We ate and drank well and he brought out a bottle of Calvados after supper. It is much stronger than it tastes. The conversation began to bounce from the one million dollars a minute spent on defence in the West to Giscard d'Estaing, owner of uranium mines. By the time I headed for bed the Calvados had gone completely to my head and it was difficult to walk. It was the only time that anyone ever tucked me up in my sleeping bag. Claude and his wife smiled down as the world span round.

'Are you all right, Jean?'

'Don't worry about me, I'm asleep.'

I could hardly think in the morning as I wandered idly in Villefort, wondering what to buy. Out of town, I walked alongside a lake to the old mediaeval village of La Garde Guérin. The village, founded in the tenth century by the Bishop of Mende, was a bizarre community of 27 'Nobles Pariers' whose job it was to protect and escort travellers on the old pasture road that ran from Nîmes onto the Serre des Mulets, the Gallo-Roman 'Voie Regardane', the only communication in the Middle Ages between the Languedoc and Auvergne, or Cantal.

The village had been well restored, the stone work repointed, the slates renewed, slotting into each other down the spine of the roof like the back of a stegosaurus. In the beautifully simple chapel, the scent of lilies was overpowering and coloured shafts of light formed patterns on the floor beneath a painting of St. George and the Dragon. Out in the courtyard, I took the stone steps up the old watchtower. Near the top they vanished. Had Stevenson perhaps been here and remembered those steps later, when he was writing *Kidnapped?* The trap door to the roof of the tower was still some ten feet above. Ignoring imminent danger of complete vertigo, I hoisted myself up through the hole, using footholds in the wall. The view was well worth the effort. On one side, in a deep crevasse, the source of the Chassezac was covered in forest, on the other was a high, grassy plateau criss-crossed by dry stone walls and grazed by tiny flocks of sheep: the Lozère.

Resting later under a tree, I consulted the map to see how many kilometres I had covered so far that day: about fifteen. I decided to have lunch and then swim in the lake. As I was tucking into bread and cheese it slowly dawned on me that I was going north instead of east. I cursed the effects of alcohol as I paced back to Villefort and climbed out of the town for a second time. That would teach me a lesson.

My feet were healed again, the hangover slept away, the Cévennes now behind me. The lowlands of the Ardèche stretched out below, the limes and chestnuts in flower, acorns beginning to form, leaves now the brittle green of high summer. All around me fruit was ripening on the trees: peaches, apples, figs and mulberries, though these were now past their best. The gardens were a mass of flowers, the earth itself that gave all this abundance a soft, reddish brown.

It was market day in Les Vans. I left my pack in a cafe to wander at ease among the stalls of craft work, dyed wools and lavender bags, eating lunch later on the wall of a hermitage that was perched in the hills above rolling vineyards and overlooked the bright dots of tents and caravans in a camping site below. The hermitage was locked, but I could just make out the simple stone arches through the bars on a small window. Holiday makers were coming and going in the woods. I understood why when the path suddenly dropped away down the white cliffs of the Chassezac gorge. I walked down and a fisherman laughed and joked as he watched me swim in the warm, shallow waters of the Chassezac river. I left him beaming, for he caught three fish while I was there. Only later did I find that the compass my father had given me had floated away down the river from my back pocket. I felt sick at the loss because it was a present and I had grown very fond of it. I would have to buy another unless I wanted to risk getting lost in the mountains.

By evening I had crossed the valley into the hills beyond. walking through endless orchards of luscious peaches, singing, scrumping, my sadness forgotten as the sweet juice of the windfalls ran over my beard, making it very sticky. The setting sun was just like a glowing peach itself.

It took longer than expected to get to

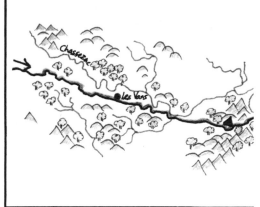

Salavas, as the path twisted a lot more than the map indicated. The road from there to Vallon-Pont-d'Arc was bordered on either side by a field of tents, a seething encampment of which Caesar would have been proud. I crossed the Ardèche into Vallon amidst a teeming mass of tourists. An English couple went by.

'Well, I'm really not going to walk into town like this every day, Fred. I thought the camping site was much closer. There isn't even a bus service and you have to wait about half an hour before ...'

The road across the Plateau des Gras was cluttered with caravans and dense holiday traffic, most of the number plates German, Dutch or Belgian, in that order. I stole into the woods with relief. The plateau began to drop down into a broad valley. In the last of the evening light I could see a wide river below reflecting a patch of blue sky and a bridge. Night came, street lights began to twinkle in villages and small towns, two cooling towers belched smoke and steam into the black sky. I had almost reached the Rhône.

I washed away the night at a fountain in St. Montant, cleft in two by a river cutting deeply through past a ruined castle. Viviers is an old town riddled with mediaeval passageways, towers, castles and other impressive buildings. The cathedral looked far more imposing from the high hills to the east, where I spent the night in the grounds of the Trappist monastery of Aiguebelle, near a grotto dedicated to the Virgin Mary, her statue impassive in the flickering candlelight. It was late by then and I was happy to have crossed the powerful, slow-moving Rhône and the *Autoroute du Soleil* that ran parallel to it. I remember standing above the motorway watching cars and lorries scream north and south, listening to the high pitched whine of the engines, breathing the fumes and smell of hot rubber. It seemed

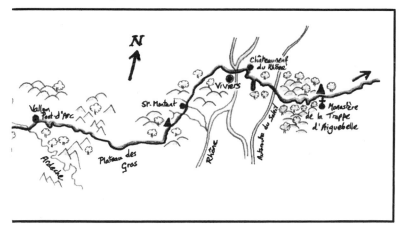

another world, foolish for its senseless haste.

Looking out from under an apple tree at siesta time next day, I could see over flat fields of ripening corn, dry pasture and slabs of purple lavender to the smooth mountains of the Massif Central. The oldest mountains in France, islands when the rest of the land was still under water, the Massif Central was behind me now. The Alps and the Pyrenees are comparatively recent, rising a mere fifty million years ago. Crickets clicked away in the stillness of the afternoon while three playful Basset puppies from a nearby farmhouse

141

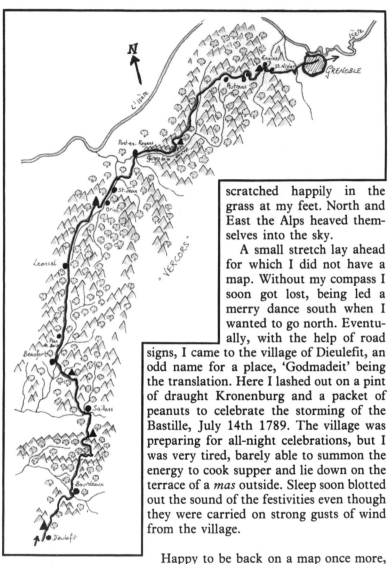

scratched happily in the grass at my feet. North and East the Alps heaved themselves into the sky.

A small stretch lay ahead for which I did not have a map. Without my compass I soon got lost, being led a merry dance south when I wanted to go north. Eventually, with the help of road signs, I came to the village of Dieulefit, an odd name for a place, 'Godmadeit' being the translation. Here I lashed out on a pint of draught Kronenburg and a packet of peanuts to celebrate the storming of the Bastille, July 14th 1789. The village was preparing for all-night celebrations, but I was very tired, barely able to summon the energy to cook supper and lie down on the terrace of a *mas* outside. Sleep soon blotted out the sound of the festivities even though they were carried on strong gusts of wind from the village.

Happy to be back on a map once more, I had stopped for water within the high, protecting walls of a farm above Bourdeaux. The farmer, a little man with a fine furze on his cheeks, was crossing the yard with a bundle of greenery under one arm; his wife I could see peering suspiciously from behind the bead curtain that hung in the kitchen doorway. I drank my fill of the hard water, dunked my head in the trough to cool down and straightened

142

up to greet the man.

The greenery was for the rabbits, he said, and took me across to a barn to see. Inside there were at least a hundred brown and white bunnies hopping all over the floor.

'You get good money for them,' he said enthusiastically, 'especially the livers. I only raise them in summer, though, when the sheep are out.'

Bourdeaux lies south of an extinct volcano, the path rising gently four hundred metres to the lip of a crater covered in thick forest, a shady track leading round the inner slopes to the treeless eastern edges. A young woman in purple with a dog and donkey in tow came by, smiled pleasantly and continued her search for wild strawberries, which were plentiful and no longer a terrible chore to bend for. I climbed up the path mechanically, wondering if I would find a bank in Saillans the next day. It was perhaps time to invest in some new socks. I would do some shopping, have a drink somewhere, write a postcard or two.

I was not expecting to find myself on top of a massive weathered crag with a sheer drop of 500 metres at my feet. A further 500 metres down, the river Drôme was clearly visible, and there beside it, lay Saillans at

The crater from Saillans

the foot of mountains that rose majestically from an early evening mist, their high, spiny folds running almost parallel, converging in the north to form a primitive stone arrowhead. This was the Vercors, the final mountain fortress before the city of Grenoble and the High Alps. It was a stirring sight. I stayed awhile enjoying the view. Next to me, a magnificent grey and white butterfly with red and black spots on its wings was sucking the nectar from a wild pea, while a few feet away a long green and yellow snake raised its head from the long grass and flickered its forked tongue at me.

I had trouble finding the path down as I was tired. I talked to myself to try and keep alert, telling myself to be careful, it wasn't worth breaking my neck at this time of day. The light was fading, making it difficult to see the path which was slippery with loose white stones camouflaged by leaves from the beeches that clung to the sides. I finally reached the lower hills without mishap, fetched water from the first village I came to and camped in a meadow nearby, deciding not to go far the next day.

There were no banks in Saillans, so I hitched to Crest, west along the Drôme. No sooner had I lifted my thumb than a young woman stopped. She would have taken me as far as Paris had I wanted to go. She was a social worker there, specialising in child delinquency, with some hair-raising tales to tell. The man who gave me a lift back invited me to a drink at his house. The drink became lunch which we ate in the kitchen while his two children played semi-naked on the tile floor. He was a road engineer, so I soon knew all about the different kinds of road surfaces necessary for modern traffic conditions. He passed over a copy of *Le Monde*, pointing to a photograph on the front page of gutted London houses. The race riots in Brixton were in full swing.

After a visit to the post office late that afternoon, I took the track to Vaugelas, arriving as the church clock struck eight. A shaggy dog with a very wet nose and a wagging, friendly tail had followed me nearly all the way, trotting along contentedly. At Vaugelas I shouted at her to go home but she wagged her tail all the more, so I hardened my heart and threw stones in her direction until she turned and ran. I felt beastly and was sad to see her go because she had been good company, but I couldn't let her follow me indefinitely.

An old man with flowing white hair came up to me as I was filling waterbottles.

'There's a spring just up there, you know, where the water's much better than this public fountain muck. Where are you going?'

'Towards Beaufort. I think I'll climb that hill and camp there tonight, get to Beaufort in the morning.'

He looked up at the track and began to reminisce.

'There used to be a time when one would see thirty horses or more going up there in a long file, carrying stores and other goods over to the valley [Isère]. That was when I was a boy, of course ...'

He was seventy-six years old.

I was glad to have the mosquito netting that night as I lay back watching hordes of the frustrated bloodsuckers trying to get at me. As I drifted into sleep I could see the full moon rising even before the last rays of the sun had vanished.

There were always little domestic chores to be done: boots to be greased, clothes mended, pots and pans to be scoured and, above all, socks to be washed. If I was good I did this once a day. I was engaged

144

in the Zen of sock washing at the pump in Plan de Baix when a teenager approached. We struck up conversation while he kindly turned the handle of the pump so I could rinse things a little more easily. He was called Jérôme.

'Have you had any breakfast yet?' he asked.

'No. I was waiting for the shop to open.'

'Why don't you come to my house? I'll get my mother to cook up something for you.'

I was soon stationed at a table in tremendously messy surroundings as his mother made me milky coffee and spread butter and honey on a large chunk of bread. I felt terrible, because she already had quite enough work on her hands with four semi-naked children wandering around sleepily demanding breakfast. She took her elder son's whims in her stride with a smile, taking a photograph from the mantelpiece and giving it to me to see: a young man with a donkey. For a second I thought it might be Stevenson.

'He's a Swiss type who came through here with a donkey once. We gave him breakfast like you and then he sent us the photograph when he got home.'

'He used to cover almost twenty kilometres a day,' piped in Jérôme. 'How many do you cover?'

'Difficult to say really, it depends on the terrain and how much energy I have left in reserve. About thirty or forty probably, but then I've been at it for a while now.'

We talked of agriculture, Ireland and the boy's uncle, a baker, before I thanked them sincerely for their hospitality and set off up to a chapel dedicated to St. Edmund, which was situated at the top of the cliffs above the village. A snake slid off into the grass soundlessly and there were masses of ripe wild strawberries beside the track which headed north in a pleasantly straight line along the westernmost ridge of the Vercors. By coincidence the man walking ahead turned out to be Jerome's uncle, the baker. He told me all about the bakery business as we walked along to Léoncel and about the British firm that had tried recently to take over the market using mass production methods. That they hadn't succeeded, he said, was due to the local people being used to having their bread fresh twice a day and rejecting the prepacked, soft doughy footballs they were trying to persuade them to buy. What saddened me most were the tales of wasted cakes and tarts that had to be thrown away after a limited period to maintain the baker's reputation for fresh produce. My mouth watered at the thought of all those cream and sweet sponge cakes going begging.

About an hour the other side of Léoncel it began to rain heavily. It had been too hot, the temperature rising into the high twenties centigrade. The woods were soon dripping, steam rising from the hot earth to the cloud-hidden peaks above. The high-wooded walls on either side gradually flattened out into rolling hills and a vista of pastoral land set with tall, graceful walnut trees opened ahead of me. When the temperature began to drop dramatically and the rain showed no signs of abating, I kept my eye out for possible shelter.

I had just set down my load on the straw in an open barn in the centre of a dilapidated village when a farmer appeared, carrying a pail in either hand.

'Do you mind if I sleep here tonight?'

The bushy eyebrows rose above his piercing blue eyes. He was a chubby man of about fifty, with a fine set of gold teeth.

'Well, I suppose you can if you have to. There's a hotel not far from here in Oriol, though.'

'Is there? The trouble is I can't afford hotels.'

He didn't say yes or no.

'Do you smoke?'

'No, of course not. Not in barns, anyway.'

'I wouldn't like to see that lot go up in smoke.'

'No, Sir. That would certainly be a disaster.'

I followed him to the cowshed, where he sat astride a three legged stool to milk, while the cows patiently chewed the cud. Two of the four he had were in calf. They were his livelihood, not much, but enough to survive, as he said. The local co-operative sent a lorry up every morning to collect the milk which went to make cheeses. He lived on that plus whatever the walnuts had to give. He said it was difficult to compete with the big producers who had thirty or forty cows, more sometimes. Still, the walnut harvest this year was going to be good.

His name was M. Fougier. We had made friends. He untied a bale of straw for a bed next to a chicken and her brood, and watched with curiosity as I stepped into my sleeping bag before saying good night.

Mother hen took her children for an early morning walk across my back, waking me at an early hour. I was ready to slip away when M. Fougier appeared to invite me into his kitchen for a large bowl of hot, fresh milk with bread and cheese. On a side-table stood a photograph of him as a young man, standing stiffly beside a pretty woman in a long, lacy dress.

'My wife,' he said, when he saw me looking at the picture. 'She's dead now.'

They had had no children. He lived with his mother, who was paralysed and bed-ridden. Nurses came twice a day to look after her and treat her bedsores, he said. His voice had flattened with

146

resignation.

'Do you have the same diseases in England?'

'Very similar, yes. How many people live in the village?'

'There's my mother and myself and a couple who live over the way. They had six children, but none of them have stayed on. In a way I'm glad that I didn't have any myself, it would make me so sad to see them leave.'

We said goodbye. The woods were still soaking so I kept to the road as I made my way into the valley of Royans, turned over in the main to maize and tobacco. The cars were much more dangerous than ever a wolf or snake had been, but somehow I reached Pont-en-Royans without being knocked over. It is a picturesque place built onto the sides of the Gorges de la Bourne. I crossed the old bridge over the deep ravine and found myself in a narrow, cobbled high street full of little shops selling trinkets and souvenirs to the few tourists. The weather had dampened their enthusiasm considerably.

It looked as if it were going to rain once more, so I followed the road rather than the path into the mouth of the gorge, thinking it would be easier to find shelter off the road. It can't have been far away that Hannibal started his ascent into the Alps with the elephants. He too had camped at the entrance, sending scouts ahead to reconnoitre. From them he learned that a hostile tribe, the Allobroges, were lying in wait further up the gorge but that they abandoned their positions at night to go and sleep in a settlement, probably Villard de Lans. On the second day he advanced to the most difficult part of the gorge and camped again. To the Allobroges, as they watched Hannibal and his men light fires and appear to settle down for the night, it seemed certain that he meant to force his way through at dawn.

Hannibal, however, had different ideas. During the night he personally took a column in to occupy the enemy positions. At first light the Allobroges found out what had happened and angrily began to harass the columns slowly winding through the gorge. Hannibal drove them off, rallied his men and went on to seize the settlement where they were encamped. He rested there for a day before continuing his march up the Isère, undisturbed further by the natives who had taken to their heels on hearing of his victory and the approach of 37 grey monsters.

I had only covered a few hundred yards from the cafe in Choranche when the rain came pouring down. I doubled back to the awning of a shuttered restaurant, sheltering there with another six people, exchanging the necessary platitudes about the state of the weather. Subsequently we were joined by two soaked, bedraggled hikers who appeared out of the woods from the path. They were

147

heading for a *refuge* in the forest, up above the gorge, marked on their more detailed 1:50,000 map. They were Dutch, called Eva and René, with an excellent command of English. We set off together when the rain had eased somewhat.

The cliffs we were to climb towered above us, rising half a mile almost vertically from the road, the path zigzagging up the side. At one point it became a wall up which we had to haul ourselves with great care, holding on to tree stumps and branches while groping for footholds in the wet, slippery rock face. I was glad we were not going down. Without a pack it would probably be tiring yet relatively easy, but with the pack to balance it was altogether more treacherous.

'Flicking path,' muttered René, from time to time. It was good to have my thoughts thus echoed.

We stopped to rest in the drizzle—it was their first day out—a worthy test—but I wanted to get to the *refuge* as soon as possible to light a fire and warm the place up before it got dark, so I pressed on.

The *refuge* was in the middle of a long-abandoned village, obviously built on the foundations of one of the ruins. Inside the wooden hut there were a couple of tables, benches, a stove, some candle butts and room for sleeping up the stairs under the roof. By the time I arrived, I was soaked through and cold, but found kindling and branches in the cellar, much to my relief. When the fire was crackling I went off in search of water but there was no well or spring that I could find, so I spread my plastic sheeting beneath the eaves of the roof to catch the rain water. A large pool had formed and hot tea was brewing when Eva and Rene arrived, thankful to get into the warm by the fire, where wet clothes were soon steaming.

We made supper while they kindly shared a flask of brandy. They were both psychology students but loath to talk about it. The rain poured down all night and didn't look like letting up when we woke in the morning. They left after breakfast while I stayed to take a complete day off. It was Saturday, 18th July, two weeks since I had left Le Puech and I needed a rest badly. I felt intensely lonely just before they left, but settled down afterwards in the hush to write letters and read.

* * *

The blood on the doorstep. Panturle had been gutting a fox when he heard the sound of footsteps on the path down to his house. He was suddenly conscious of the fact that he had his hand right up in the creatures entrails, that he had been shivering with pleasure at the viscous squelching. The spring sap was rising, plaguing him with restless dreams. In shame he rushed inside, closed the door and went upstairs to see who was coming. What he saw made his blood race: there were two people, one of them a woman, a young woman.

He stumbled out of the room, but banged his head on a beam as he went. Stars exploded as he crashed downstairs and fumbled with the key to open the door—nothing. He couldn't be sure that the solitude was not driving him mad until he saw a branch moving from left to right. If it were simply a current of air, it would move up and down. The hunt was on. He would catch up with them by taking the short cut over the falls, but there a supporting branch gave way, he fell and the strong current pitched him over the edge unconscious.

When he comes round it is night. He is lying face down on cold stone with grit in his mouth. He turns over. The woman is sitting beside him, her features sharp in the moonlight, beautiful. They dragged him out, she says, pointing to Gédemus asleep under a nearby tree. In a tender scene he proposes: 'I am as good as any man ...' She remembers the wind caressing her, full of flowers. When Gédemus wakes, they have gone.

* * *

My solitude did not last long. A couple with a friend and child in tow arrived, up from La Chapelle-en-Vercors. They began a picnic, *casse-croûte*, kindly giving me a piece of cake, some chocolate and a glass or two of wine, telling me of an old lady of 81 who still insisted on walking everywhere. She even went camping, saying it kept her body awake. She sounded a remarkable woman indeed.

The day came to an end with a pleasantly weightless walk in the woods. The rats had a merry time that night, scuttling around, rustling and banging. I thumped on the floor to drive them away but they just danced more merrily.

The rest had done me good. I set off in the morning at a cracking pace down into the valley and up again over the rocky spine of Clapiers Forest, with just one thought in mind: I wanted to get to Grenoble. A group of scouts who had lost their way listened sheepishly to instructions on how to get back to base. Autrans lay below. It seemed strange that many of the houses in and around the village should be roofed with a mixture of different tiles, slates and corrugated iron. The houses themselves looked as if they had at one time been demolished. The story goes back to the eve of D Day, 5th June 1944.

The Vercors was an ideal place for resistance forces and there had been Maquis there since 1940. Until September '43 the region was occupied by Italian troops who frequently got annoyed with the

Maquis for stealing supplies and ammunition from under their noses, and made regular sorties up into the valleys through the only weak spot in the natural defences, the gap at St. Nizier, above Grenoble.

When Italy capitulated, the Nazis took over control in the region. In mid winter, January '44, they stormed St. Nizier with the loss of ten men. In revenge for their deaths they burnt down two villages and the greater part of another. The Maquis began to plot. Ideally, these men wanted to hold the Vercors, to 'fly the French flag over at least one corner of France'. A plan was agreed with the Free French top brass that the groups in readiness would assemble when allied landings began on the south coast. All depended, nevertheless, on the arrival of Force C, an airborne French division from Algiers which would be parachuted in to back up the resistance. The plan was codenamed 'Operation Montagnard'. In March, the B.B.C. broadcast a special message: 'The Montagnards should begin to scale the heights'. The plan was on.

On the eve of the D.Day landings signals were sent out calling for limited tactical strikes by the resistance to confuse the enemy. The landings had indeed begun, but only in the north, yet the men in the Vercors thought the time had come for Operation Montagnard. By the 9th over 1500 men had assembled and the number was increasing daily. Their first test came on the 13th June, when the Nazis attacked St. Nizier with 1500 men. Two hundred and fifty Maquisards held them off. They tried again two days later with double the number, taking the village this time and burning it to the ground. The Maquis fell back behind the Gorges de la Bourne, while the Nazis returned to Grenoble. For a month the French flag flew over the 'Republic of Vercors'. They even celebrated the Day of the Bastille, the U.S.A.F. dropping red, white and blue parachutes, for which the Nazis retaliated with a bomb attack. All seemed to be going according to plan. The airborne troops should soon be on their way.

On 19th July the Nazis surrounded the Vercors with 20,000 crack troops. The assault began on the 20th in pouring rain, one column taking the St. Nizier gap, seven others forcing the passes. The Maquis were slowly pulling back when they heard the throb of airplane engines. Twenty gliders, Force C on the way. Morale soared as the parachutes opened and a thousand well-equipped soldiers floated down into the heart of their defences. But they were not from Force C; they were Nazi S.S. troops. More followed and the Maquis were blasted off the Vercors in two days, leaving only villagers to bear the brunt of Nazi anger. 'Terrorist' purges and torture began over the whole area, a familiar pattern best left to the imagination. Execution Wall in La Chapelle will always be there to remind those who pass of what happened. Forty years have gone by. A poll published in *L'Exprès* in 1979 asked which country was considered the best friend of France. Germany was easily top of the list with 33%, while the Allies got 22% (U.S.) and 16% (G.B.). Lamb wars are what make the news now.

Autrans has become a thriving holiday centre full of clean, well-dressed tourists, bicycles, restaurants, tempting shops and a bakery where I bought fresh bread for the first time in three days. French bread is delicious for a few hours but then goes stale, soft and rubbery so it is no good for travelling. The *biscotte*, a dry toasted bread, is much better, lighter and equally nourishing.

After lunch outside Autrans, I panted up a wide chimney to within striking distance of the Pas de Bellecombe at 1636 metres. The weather had turned filthy again and clouds had come in low reducing visibility to a few yards. I thought as long as I kept going I should have no problems as the ridge ran plainly north/south, but I would dearly have liked to have my compass with me. The imprint of boots in the path I had chosen from among many, bolstered my confidence, though I made it to the pass more by instinct that judgement. A flock of sheep were grazing on the crest where the slopes broadened out to form an alp bordered by pine woods. My poor boots were squelching, awash in the long, wet grass and I was feeling dispirited, when I noticed the door of a shepherd's hut open and no one in sight. I took a good swig of red wine from a bottle on the table before taking a path down.

It was getting late as I approached Engins and it was still raining. A wooden shed on the outskirts looked like paradise. The farmer said he didn't mind if I slept there, showed me the fountain and went about his business. I warmed up with soup, pasta and a hot cup of tea before lying down beside a plough to listen to the rain pattering on the tin roof.

It was still drizzling in the morning when I enjoyed a certain masochistic shiver of pleasure pulling on cold, wet socks and boots as my others had had no chance to dry. The sky cleared a little as I tackled the stiff climb to modern St. Nizier. The wide valley of the Isère lay below, covered in a blanket of soft cloud that swirled up at times to reveal the urban sprawl of Grenoble. On the other side of the valley towered the first mountains of the High Alps.

THE ALPS

GERMANY

FRANCE

SWITZERLAND

AUSTRIA

ITALY

1 : 3,000,000

50   100

(miles)

PART THREE

The Alps

'I should like the Alps very much if it were not for the
hills.'
(John Spence, 1730)

'The Alps are too big to be of any use to us.'
(Gustave Flaubert, 1821–80.)

'The Helvetic Confederation has a population of over six
million, which is less than 0.03 per cent of the population
of the world.. It is the world's leading market for gold,
money and insurance, the world's third largest financial
power, the eleventh industrial power and the home of the
world's largest food processing industry. The Swiss
people are the second richest in the world. The total land
area of the country is 41,295 sq.km., about a third of the
land area of England.'
(Adapted from Fritz Horn, *Switzerland Exposed*, 1975.)

153

France

A cable car brought cool, unperspiring tourists gliding up over the Isère to the restaurant terrace of the great fortifications of the Bastille above Grenoble. In the middle of the nineteenth century, a group of brilliant French engineers began experiments on creating electricity from the nearby waterfalls, a new idea at the time. Initially famous for its gloves and textiles, the abundant electricity generated in the mountains made the city an ideal location for chemical, engineering and plastics industries. Grenoble never looked back. The population after the War was 80,000. By 1975 this had increased to 400,000; the city was booming, the home of some of the most advanced scientific research centres in Europe. Even the City Council is controlled by the boffins, which is unusual in France.

The nuclear power station beside the river on the outskirts of the city is one of twenty in service in France, a surprisingly diminutive box structure painted yellow. The anti-nuclear lobby was expecting Mitterand to cancel work on the other twenty in construction, but in the end he only halted work on five.

My plan was to follow the line of the Massif de Chartreuse north from the Bastille, to the Bauges, past the southern tip of the Lac d'Annecy, then over the mountains to Lac Léman and Switzerland, a trek of a hundred miles, at least, which meant a week's walk.

I stopped for the night beside an empty house in a sheltered position overlooking the city. The broken knuckles of the Belledone chain rose up on the other side of the valley, the Grand Pic itself jutting up to 2752 metres, patches of perpetual snow showing between its crags. As the light faded from the sky the valley came alive, pulsating, the roads becoming arteries of sparkling orange, merging at the centre to form a monstrous, spidery creature of great beauty. It is easy to understand the fascination the city holds for the peasant who has spent all his life in some tiny, forgotten village.

I slept well and made good headway in the morning. A group of

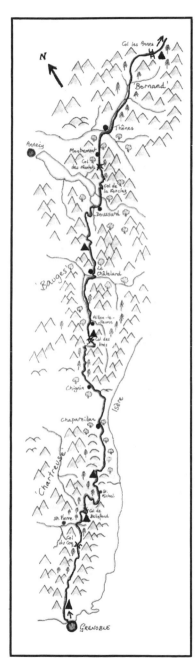

children passed, making lots of noise to frighten away the snakes, they said. Their leader was an English teacher, off to visit Salisbury on the Friday.

'It will be interesting to practise my English,' she said.

The conversation came round to dogs. The French do not treat animals as the English do. Dogs are not their best friends but guards with a job to do. They have much to lose, they think. She knew one family who would not even go on holiday for fear the house would be stolen.

The children looked on in admiration.

It was difficult to keep out of the puddles on the path to the Col du Coq. Large, thundering grey clouds rolled in to hide the sun, the temperature dropped sharply. It was only a cloudburst, though, the rain only settling in for good that evening when I stopped to rest by a large, covered fountain in a remote hamlet called Perquelin, up river from the Chartreuse monastery. 'Cabane de Bellefond' said a sign. I was tired, loath to tackle yet another slope, but the hut might provide shelter. A bar of chocolate gave the necessary energy for the climb, which took little more than an hour up a slippery, waterlogged path. A shepherd was surveying the jagged rocks on the crest of the Bellefond where some 800 sheep had their summer grazing grounds. 'Is there any chance of spending the night in your cabin?' I asked him.

He lowered his powerful binoculars.

'Are you alone?'

'Yes.'

'That should be all right, then. Wait for me at the cabin. I won't be long.'

He arrived with the rain. I moved my things inside, where a large trough bed took up half the available space, a table, benches and a stove the rest. They are remarkably efficient, these stoves, upright cast iron cylinders set into the cabin, radiating heat quickly, with rings on the flat top that you can remove so the flames play directly on the base of the pot when you are cooking. His wet, woolly grey dog trotted to my feet, her tail wagging.

The shepherd was a gruff man of few words, which was natural enough as he spent half his life by himself in the mountains. He had come up with the flock on 8th June to stay until the first heavy snows. From time to time he would swear and mutter at the weather.

'Adieu les beaux jours' (the good days are over).

He was fifty-two years old, with a withered right arm that made all his actions lopsided, and a leathery face that was lined and careworn. He banged around making supper on the stove, treating me to a bowl of hot soup.

'You take that.'

'Are you sure you've got enough for yourself?'

'Of course. I made enough for two.'

He reached up to the shelves of provisions.

'Here, take some cheese and grate it into the soup. It'll do you good, it's Cantal. Take some bread too. No, no, more than that, lad, take a real piece. Drink?'

'Thank you.'

The light had faded, so we went to bed. The night brought storms, thunder, heavy rain and a violent wind that tore at the cables which kept the cabin from being knocked down into the valley. It was still blowing strong in the morning at seven, when he turned on the radio for the weather forecast. The news came first, a policeman and all his family murdered, the Queen on a state visit to France, finally the weather—foul until the weekend. It was a Thursday. I turned over and went back to sleep, wondering that the hell I was going to do. At about nine, he got up to heat two bowls of milk for breakfast.

'I don't mind if you stay, but the boss may be coming up today and he doesn't like it much. We'll hang on anyway, see what the weather does this afternoon.'

I took out my book to while away the hours.

* * *

156

Things have changed at Panturle's house now that his lonely, bachelor days are over. Everything is clean, tidy, washed and scrubbed. The firewood is kept outside and Arsule, now his wife, has made him a new jacket and trousers from those of his father she found in an old cupboard upstairs. She found sheets, too, made him carry the straw mattress upstairs, put up the bed and wash before getting in. The only thing they lacked was bread. Perhaps his friend Amoureux would lend him a horse and seed corn while Gaubert, the old cartwright, could make him a plough. Amoureux agrees to his request, but Gaubert he finds paralysed, incontinent, depressed. Panturle's dreams are shattered, yet Gaubert can sense the rebirth of the village. He has Panturle take a key from his pocket, the key to a cupboard in his old forge.

'There's the last plough I ever made in it. Take it. Plough the strip on the slope above the village. The land will yield a good crop.'

Winter was approaching as Panturle ploughed the first furrow, the share cutting through the fat, black earth like the prow of a ship in still water. The battle was on.

He found what was left of Mamèche that winter up on the plateau. Returning to the village for the winding sheet that she had carefully left behind on her kitchen table, he found it had been destroyed by the rats, so he took a sheet off their own bed instead, wrapped her body in it and dropped the light bundle down the well. It was where she would have liked to go, he thought.

Summer comes. The local town is packed with country people down from the mountains for the great market. It has been a terrible year, the crops are poor, ravaged by storms, the yield low.

There is one man, though, who has good grain to sell. He is standing behind six sacks of spotlessly clean, golden, healthy wheat. Beside him stands a little woman, youngish, quite pretty really, cooked by the sun.

'Don't touch it,' he says to those who come and look.

M. Astruc, the grain merchant, understands. He asks the man if it was threshed by machine. Panturle holds out his hands. When he opens them, the scabs crack and bleed.

'Shut your hands,' says Arsule.

Astruc gives them 130 francs per sack, seven hundred and eighty francs in all. Panturle has never had so much money in his life. Together, they wander off to do some shopping but they can't decide what to buy. Finally, Panturle gives his wife all the money. That way, things work out very nicely.

The shouts, the fire crackers, the salesman's cries, the drinking, the incessant grinding of the barrel organ is suddenly too much for them. Amoureux said that he would give them a lift but they don't want to wait. Accustomed to the wide fields living slowly beside them, they feel the noise between them, cutting them apart. They need to be alone in their own silent world together. They set off home on foot.

★ ★ ★

A group of dripping hikers invaded the cabin as we were eating lunch, two couples, four children and two steaming dogs. I took my leave at about one o'clock as the weather seemed to be clearing a little. The shepherd brought out a bottle of *marc* and poured a full glass.

'Drink that, you're going to need it, I think.'

We went outside.

'Now listen carefully. You have to climb up to the end of the pastures where the rocks begin, then follow the line of the crest till you see a cross above you. Head for it. It marks the path that will take you down into the valley. You understand?'

I repeated his instructions and he nodded.

'It's a good thing you understand French.'

We shook hands, left hands, and he smiled a genuine smile, dropping his defences for a moment to reveal just another lonely man in the world. I never found out his name.

'*Allez, au revoir, bonne chance,*' (good luck to you).

'*Merci, au revoir.*'

At 1950 metres the wind was driving the rain at me horizontally, threatening to knock me over, finding every gap in my waterproof armour. Luckily the cloud that had drifted in cleared long enough for me to spot the wooden cross on the ridge above. Much relieved, I stumbled over the rocks and sparse scrub towards it. From there a good sheep trail led down to St. Michel. I marched along the road singing happily, ignoring the rain which came in sweeping gusts —thick sheets of water bouncing off the surface tarmac—until I finally had to admit defeat and take shelter in an open barn. I rested, but had to jump up and down to keep warm when it made no signs of easing off. In the end I decided to knock at the door of the farmhouse across the way to ask if I might hole out in the barn for the night.

The door opened before I had even knocked. A neat, tidy woman with round steel-framed spectacles was looking up at me.

'Would you mind if I sheltered in the barn over there tonight?'

'You can't do that. Come inside instead and get warmed up. You look soaked, your lips are blue. Where have you come from?'

'I've just come from the Col de Bellefond.'

'Oh, you poor thing, in this weather too. Come in, come in.' Strange how it is always at times when you are wet, cold and very miserable that Lady Luck smiles again, the wheel turns, sitting you in a warm kitchen when you were least expecting it. When she found out I was English, she brewed a pot of Earl Grey, produced a plate of bread, butter and jam, sat me down next to the fire and told me to tuck in.

She was called Clothilde, wife of Jacques, mother of Micheline who herself had a baby to look after. They made me very welcome: they put the bathroom at my disposal, hung my wet clothes by the stove to dry, set my sodden boots near the fire, lent me a warm pullover, showed me a bed where I could sleep in the playroom and invited me to supper.

'For what we are about to receive may the Lord make us truly thankful.'

'Amen.'

I had seldom said that word with greater conviction. They were all members of the *Communauté de la Sainte Croix*. After supper we sat round the fire while M. Falaise talked knowledgeably of local history. It was an opportunity to clarify something that had been puzzling me.

'Do you know Autrans?'

He nodded.

'I noticed that all the houses there seemed to have been knocked down or demolished somehow. Was it during the War?'

'Autrans in the Vercors? Yes. It was the Americans, bombing from high altitude. It didn't seem to matter to them if there were civilians. Their logic was simple: if there was a nest of machine guns in a town, wipe out the town. The same sort of tactics that they used in Vietnam, really.'

I fell asleep to the sound of occasional bumps and cries from the baby and awoke next morning to the rattle of the stove being raked out. Clothilde was in the kitchen.

'I'm afraid we don't have any porridge, so I've made semolina for you instead, which is as close as I can get.'

There was tea, bread and honey, yoghurt and fruit to follow. They gave me a booklet called *Paix, Vérité, Amour* to take with me, the Gospel of St. John in French. Inside was written 'Matthew 7 v7'. 'Ask, and it shall be given you; seek, and ye shall find; knock and it shall be opened unto you.'

As I was about to head off into the fine drizzle, Micheline handed me a bag.

'I've made you a *casse-croûte. Bon appétit.*'

'Thank you. I shall not forget your kindness.'

159

I kept to the roads before crossing the valley south of Chambery, not wishing my dry, newly greased boots to get wet again, passing two sleepy villages and a decrepit château with lovely, soft red tiles, a pleasant change from grey slate. From fields of maize, tobacco, wheat and vineyards I climbed to the Pas de Prés to sleep beneath my plastic on the lawn of a vacant chalet, back once again among wet meadows, breath misting in the steady rain that fell all night.

It could have been a morning in late autumn it was so chilly, misty and damp. Buildings were haphazard, usually either old farmhouses with spacious hay lofts beneath wide roofs of corrugated iron, or holiday chalets scattered among the wooded hills. Cannibalistic slugs sucking the remains of their dead companions committed suicide all over the road. I could not help thinking that their remains looked remarkably like burnt custard. A farm labourer in a dirty beret hailed me from the doorway of a cowshed where we stood chatting. He had been a prisoner of war for five years, one of those who didn't escape the dragnet for forced labour.

'I don't talk about it much. Young people these days just laugh at me. They think I'm inventing stories to frighten them.'

He told me of a short cut down to Le Châtelard, which I remember most for its supermarket and the postcard I sent home. It was Saturday, so I would have to stock up for the morrow. The sun came out briefly to evaporate the damp from my clothes, but otherwise it continued cold, wet, windy, misty and horrible, despite the weather forecast I had heard in the cabin on the Bellefond.

I reached the Lac d'Annecy by twelve o'clock the next day, tearing along after a very long sleep. I drank a little too much wine at lunch in a cafe in Doussard and paid for it dearly on the way up to the Col de la Forclaz. I suddenly found my head buzzing, while the sweat pouring off my body was freezing instantly and my heart was thumping so hard I had to sit down. I recovered soon enough, though, continuing on the soft, leafy path between hazel, beech and pine, wondering as I went if I had just suffered a heart attack. The Col was packed with weekend holiday makers milling round souvenir stalls beside the Hotel Edelweiss. The hang-gliders were the centre of attraction; they would take off from a rocky perch, shake around a little, level out and float gracefully down into the valley over the calm waters of the lake. One man even took his dog with him, a small highland terrier with a special harness all to itself. A ripple of wonder spread through the crowd as the pair disappeared into the void.

From there it was further up to the Col des Nantes, where an aggressive cow with menacing horns chased me over a fence. Perhaps it was her calf that a peasant couple were driving down a thousand metres to Montremont and she hated all mankind for it. The calf could sense it was going to the butcher's and stubbornly resisted all the way while the man and woman beat and prodded it, swearing and cursing its reluctance to be led to the slaughter.

The horns of a nearby scout camp sounding reveille nearby woke me in the morning, followed by a great rattling of forks on tin plates and cries of *Sur la Ferme*. After breakfast one of the scout masters appeared in a track suit carrying a spade, peered round and began to dig a regulation one-by-one. I cleared my throat noisily. He jumped up and beat a hasty, embarrassed retreat. I washed my feet in the river, put on clean socks and laced up my boots. The perpetual wet had caused cracks in the leather that would be almost impossible to mend. In Thônes the houses were all alpine, wooden with fancy joints at the corners, balconies with carved banisters and pretty, well ordered gardens bright with flowers. It was still cold and wet. I did a little shopping, then attacked the road, eating up the kilometres.

A light brown baby stoat with a white underbelly was playing up in front, frisking and flowing as if it had no bones, streaking up the road into the verge where it stood on its hindquarters like a question mark, its head out of the long grass, its beady eyes fixed on me. Then it was gone. In the orchards the apples were turning rosy, while the blackberries in the hedges were almost edible.

It took me by surprise when I realised I could probably get over the Col les Annes before camping, as I had already covered a good thirty kilometres. The whole area of the Grand Bornand is a ski resort in winter, spawning little restaurants and smart modern chalets everywhere which contrast sharply with the older, weather-beaten cabins that have wooden tiles and chimney stacks.

It was lovely to escape from the wind and sip a hot coffee in a primitive *buvette* on the leeward side of the Col. Three men and a woman were sitting round the fire in the middle of the room watching me as I added ten lumps of sugar to the cup.

'Don't your legs get cold in shorts?' they asked.

'Not when I'm walking. Sometimes a little when the wind is very strong, but when it's raining I prefer to get my legs wet rather than my trousers. They dry quicker.'

The young woman smiled charmingly. I pocketed some more sugar lumps for porridge in the morning and set off down the pass, camping beside a mound of pine needles which turned out to be an ants' nest. A breeze was beginning to take the clouds away, opening chinks of pastel blue and pink in the monotonous, grey blanket overhead.

The arrival of my old friend the sun at mid morning the next day made me so happy that it didn't matter I was lost. A sign to Romme made me chuckle. I duly ended up there when I had, in fact, intended to cross the chain of the Aravis mountains. I resigned myself, not unhappily, to a day's walking on tarmac. At Nancy-sur-Cluses an old woman with a bulbous nose and chronic rheumatism waved to me to come and sit down on the bench beside her, outside her house, which had bright red geraniums in the window boxes. She said I was lucky to be seeing the world while I was still young enough to enjoy it in good health. It was definitely the right time. There was no sense in waiting for retirement when you can't enjoy things physical to the full any more.

'Wait here. I'm going to get two glasses and a bottle of wine so that we can drink to your journey and a safe return home.'

'Ah, I do love the sun,' she said. 'I can feel it warming my old bones. The winter here is so long and cold, it will be the death of me soon, no doubt. Would you like a tomato for your lunch?'

She lumbered heavily into her garden, coming back with an apple as well.

'Thank you very much. Do you do all the gardening yourself?'

162

'Not quite. My son comes up sometimes from Cluses to do the digging. The rest of the time I live alone, so it's nice to have someone to talk to.'

'I know how you feel.'

There were no short cuts possible on the steep, twisting descent to Cluses, which lies in an industrial valley beside the river Arve, a wide motorway cutting past the town. I covered twenty-seven more kilometres that afternoon, though I doubt I would have gone so far without the company of a young man on his way to a holiday home to do the washing up. His motorcycle had broken down, so he had to walk. At least the conversation kept me from dwelling on tired, sore feet.

In Morillon, where he worked, he offered me a beer and gave me the remains of his lunch, wrapped in silver foil, saying he could get plenty of food at the house.

'There's not much there, anyway, just a little roast beef and some cheese. You look as if you need it more than I do.'

I was certainly not putting on any weight. My mouth watered in expectation of what turned out to be three sizeable chunks of lean *rosbif* which I ate at the side of a field by the river Giffre, at the edge of the mosquito-ridden wood where I slept.

I lay watching the sun rise slowly until I could feel its warmth seeping through the sleeping bag, the first time I had seen it rise for many a day, twelve in fact. It had been raining almost incessantly since the 17th. Could it be that the bad weather was over for a while? I hardly dared hope so in case my hopes were dashed. I fetched water, made breakfast and wandered late into Samoëns, where I paid a visit to the bank before buying a pair of canvas boots in case my faithful Trickers should give up the ghost in the Swiss Alps. The prices for such things would undoubtedly be higher in Switzerland, even if only marginally, and that could be the price of a beer or two.

By about six I had reached the Col de Coux where the path entered Switzerland for a few miles. The Swiss flag fluttered over a well-locked border hut while cows and goats grazed peacefully round a hamlet lower down and the happiest, cleanest pigs in the world grunted and charged around in the long grass. Now, for the first time, there was something to look at in the distance, something that filled my heart with wonder, for directly opposite were the rearing peaks of the Dents du Midi, and south-east across high ranges the icy, imperial summit of Mont Blanc itself.

I camped by a ski lift, gently rocking in one of the empty chairs as I finished reading Giono's *Regain*.

* * *

Panturle can hear Arsule singing happily in the bedroom above when a man appears at the door, timidly creeping into the house to find Panturle waiting for him with a long knife at the ready. It is Gédemus, the knife grinder. Panturle, who has been expecting this visit, allows him to sit down and have his say.

'It is hard for me now that Arsule has left, I am an old man, the grinder is a heavy weight to pull. Do you happen to know what became of her? She was poor company, anyway, not a good woman by any standards, picked up from the gutter, a poor cook, lazy and ungrateful as well, not worth a rabbit's fart in fact.'

Panturle listens in silence until the old man runs out of steam.

'She is here,' he says. 'If she was as bad as all that, you must be happy to have seen the last of her.'

He goes over to the mantelpiece and brings back 60 francs in notes.

'Buy yourself a donkey to replace her.'

Gédemus leaves. Arsule is still singing softly upstairs, unaware of the scene.

Autumn comes. Panturle is ploughing when he sees a short, strapping man coming over the field towards him. He anchors the plough to hold the horse and leave his hands free in case of trouble. The man approaches, introduces himself as Désiré. He is to be Panturle's new neighbour. He, his wife and their three children will be moving in shortly. Neighbours. Arsule and Panturle can hardly believe it, but word of the only good wheat at the great market had spread.

The spring wind arrives. Panturle is sitting under a tree smoking his pipe and listening to Delphine calling the children as Désiré puts the finishing touches to a new door for his barn. He and Arsule have still not got used to hearing the sound of other people in the village. She is coming down the path towards him, playing with a sprig of may. She seems to have got heavier, slower, her feet drag a little. Their eyes meet. Her face is radiant.

'Now you know,' she says.

He is to be a father. Panturle has to walk. He stops at the edge of his fields, bends, takes a handful of earth and rubs it between his fingers. Standing stock still, merging with the landscape, happiness washing over him, an image of the old, leprous, deserted Aubignane flashes before his eyes. The village is coming back to life. He knows, now, that he has won.

*　*　*

I closed the book and listened to the hiss of the stove cooking supper. If only Panturle could really win.

164

The morning was bright and clear, the air crisp and fresh, the peaks touched with the rosy fingers of dawn. For the first time on the trip, the path rose about 2000 metres as it crossed back into France over the Col de Chéserey and I paused a while, remembering how pleased I was the first time I went over 1000 metres, in Portugal the day before Piers left for Coimbra. From the Col I followed a high ridge of barren rock above pools of bracky water before dropping down to La Chapelle d'Abondance and a welcome sign: 'food'.

A man was climbing up towards me, looking worried.

'Have you seen two young women up here?'

'No, I'm afraid not.'

'Well, I suppose I'll have to check. Ruddy women,' he went off muttering.

I came across them a little later, sitting happily by a stream eating peaches.

'Are you lost?'

'No, we just got tired. We're waiting for our friend to catch up.'

'He's gone up to the top of the mountain looking for you.'

They laughed.

'We'll just wait for him to come down, then.'

A narrow valley sloped gently up from Abondance to the foot of a sheer wall of rock, the Cornettes de Bise. I was tired. It is difficult to know how far you have come in the mountains. As the crow flies it was about 17 kilometres but I was no bird. I struggled manfully to the pass and cantered down the other side, overtaking some very surprised hikers who were picking their way gently down. They were being sensible, of course, while I was being foolish, but fatigue has that effect. The bowl of the valley was marshy, full of mosquitoes that I hadn't expected to see at such an altitude. Mountains loomed on three sides, a stream running out to the west where the sun was sinking. A generator throbbed in one of the long, low barns where they were milking the cows. The *refuge* was smart, more like a hotel. As I would have to pay, I camped the other side of the stream while goats and ducks looked on indifferently.

My last day in France had arrived. I was up early to tackle the Dent du Volan, thinking too much of reaching the frontier, too little of the path, which I lost. Seeing the crest above, I decided to take it by storm. My motto wasn't 'Climb a mountain before breakfast' for nothing.

It was a foolish decision. After an initial period of confidence, I found myself unwittingly climbing properly, feeling for footholds, handholds, anything to hold, even knots of coarse grass that grew from fissures in the smooth rock, knowing full well that they would give way if I had to put my full weight on them. With my face right up against the rock to counterbalance the pack, I could smell the earth. There was no way that I could turn round without falling, breaking a leg if I were lucky, dashing my brains out if not. I was afraid to look down anyway. I had to keep on climbing. I edged my way up slowly, with great care, taking my time. The crest I had seen was not the true crest, but at least it sloped more gently from there. I had only to take my time. I found a secure position to rest and clear my head of panic. This was certainly dangerous, it was frightening to feel so close to death, small, fragile, unimportant. I had been in danger before, though, during the lightning storm in Galicia. Then I had been conscious of being totally powerless, whereas here, at least, I could fight.

I fought. The gradient became less steep, the bare rock gave way to coarse grass. I scrabbled up to the true crest like a wild animal, taking huge breaths as sweat poured from me, until I finally collapsed on the ground, my whole body trembling from the exertion and shock, both physically and emotionally drained.

Looking up, I saw the placid waters of Lac Léman while below, my gaze dropping 1700 metres to the terraced vineyards on the further shore and the blue shadows of the Jura mountains beyond. I floated down, my legs unfeeling, and crossed the border into Switzerland.

Switzerland

The Swiss flag was flying proudly from the roof top of almost every house in St. Gingolph, fluttering in the breeze that ruffled the grey waters of the lake. On the morrow, they would be celebrating the First of August, 1291, when the leaders of three alpine valleys, Uri, Schwyz and Unterwalden met at the Rütli on Lake Lucerne to form an alliance against the Austrians, who were threatening the independence of a traditionally democratic, Celtic people by sending in judges from outside. They had no desire to become vassals of a centralised, Habsburg monarchy. They called themselves *Eitgenoze*, or 'Sworn Comrades', which later became corrupted to Huguenot.

The Alliance was soon put to the test at the battle of Mortgarten in 1315, when Leopold 1 of Habsburg sent 7000 men and 2000 mounted knights against a mere 1330 Schwyzers. By clever use of surprise tactics and their knowledge of the terrain, they won the day. After the Habsburg threat came that of Charles the Bold of Burgundy, who was also roundly defeated. The Confederation began to grow. By the time Napoleon invaded, it included fifteen different cantons. At present there are twenty-two.

I waited for one of the fast paddle boats to take me effortlessly across to Montreux, a birthday treat. It was nearby that Byron and Shelley were 'most nearly wrecked in a squall' while on a tour of the lake in a rowing boat. I sat watching the well-oiled pistons pumping in the spotless, gleaming brass engine room below deck as I ate sardines, bread and cheese and looked out over the lake to the mountains rising sheer from the shore on either side of the flat mouth of the Rhône. Cameras clicked and whirred amidst exclamations of wonder as we passed the castle of Chillon, where the galleys of the Counts of Savoy once moored, a fortified palace beside the lake housing barracks, law courts, a chapel, the treasury and the dark dungeons where Bonivard was kept in chains for six years before the Bernese came to his rescue. According to Byron's poem, he was not really sure that he wanted to leave at all.

167

With spiders I had friendship made,
And watch'd them in their sullen trade,
Had seen the mice by moonlight play,
And why should I feel less than they?

...

My very chains and I grew friends,
So much a long communion tends
To make us what we are:—even I
Regain'd my freedom with a sigh.

The castle of Chillon

We docked at Montreux not long after. 'A stupid, temporary town', says Russell, 'with nothing interesting to say for itself'. It is built on a series of steep slopes, the main street dominated by hotels and expensive shops, the people mostly tourists, elegantly dressed in the latest French fashions. It was just a simple fishing village until the eighteenth century, when it became the thing to view the mountains and glaciers inland. The cemeteries testify that most of these early visitors were British.

If the French had seemed efficient, the Swiss were hyper-efficient. The young woman behind the counter at the post office was most polite and kind, taking great pains to ensure she had all the post that was waiting for me, smiling courteously as she handed over a parcel and a bundle of letters. I handled them lovingly before stowing them away unopened. They would make good company on my birthday, a treasure to look forward to.

Next, a visit to the bank to cash a cheque. There are some four thousand banks in Switzerland, no bank robbers to speak of either. After all, you don't rob a bank if the money in it is yours. I came out fifty pounds richer and went shopping in a vast 'Migros' supermarket, the equivalent of the English 'Sainsbury's'. I would have to be careful with my money because the standard and cost of living were very high. All the packaged food was marked with the amount of protein, fat and carbohydrate, as well as the calories per 100 grammes, so I spent a pleasant hour trundling round with an enormous trolley working out the cheapest 4000 calories that could be carried. I had to provision for the weekend, so I was carrying a fair weight by the time I left the town to start the 500-metre climb to Glion, a taste of the mountains to come.

A lightly gravelled path led up across the lakeside motorway into woods of umbrella pine that gave way to pasture higher up, dotted with holiday and weekend chalets. A middle-aged German tourist stood on the path above, his cine-camera focussed on me as I

168

struggled up the hill, head down, puffing, sweat dripping over the lenses of my glasses.

'You'd better preserve those pictures, Monsieur. They're historic.'

'Where are you going?'

'Istanbul.'

'Pardon?'

'To the city.'

'Oh.'

From a bench in the evening sun, I watched the Glion cafes fill with people relaxing from the week's work in front of frosty glasses of beer. I was sorely tempted to have a bottle myself, but I already spent my allowance for the next three days. The longing to join in was difficult to resist, for this poverty of mine was not real, but self-imposed. Perhaps it gives an edge to life. The night was close and heavy, with intermittent drizzle, but August dawned bright and sunny. My destination for the day was the Lac d'Hongrin, not too far away. A well-marked path meandered over the Col de Jaman, past a lake 'in the very nipple of the mountain' as Byron put it rather inaptly in 1817, when he passed by on horseback with a mule to carry the baggage and a guide to show him the way. Now that was definitely the way to travel.

With a last look over my shoulder at the Lac Léman, I headed down, then gently up again, following the river Hongrin to the dam, pitching camp in a stand of pines on a knoll above the lake. There was just enough time to collect pine needles to make a good bed before light faded. I went to sleep happily, wondering how it would feel to be twenty-eight when I woke up.

I woke suddenly in the middle of the night. The wind had dropped and there was not a sound to be heard. Then voices began to drift up from the lakeside, the sounds of chinking glass and muffled laughter, a group of Swiss celebrating the birth of the Confederation. One of the carousers lurched past the tent later.

'Is that a tent I see before me?'

I poked my head out sleepily.

'No, it's a cow.'

'Oh, I'm serribly torry.'

Imagine waking to a very soft green light, the blue shadows in the valley gradually changing, turning green, the reflection of the mountains on the surface of the lake slowly crystallising, the sun about to break out over the tops, the spot peaceful and quiet. Twenty-eight years old, another seven-year cycle beginning. Life was good. I felt confident, holding no doubts as to the validity of the trip. The future was, as ever, hazy but I was content to know my direction if not the way that would lead there.

I plunged head first into the snowy reflection, came up gasping at the cold and struck out, crawling hard, feeling fit, strong and happy. The day stretched before me, long, pleasant hours of rest with plenty of food to eat and letters to read, that had to be opened slowly, with care, so that I could savour the words and picture family, friends and loved ones. The parcel was a book from Frederick, who also enclosed a letter to say he had contributed fifty pounds to the travelling fund, another two week's grace before the bailiff began to hammer at the door. The book was *Jupiter's Travels*, by Ted Simon. I lay reading avidly, following him round the world on a motorcycle, roaring across the sands of the African deserts, carrying the dreams of those he knew with him.

The day wore gently to a close, the reflection in the lake dying away, though the ghostly silhouette of the mountains remained as the stars came out one by one. I had had plenty of time to study the map I had bought in Montreux in a small stationer's shop. It was a good map, the salesman had said, only published that year.

'You'll find all the paths you need marked on it, even though it's 1:300,000. It's waterproof too, printed on special paper tested for wear and tear. They put it in the mud and ran lorries over it just to make sure it would survive the toughest treatment. If it gets dirty, a wipe with a cloth will clean it in no time.'

'I'll take it, thank you.'

The plan was to follow the well-worn path on the northern side of the High Alps that headed roughly east-north-east via Gstaad,

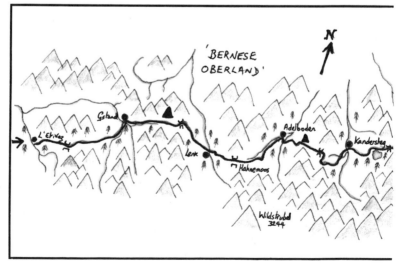

Adelboden, Lauterbrunnen, Meiringen and Altdorf, all convenient points for refuelling. Then I would have to think of Austria and Italy, planning the way on to Turkey. I had my work cut out to reach Italy before the twentieth of the month, although sixteen days to cross Switzerland did not seem impossible. I was certainly fit enough.

I found out all about Swiss cow bells that night, vast things a good six inches across that can be heard from way across the valleys. A herd of the cows came grazing peacefully towards my tent that moon-lit night, their tongues rasping as they curled round a tuft of grass and ripped it up, the sound of munching and grinding molars pleasant in the silence. But the bells... the intermittent clanging was loud enough to make all sleep impossible and I had no desire at all to spend the night in a belfry. First, I tried sticks and stones to drive them away. They retreated, I relaxed, but they wandered back once more, forcing me reluctantly from the warmth of my sleeping bag to chase them away. As I charged around in the moonlight shouting at the quadruped spectres, naked and furious, I slipped in the mire and was forced to go down to the lake and wash my feet before I could get back to my sleeping bag. At least they kept their distance after that.

I set off at dawn to the still village of La Lecherette, but the general store in L'Etivaz was open by the time I arrived there. A matronly woman with grey hair tied back in a bun watched as I wandered round the open shelves loading up with powdered milk and other essentials. She came out into the warm sunshine afterwards to show me the way on, to an alp which lay between two peaks at an

altitude of about 2000 metres, a climb of almost a kilometre. I would need a good breakfast before tackling that one; the usual porridge, half a litre of milk, two eggs, four rashers of bacon, cheese and chocolate eaten with a loaf of crisp, fresh bread. I gloried in the taste and texture of the bread, relieved to have escaped from the land of the *baguette* at last. With my stomach full and heavy, it was an effort to start off, but the rhythm returned soon enough. The day was fine, the views changing every minute. Exact memories of the scenery have disappeared, but two Canadians I can still see sitting beside the track on a boulder, eating their lunch. They were out on a walking tour of the Bernese Oberland and kindly shared their packed lunch with me as we chatted, offering me unwanted tomatoes, an egg, bread and cheese as well as a very welcome glass of wine. The pass marks the frontier between the French speaking Vaud and German-speaking Bern. The French Swiss are *Welsche* to the Swiss Germans, a word meaning 'foreigner'. I strode down to Gstaad singing happily in the clear, elastic air, snatches of 'Oh, Danny Boy', which bounced back to me off the rocks. I was looking forward to trying to communicate in German, a language of which I knew only a few words. I would have to wave my arms around in the air, point at things, making up nonsense as I went.

The hay had been cut in the meadows around the houses and barns in the long, gently sloping river valley. The old farmhouses are very fine buildings, often enormous, with long balconies under wide, overhanging roofs that come down almost to the ground. The most precious have dates and beautiful, flowing gothic inscriptions: *'Zur Herberg hier fur kurze Zeit, die Heimat ist die Ewigkeit'*, which I am told means 'This is our abiding place for a moment, our true home is in Eternity'.

They used long trucks with a very low wheel base to collect the hay, which was flicked automatically onto the trailer from behind, then taken to be sucked up by a giant drier and blown into the barn. All very practical and tidy: very Swiss. It cannot be pure coincidence that one quarter of the country is unproductive, one quarter arable, one quarter pasture and one quarter forest. You need legal permission to cut down woods in Switzerland and you have to reforest the equivalent amount elsewhere.

There were quite a lot of hikers around, mostly small family groups out from Gstaad for the afternoon. I hummed instead of singing in deference to their sensibilities.

'Guten Tag,' I said.

'Gruetzig,' they replied.

I wondered what that meant. It was the first time on the journey that I was confronted by a language that I did not know.

Gstaad was full of tourists. A popular skiing resort in winter, a centre for walks and easy climbs in summer, it is difficult to imagine what this sort of place was like before the invasion. An untidy cluster of houses round a church more than likely, with a tough local peasantry who sensibly found that they could earn more money in a week from rich tourists than they could earn in a year breaking their backs working on their smallholdings. At least it has stemmed the rural exodus. Some six per cent of the working population now work in the tourist industry while seven per cent work in agriculture, a lot more than in England where the figure for agriculture is a tiny three per cent.

I found little of interest to detain me in Gstaad, so I did some shopping, posted a card or two, bought petrol for the stove and followed the river out. It had surprised me that they wouldn't sell me petrol at the petrol station. It was against the law, they said, so I was forced to follow directions to a carpeted chemist's displaying magnificent arrays of toiletries and suntan lotions, in order to ask humbly for fuel. Here we had a linguistic problem, for they weren't sure whether I wanted petrol, benzine, essence, alcohol or what. They eventually let me have some pure *Benzin*, insisting on sticking a typed label with a skull and cross bones onto the bottle before I could leave. I sincerely hoped the fuel would burn and cook my supper that night. Fortunately, it did, though the stove didn't seem to like it very much. It was probably too pure.

By eleven o'clock the next day I was in Lenk, famous for its sulphur baths, another tourist centre crammed with jostling holiday makers. I remember the bakers had a selection of more than thirty kinds of bread to choose from. By evening, I had climbed over the Hahnenmoos pass, taken the path down to Adelboden and camped above the valley on the other side. The sun had set, the slopes were in shadow, but a range of jagged pinnacles were still outlined against the silvery blue, late evening sky, the snowy, soaring crags of the Tschingelhorn and the Wildstrubel still holding the sunlight. The cooker hissed. I might have been in Tibet.

Another day, time to move on to Kandersteg, over the Bonderalp a thousand metres above. The climb to the pass was not difficult or particularly steep, but long, gradual and tiring. From the pass I gazed straight over the next valley to a high, green lake, the Oschinensee, which was tucked into the folds of mountains that rose on three sides. It was about ten kilometres as the crow flies and it would have been pleasant to float over and escape the town altogether, for I had no wish to join the other tourists. There were too many of them, reminiscent of Oxford Street in summer, when it's a job to spot a local. Let me entertain you with some figures while I pick my way down to Kandersteg; the figures are for 1975 but things haven't changed much since then.

In that year foreign tourists brought in a total of 5.35 thousand

173

million Swiss Francs, making tourism the third biggest industry behind the chemical and machine industries. The positive trade balance was 2.4 thousand million S.F., the equivalent of £20,000 for every square kilometre in the country. The consumption figures are also fun. Between them, the tourists consume 94,000 head of cattle, half a million sacks of flour, 27 million litres of milk, 4.7 million kilos of cheese and 68 million eggs.

The path ran down through a farmyard where a man was standing in the doorway of his house, the smoke from his pipe drifting up over the lintel into the eaves. I walked over to see if he would sell me some milk. He had just finished churning butter, which he did in a thin wooden cylinder with a pestle that he pumped up and down.

'*Gooten Morgan. Do vous haber a kleiner bitter milch?*'

Put the stress on the last word and hope the message gets across. Untie the tin cup from its lace and hold it expectantly. He understood, retiring into the dim interior of the house, returning with the cup filled to the brim with rich, creamy white, warm milk. No brucellosis there, I hoped, as I rummaged around for a franc in the pack pocket.

He took it, nodded and went about his business as I collected water from the trough beside one of the wooden barns. His wife came over a little later, when I was tucking into porridge, followed by a loving cow which insisted on chewing her arm. She took my cup and went back to the house to refill it. She did so surreptitiously, when her husband was out of sight, smiling conspiratorially when she brought it back.

There were more English-speaking people in Kandersteg than Swiss; there was even a Girl Guides' camp complete with Union Jack. The Kander river was a murky brown colour, and rushed in tight waves through the fields, down from the glaciers behind the Blümlisalp, one of the solid walls of rock that I had seen beside the lake. I did some shopping and headed straight for the Oschinensee, sweating heavily in the afternoon heat as I did so, and sharing the path with many other walkers. They all appeared to be well-booted, flannelled and rosy, with regulation breeches, long, red woollen socks and light picnic packs. I stood out from them like a sore thumb, a shabby, dusty wreck in white shorts grey from cold water washing, black tar stains on the seat, a T-shirt instead of a check shirt, a monstrous green pack, a long bamboo stave and boots that were so worn they were beginning to crack, developing little holes so my feet could breathe more easily.

The lake shore was crammed like Copacabana beach on a Saturday. I swam in the icy water, soaked in the warm rays of the sun, ate lunch and headed for the second pass of the day, the

174

Hohtürli which at over 2000 metres was but a climb now of little more than 550 metres. Where the path became dangerous and skirted a vertical face of rock, a cable was kindly provided by the Club Alpine and led over a ledge into a narrow valley cut by the tongue of the Wilde Frau glacier. From the path, I gazed down on the ice, an eerie blue green, the cracks at the side stained with the ashy black deposits that turned the water in the valley below that grey-brown colour. It was useless for drinking. With the glacier to contemplate, I rested and consumed the third Mars Bar of the day. Normally, I ate nothing but the cheapest black chocolate which has more cocoa and thus more iron, but a longing for the familiar taste of a Mars Bar had been too great to resist. I bought three in Kandersteg in a special offer pack, thinking I would have one a day as a treat. They had lasted the afternoon. As a matter of interest Swiss chocolate production amounts to 69,474 tons a year, of which they only export 17%, leaving them with the equivalent of ten kilos per head of the population per year, not that much, perhaps. I was eating about half that amount every month.

The Mars gave me the necessary energy to reach the pass. I could feel my body digesting the sugar instantly, burning it away as I climbed. As I crossed the snow and ice at the top, I could hear the sound of running water beneath the crust, and then made a careful descent on the slippery grey-black slag treacherous in the half-light. Far away to the north, light was just fading from the surface of the Thunersee by Interlaken, green pastures and pines on the higher slopes catching the last slanting rays of the sun. Goats bounded around on the rocks and I felt as agile myself, as I enjoyed a level part of the descent to the Griesalp. On my way down, I passed an isolated hotel where people sat cosily inside eating their supper in the warm, subdued electric light. I felt no envy. The stars shed enough natural light to find a place to camp in the shelter of a boulder further down. I was warming to the mountains and slept better than I would have on any bed. When the weather was good, what better life could there be?

From a perch on the other side of the Griesalp, the smooth, rounded boulder behind which I had spent the night looked small and insignificant, as if tossed there by some giant. A large breakfast gave me strength and the will to tackle the next pass, the Sefinenfurke at 2600 metres. A tired Englishman sat resting against a rock at the foot of the pass. I remember his black army boots and expression of sad exhaustion. No doubt I looked much the same at times.

'You shouldn't stop you know. It'll make you feel more tired.'

The pass was a mere crack in the chipped, eroded granite wall that

175

loomed above. This was going to be a tough one. The gradient began to steepen sharply. I began talking to myself 'Steel your will, measure the pace. Just take small steps now. Breathe deeply. Poise your body ready for the assault.' Balance was all-important and to achieve that I had to crouch slightly in order to pull the weight of the pack forward so as not to lose that precious, slow momentum. 'Head down now,' I chuntered on. 'Keep your eyes on the ground, guide those feet; there'll be time enough later for the views.'

It was getting very steep. My heart was thumping and my lungs were working like bellows to haul in the sharp, crisp oxygen; they felt as though they were going to burst. The sun beat down and I noticed I was leaving a trail of drops on the path as the sweat trickled down the end of my nose. Every so often, I looked up to see how things were going, but not for long. Concentration. If I could just keep going, the pass would come to me. 'Up, steeper, slip, keep that momentum, dig in the staff, a third leg to help you up. Keep your balance, boy!' I muttered.

A flash of red and white went by, a path marker, reassuring. I slowed for a second to admire a tiny, delicate flower with blue and white petals, but frightened of losing the momentum, I could not stop. Now all I could hear was the sound of my own heart thumping and the rattle of a loosened stone on the slippery, matt grey shale. The last bit was coming. 'Start scrabbling on your hands and knees, let the instincts take over. Careful of that rock face staring at you, watch out the pack doesn't get snarled, the tin cup is banging a warning on the rock; hold on to the stick, don't lose your balance, sound like a steam engine. Salt stinging the eyes, running into your mouth. Lick it, you're almost there.' Then I was.

On a ledge high above the world, I sat back ecstatic, closed my eyes and rested. Deep, smooth breathing returned and I could feel the blood coursing free again. My whole body glowed. Opening my eyes, I looked down to where I had come from and there was the town of Kandersteg now no more than a toy village. Looking to the east, the earth dropped away and I could see the path further down across the ice flow. A new valley had opened up before me, an immense panorama of mountain crags and clefts with little lakes cupped in the gentler folds, and there, ten miles distant, were the dazzling peaks of the Mönch, the Jungfrau and the Eiger, an impressive trinity, stark, merciless and indifferent, guarding the wastelands of perpetual snow and ice. Those mountains sang in my blood.

Jackdaws circled playfully in the air currents, one perched on the sign 'Sefinenfurke, 2612 metres.' Someone had daubed the rocks with 'Jesus Lives' in German.

The descent was not difficult after the initial bends and patches of

176

icy snow, but I felt weak and exhausted and had to stop at the first water trough to eat lunch and gather strength in the sun. It was just over a month since I had left Le Puech. Most of the time I had been walking in mountains and I had only taken two days of complete rest. As I was carrying no reserves of fat, I had to eat to keep going; a very simple life. The towns were little more than stations along the way where I could refuel, even though Lauterbrunnen and the other towns that lay ahead were full of history, haunted as they are by the literary ghosts of the Wordsworths and their friends.

The water trough made from a tree trunk

Lauterbrunnen lies sunk at the base of a great fissure in the chain that I was following. I had to descend nearly a mile and a half into the gorge, ever downwards on the steep cliff sides. The lower I went, the more tourists I met. I indulged in a ridiculous conversation with a kindly, middle-aged German couple about the strain the descent was having on my knees. I had to say something. I hadn't spoken to anyone for what seemed like days. It was refreshing to hear my voice for once rather than my thoughts. I love the mountains, the sense of wild freedom that they give, the ever-changing perspectives, the air so clean it clears the mind completely, but their company is silent, vast, forbidding, inhuman.

Lauterbrunnen is the home of the *Staubbach* falls, the 'torrent of dust' a thin waterfall that sprays over the side of the gorge, breaking into a mist on the long 240-metre drop to a projecting rock where it forms once again into water. Byron describes it nicely as 'the tail of a white horse streaming in the wind'.

Once down, I followed the signs for the Wengernalp below the Kleine Scheidegg pass, past a busy campsite to a thundering great waterfall, the *Trümmelbachfälle*, that cut through the vertical wall of granite above, and plunged down into a pool that was a writhing mass of foam, the spray drifting out over a sward of green pasture at its base. I had thought to climb to the Wengernalp before night fell, but one look at that sheer wall put paid to that idea. I camped early instead, dropping my stuff under a nearby maple before going back to fetch water from the nearest house.

'*Wasser?*'

My German was not improving. The middle-aged woman who

opened the door showed me to a trough and tap, pointing out the date on the cement as she did so. I was reading more of *Jupiter's Travels* after supper when she came walking over the meadow towards me, carrying a large thermos flask.

'For your breakfast, some coffee.'

'*Danke, Fraulein, danke.* What shall I do with it when I have finished the coffee in the morning?'

She pointed back to her house and retired. It was good to feel cared for. A glow of happiness and contentment spread slowly through me. It was such a small thing, yet she must have appreciated that it would mean a lot.

It had been threatening to rain and suddenly poured down. I scampered over to the maple tree to set up tent, an elementary camping lesson learned: 'never read when you should be putting up your tent'. I slept soundly, too tired to even notice the thundering of the Trümmelbach, fed by the silent Jungfrau three thousands metres above.

The first zigzags of the path up to the Wengernalp the next morning were tricky, but again there was a cable to hold on to when the ascent became in any way dangerous. The path rose through woods cupped in the hollows beneath the Mönch, before descending slightly to cross the Trümmelbach on a small, wooden bridge. The river had cut through the rock, and formed a chimney no more than a metre wide. I leant on the parapet of the bridge to watch the water coming towards me at incredible speed at stomach height, dropping away just before the bridge, plunging in a giddy rush down, alive, relentless, an artery of Gaea, the 'Universal Mother, firmly founded, the oldest of the divinities' (Homer). According to Hesiod, in the beginning was Chaos, a vast, dark, gaping space. First Gaea appeared, then Eros. Gaea bore Uranus, the sky crowned with stars, 'whom she made her equal in grandeur, so that he entirely covered her'. Then she created the high mountains and the sea and the Earth was formed. From the union of Gaea and Uranus came the first race, the Titans.

I had never felt so close to a power over which we petty, squabbling mortals have absolutely no sway. I went on eventually, reluctantly, feeling strangely drawn back, never really wanting to leave Mother Earth.

I rested the other side of the Kleine Scheidegg pass, where the soft green turf cut with bubbling brooks was drenched in sun and bright with gentians, yellow arnica and tussled thistles. It was a placid, rural scene, but only if you kept your eyes on the ground, for directly in front, a massive wedge of rock rises smoothly for a mile into the sky above: the north face of the Eiger. Way above me, it joined the peaks of the other mountains, all licked by wisps of cloud, some sides with jagged, gloomy fissures, others bright and dazzling white; a world of sudden storms and cold, lonely deaths.

The North Face was first climbed by two Swiss men on 1st August 1932. This left the Eigerwand to be conquered, the north-west face at which I was looking. It is really dangerous. Two Germans tried it

The Eigerwand

in 1935, but failed. The next year a party of two Germans and two Austrians set out for the summit. They spent three unsuccessful nights on the mountain before a storm drove them down to a point just above the Eigerwand station of the Jungfrau Railway. The traverse that led to safe ground was iced, so their only hope lay in abseiling down. An employee at the station heard their shouting and telephoned for help. The rescuers emerged from a tunnel 100 metres below where Kurz was hanging on a rope, the only member of the party to survive the abseil attempt. Rainer froze to death, Hinterstosser fell to his and Angerer throttled himself in the ropes. As it was growing dark, there was little they could do but shout encouragement to Kurz and wait for the light to return.

Kurz hung there all night, bombarded by falling stones and drenched by the freezing water that poured down the smooth mountainside. Incredibly, he was still alive next morning when the rescuers managed to reach a point some 40 metres below him. He needed more rope, so he climbed back to the body of one of his companions, cut the rope that bound him to the corpse and used this to lengthen his own, an operation that took him six hours. His hands were frozen, the cliff so smooth he could find no secure footholds.

When he was ready, he lowered the rope to his rescuers, who attached a 30 metre rope to it plus pitons and a hammer. He pulled

179

them up, drove in one of the pitons and slowly began to lower himself past the overhang that lay between him and safety, using his very last reserves of energy. The rescuers had just seen his feet appear above their heads when all movement stopped. Kurz had died.

The Eigerwand was finally conquered in 1938. In the next twenty years, thirty-one people attempted the climb. Of these, only fourteen succeeded and seventeen died.

I walked down the steady slope to Grindelwald with a Swiss-German who called himself Bertie. The town lies in a pastoral basin below the alp, surrounded by mountains, the slopes on the way down dotted with chalets, a lake glistening ahead. Bertie spoke good English and so for the first time in days I was able to have a proper conversation. He was taking his final exams in Law that year and spoke of the recent riots in Zurich; not something I immediately associated with Switzerland. They appear to have started with the voting of sixty million Swiss francs for the building of an opera house. The Left had been promised a youth centre at half the price and when the money wasn't forthcoming, all hell had broken loose. They had the centre now, but they wanted it to be outside the law with no access by the police. 'They just wanted to smoke cannabis and get high in peace, instead of being busted all the time. There have been twenty-two deaths from heroin abuse already, now there are more riots. It's all international terrorism, of course,' he added.

We had come to the outskirts of the town, where we parted, picking our separate directions through the crowds of Japanese and American tourists that swarmed around the centre. I rested on a bench, tired, watching the faces. There were white stains on my black T-shirt from the salt of my exertions in the mountains. As my strength returned, I decided there was still time enough to climb the Grosse Scheidegg. It would not be difficult, a long, gentle rise of a thousand metres. 'This must be the equivalent of going up Snowdon twice in one day,' I thought to myself, as I set off.

The pass was a humble affair between the two huge massifs that overshadowed it on either side. The Wetterhorn was covered in low cloud which was not a good sign. It is known as the 'Barometer of Grindelwald'. When obscured by cloud, the message is simple: it is going to rain. It was first climbed in 1854 by an Englishman, Alfred Wills. who later presided over the trial of Oscar Wilde as Justice Wills.

I ate lunch unmolested by the storm clouds that were gathering in the north and blotting out the sun, but later, as I crossed the pass and headed down once more, the wind changed direction and they came towards me. Thunder rolled, the sky grew ever more black and fat raindrops began to spatter on the ground. I took shelter in a low barn with wooden tiles and leaned on the half door as I watched the heavy downpour. Within minutes the valley below was lost in the mist and visibility was down to a few yards. I turned to investigate the shed.

It was empty, though the clothes hanging on a line from the beams suggested that someone would be along soon. I was wondering who owned the moped that was standing in one corner when Fritz appeared, smoking a small cigar, a stumpy old fellow wearing a blue woolly hat with a tassel, a red-and-white checked shirt, baggy trousers with braces and green wellington boots, his wrinkled, weather-beaten face sporting a long, curly, whitening beard and whiskers. Using sign language, we understood each other immediately. I learned that he had 101 cows, not milkers, young ones, little ones, if I had interpreted him correctly. In turn he learned that I had walked from Portugal, that it had taken five months, and that although it was very hard, yes, I considered it good for the head. 'How many kilometres?' Who knows . . . many.

The rain had stopped, but the sky remained black and menacing. Fritz beckoned me with a crooked finger. I followed, ducking beams under which he passed with a good six inches to spare, a fact that he noted with a wry chuckle. He pointed to a pile of hay in the far corner beside the mangers, put his palms together, raised them to his right ear, cocked his head sideways to rest on this pillow of gnarled knuckles and raised his eyebrows in a question.

'*Ja, danke*, Fritz. *Danke* very much indeed, that's just what I need.'

His living quarters were built onto the far end of the barn, a tiny window giving light to a cluttered kitchen with a table and chair wedged in and a log for visitors to sit on. I noticed he kept all his knives pinned in the cupboard door. Three steps led up to his bedroom from which his dog came bounding out to lick his hand and snuffle excitedly round my feet.

Supper I cooked outside near the trough, sitting beside the dung heap in the light drizzle, perfectly content at the thought of having shelter for the night. The hay would smell sweet and heady, I would drift into sleep listening to the patter of rain on the roof, the occasional sharp metallic crack of thunder from the glaciers on the Wetterhorn and the long roll of avalanches muttering behind the mist.

I woke to a cry from Fritz.
'*Kaffee. Johan, Kaffee.*'
In his kitchen he pushed a large cup, the size and shape of a small chamber pot across the table and filled it right to the brim from a steaming jug of milky coffee. He produced bread and cheese as well

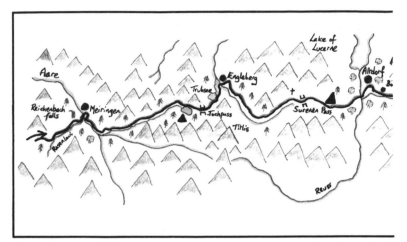

and motioned me to help myself, filling the bowl again when I had
finished the first. The sky outside was turning a thin blue over the
horizon, the sun would soon be up. I washed, brushed my teeth,
shook hands gratefully with Fritz and set off down to Meiringen, sad
that I had been unable to talk with him properly. He could easily
have modelled for Heidi's grandfather and I was sure that he had
some stories to tell. His eyes certainly twinkled enough.

I gloried briefly in the warmth of the sun, though there was still
mist around the peak of the Wetterhorn, and followed the rushing
waters of the Rosenlaui into the Aare valley. Here I stopped to gaze
at the Reichenbach falls where Sherlock Holmes met his first death
at the hands of the infamous Moriarty. Hilaire Belloc passed through
Meiringen on his way to Rome, describing the scene thus:

'... I thought that there I would eat and drink a little more, so
I steered into the main street, but there I found such a yelling
and roaring as I had never heard before, and very damnable it
was, as though men were determined to do common evil...
bawling and howling and saying "This way to the
Extraordinary Waterfall." My illusion of being alone in the
roots of the world dropped off me very quickly...'

Nothing much had changed, though the art of attracting tourists
had been discreetly perfected. I wanted to rest on a grassy spot by the
river Aare, but sleep was impossible as there was target practice
going on in the hills. Military service is compulsory for all men who
are fit and they are sent to prison if they object. It is not considered
a duty but a privilege to serve in the army and every man keeps his
uniform, kit and automatic rifle at home. The system is ancient,
dating back to the middle of the fifteenth century. Even the names

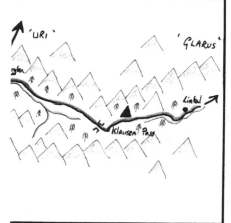

remain, the *Auszug* for the young men up to thirty, the *Landwehr* for those from thirty to forty-five, and the *Landsturm* for those who are older. They have to do two weeks and a certain amount of shooting practice every year to notch up the correct number of points or they are given an extra course. Lenin, when asked by Ernest Nobbson where he thought the Revolution would first break out, replied:

'In Switzerland, because in your country every citizen keeps his army rifle at home, so that you start with the advantage of an armed proletariat. Shoot the town councillors and take possession of the town.'

He didn't know the Swiss or their history very well. It is a measure of how happy—some might say complacent—they are with their system that they would probably say that was not what the gun was for. I can think of many governments, perhaps most, that would topple within hours if all the healthy men of the country possessed a rifle and received free ammunition as well.

A rest, then, but no sleep as I listened to the guns fire in the mountains above. I dug deep into my pocket and paid the three franc toll to walk the gallery built onto the sheer sides of the impressive gorge called 'Aareschlucht'. This magnificent cleft of smooth granite carved out by the river over the ages has been tamed, like the Jungfrau. Someone had even written 'Jerusalem U.S.A.' with pebbles on the central island to remind the passer by of the reality of the outside world.

I had been walking for a week now without a break and thought it sensible to have a day off before I did something silly. My next stop would be Engelberg, the other side of the Jochpass, an easy name to remember. There was a lake up in the mountains below the pass which would do nicely for a long camp.

There was a road up to the lake but I took the path which was more direct, heading slowly up with a heavy load in the sultry air, feeling tired and grumpy, longing to reach my destination and flake out.

I was still some way from the target and feeling pretty miserable

183

when an emerald green VW Golf pulled up. The driver, a woman, leant out to ask if I would like a lift. There was nothing in the world I wanted more at that moment, but I was embarrassingly dirty and hesitated to spoil the air inside their car. I warned them in French, which they understood, but they said it didn't matter, so I clambered in happily. The two women were on their way to the lake to have a bite to eat at the restaurant.

The way on

'I saw you in Meiringen,' said the driver. 'You are unmistakeable, you know, with that baton of yours. Why do you carry it?'

'Because it's very useful. It's good for jumping small rivers, clonking dogs on the head, balancing on a steep pass or path, rhythm . . . it forms an integral part of my tent too.'

I explained further as they spirited me up to the lake.

'Would you like drinking a beer?'

'That would be very kind indeed, thank you. If you don't mind, I'll tidy myself up a bit before I join you.'

I was still wearing the salt-stained T-shirt, so I changed into my other on the terrace, then put my trousers on unashamed and oblivious of social niceties. The trousers were getting frayed. Darkness had fallen and it was beginning to drizzle, the Wetterhorn doing its job well. The last time I had been in a restaurant was in Spain. This one was the very height of luxury, with wooden panelling inset with mirrors, white linen tablecloths and napkins stiff with starch, silver cutlery, discreet service and low lighting, which was a blessing. I felt like a cave man entering the palace of a King.

184

A fire crackled in the grate. They ordered beer and *fromage croûton*, a speciality which arrived on a silver salver. I was incredibly hungry. Alone, I would have wolfed the food down in a few seconds, leant back carefully, washed the snack down with the beer and licked my lips. I hoped that I was not about to confirm Richard Ford in his prognosis that all walkers will be reduced to the level of the brute animals. Thankfully, my social graces were rusty, but not lost. I did my best to hold my knife and fork correctly and eat elegantly, without haste, hoping they hadn't noticed that my nails were too long and dirty.

They introduced themselves. They both worked at the hospital in Meiringen. The elder of the two was the directress, a matronly woman, firm but friendly, while her companion was in charge of the accounts department. She was a slim, sophisticated woman with fair hair and blue eyes who exuded a cool green elegance in her tight white skirt. I introduced myself in turn, thinking as I spoke that they must see me as a strange creature indeed, a patient perhaps, a specimen worth an hour of scrutiny. They were certainly a well-educated and informed pair, quick to appreciate how much I wished to talk and learn about their country.

The conversation came round to the problems of what they called the 'Guest Workers', a euphemism for the eight million foreign immigrants in industrial Europe doing the dirty jobs no one else will touch. They have few rights within the Swiss system, having to have lived in the country for ten years before they get any kind of social security. In 1914 they made up 15% of the population of Switzerland. By 1975 the figure had risen to 20% of the workforce, a situation that had begun to cause an amount of hysterical xenophobia in the German speaking majority. The balance in Switzerland between the different language groups and the two religions, Protestant and Catholic, is a delicate one. Almost half the immigrants are Italian speaking Catholics, who thus threaten the juggling act they call the status quo. A referendum in 1970 which would have meant the expulsion by law of over 200,000 men and their dependants was only narrowly defeated. The percentage in favour of expulsion dropped substantially the next year when women were given the vote for the first time. Many of these workers had to leave anyway during the economic slump in the mid seventies, so the problem was resolved without loss of face. The percentage of immigrant labour is expected to be kept at around 10% in future.

We were in the middle of earnest conversation when a group of people who had come in earlier started to sing Swiss folk songs. All conversation stopped, an accordion appeared from a corner and a spontaneous choir formed, weaving fine harmonies over a lusty, powerful bass. Then one of the girls at their table came in with a clear, impressively held yodel. I sat back, letting the music flow, privileged to be there. They bought me another beer.

My hosts got up to go eventually and I followed them out into the darkness. It was cold and raining heavily. Sharing an umbrella they ran for the car and drove off with a wave. I turned away to a knoll above the lake where I pitched camp, cooked another supper and crept contentedly into my sleeping bag.

Next day was one of rest and solitude. It was lovely to wake and lie listening to the sound of water from somewhere behind the mist before going back to sleep once more. The mist only lifted once during the whole day when it revealed a chink of blue over the Jochpass. As no tourists came, the only human beings around were the silent fishermen, my only encounter a curious, woolly calf that wandered up and licked the salt from my legs as I ate lunch. I spent the rest of the day finishing *Jupiter's Travels*.

As the lake was at 1500 metres, I crested the Jochpass next day with little trouble. Cloud cover was low, visibility minimal, the great Titlis hidden, the Trübsee a dew pond slowly emerging from the mist below. In that cold, bleak no-man's-land the only living creatures I saw were two slow-moving, shiny black salamanders, trying to keep each other warm. As they live at this high altitude all their lives, they have adapted to the harsh conditions. They give birth to completely formed babies, rather than hatching eggs. Eggs would never survive the cold.

Empty ski chairs moved silently through the air like ghosts, as if the end of the world had come and no one had remembered to turn off the machines. The weather forecast in Engelberg was gloomy: wet till Wednesday. It was Monday. As I could see nothing of the valley or the scenery, I rely on William Coxe, for a description: 'A picturesque plain of an oval shape beautifully wooded, watered by several lovely streams, enclosed within a circle of gentle hills and terminated by a majestic amphitheatre of cloud capped alps'. A charmless town, Henry James called it, 'a grim, ragged, rather vacuous but by no means absolutely unbeautiful valley'.

I didn't stop once on the way up and over the Surenenpass, not even to investigate a little chapel and a solitary wooden cross beneath the pass. The conditions were too miserable. The other side was a sheet of snow and ice down which I slithered cautiously on a plastic bag, using my stick as a brake. In the early fading light, I found the path down more by luck than judgement and breathed a sigh of relief. A couple of wild goats, or perhaps they were chamois, bounded

186

by as a spectral churn of milk passed on a cable trolley from some inhabited shepherd's hut above.

It was very tiring to cross two passes in the mist in one day, and when I reached the shelter of an isolated barn I lay down and fell asleep almost immediately—just aware for an instant of a large rodent scuffling in the hay.

The mist had not lifted from the high ground. I could smell ripe plums somewhere over to the left on the other side of a ruined wall and went over to pick some for breakfast. The luscious, ripe fruit wasting on the ground was a useful find as I had run out of food. Altdorf lay below in a flat depression at the southern tip of the Lake of Lucerne in the Canton of Uri. The outskirts were carefully suburban, interspersed with orchards of ripening apples and pears.

I crossed the valley to Bürglen without stopping and at the centre of the village I found a statue of a squat fellow with a cross-bow in his right hand, his left resting on the head of a small child. It was William Tell, the chamois hunter, and his son. He was a solitary, silent man of the mountains, the best bowman in the valley. One day he came into Altdorf to find that a green cocked hat had been placed on a post in the central square, in front of which all those who passed had to bow. This meant, of course, that the townsfolk avoided the square. Not Tell. He strode past it without a second glance and was duly arrested by the guards. At this moment Gessler, the local tyrant, rode up on his fine horse. He gave Tell a choice: prison or freedom if he could shoot an apple from the head of his son. The child was placed under a lime tree eighty paces away from Tell and the crowd hushed as he took aim. When his now-famous shot neatly split the apple in two, the crowd was jubilant. Less well known is the sequel to the story. When the cheering died down, Gessler asked him why he was holding a second arrow. Tell, being an honest man, told him:

'The second arrow was for you, in case I missed.'

For his frankness he was chained and taken down to the lake to be ferried across to Gessler's castle. A sudden storm blew up as they were crossing and when the crew panicked, Tell was released from his chains to hold the rudder. He saved himself and the crew but jumped boat on reaching the other side, in order to catch Gessler before he arrived back at his castle. When the hated tyrant was in range, he took careful aim and shot him straight through the heart. Inspired by his action, the people turned on the castle and burnt it to the ground.

There are echoes of Robin Hood in the legend with Gessler as the Sheriff of Nottingham in his castle, a symbol of implanted authority, a foreign Hadsburg invader in the same way that the Sheriff was a

Norman invader. Whether the story is true or not, it holds a much stronger grip on the Swiss than does that of Robin Hood and his Merrie Bande of Men. Tell is more of a Che Guevara, a figure to be invoked at demonstrations such as those in the late 60s when it was his face that led the marches. They say he died while trying to save a child from drowning. Gessler died on 18th November, 1307, in the apple season.

It was drizzling again and very misty. I found shelter on the terrace of a barn and cooked a very late breakfast before stomping up to the Klausenpass, snorting steam into the cold air. The plants and grass wore chains of dewdrops, like nature's beads. The rain was so fine it penetrated all my layers of clothing before I really noticed. All sense of time and place was lost as the white mist closed in. It had become an all too familiar world. Blind, I could do nothing but listen to my regular breathing, the crunch of boots on stone and gravel, the occasional squelch of mud, the ever-present sound of dripping water. I spent my time trying with great difficulty to distinguish between the sound of the river below and the rustling of leaves in the slight breeze.

I only became miserable when the wet turned cold. One of the two, wet or cold, is bearable, but the two together form a fatal combination in the mountains. On the descent from the pass, my sweat began to freeze, while my hands and feet went numb. I don't remember where I found shelter from the now heavy rain, only that my hands were so cold I couldn't strike a match, having to hold it in my teeth while I ran the box along the striking edge, singeing my beard in the process. I put on dry socks and the dry canvas boots, wiggled my toes and danced around while supper cooked. I had walked about thirty miles and felt about as much like dancing as an elephant. With my insides glowing warm with a mixture of pasta, rice, oats and semolina—all I had left—I turned in for the night to enjoy the pleasant oblivion of sleep.

I woke to another dire, dreadful, dark, dripping, dreary day of drudgery, so my diary tells me. I had had enough of cold mountain and cancelled my plan to cross the Freiberg, deciding to walk round it instead, which was not an unpleasant sensation, though it took a while to adjust to a flat surface. I covered a lot of ground with ease, the mist, so thick in the morning I could hardly see my outstretched hand, though later it gradually dispersed, banished to the mountains where it hung around waiting for an opportunity to come down again. I was glad I hadn't gone up the Freiberg.

I cashed a cheque at the bank in Schwanden, bought a new pair of socks to replace those I had carelessly left behind and did some shopping to stock up on basic provisions. The sun was warm enough at midday to wash in the river, which left me feeling like a new man and less depressed. I ate food all day, never having felt so continuously ravenous before. The path south to Elm was choked with small, tangy and deliciously addictive raspberries. I made slow progress between bushes, passing a sign that announced I was walking the 'Suworow Weg', and further explained that General Alexander Vassilyevitch Suvorof had come this way with his army in 1799, during the war of the Second Coalition, when Napoleon's generals were fighting the combined armies of the Austrians and Russians.

The sign gave no hint of the remarkable man that he was. At the age of seventy, he had come up from Italy with a large army, hoping to join forces with the Austrians against the then forty-one-year-old Marshal Masséna, but the allies let him down completely. He was forced to retreat over the Panixer Pass south-west of Elm, losing a quarter of his men, all the pack animals, the artillery and baggage.

Although he was old, he dressed only in the thinnest clothes with a cloak to wrap around himself when he had to sleep rough. He was pious, indifferent to appearances, unorthodox, lightly touched, forthright, disgusting, egotistic, jealous, proud, a buffoon, an animal and an arch imperialist who expressed contempt for all those beneath his precious Tsar. His men loved him like a father for he let them loot and plunder as they desired. In fourteen days they crossed the high Alps four times in terrible weather, putting up with the hardest privations, chewing leather and eating soap by the ton they were so hungry, yet arriving in Chur with 1400 prisoners. Suvurof had a particular love of English beer and also corresponded with Admiral Nelson, finding the time towards the end of the year to dash off a letter of Nelson wishing him a Happy New Century.

The quality of the morning light filtering through cracks in the hay loft where I had spent an extremely comfortable night indicated that it was going to be another dismal day, but my heart lifted when the sun passed through the cloud revealing the outlines of the mountains. Tanks rolled by from the army training camp as the winged seeds of a sycamore swirled and drifted down in the breeze, its leaves turning brown. I had decided not to continue east to Liechtenstein and Austria, but rather to head south-east to the border with Italy. It was time to cross the chain I had been following since Montreux and striked out for warmer climes. The little town of Schwanden marked the northernmost point of the journey, the apex of a triangle. The way on lay over the Segnas Pass to Flims, the Rhine valley, Chur, Davos, the Engadine, then Italy.

189

Two men were scything the grass in a lonely hamlet on the way up to the pass, while a third, wearing a white shirt and smoking a pipe, was turning the hay with a pitchfork. I wanted to talk, but could think of nothing better than 'Segnas Pass?'

The weather was not my only consideration in turning south. I had relied on casual conversation with local people to keep me from turning too far inwards and I was dispirited at not being able to speak German. I missed the long conversations I had enjoyed in Portugal, Spain and France. Italian would be easier, a Romance language like French

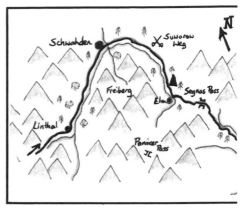

with a Spanish kind of grammar and a Welsh accent!

The man pointed out the way. My conversation of the day was over.

Now the path really began to climb. 'Grit your teeth and smash that mountain,' I muttered. I also found myself repeating a snatch of song in my head: 'Don't go breaking my heart,' step, 'I couldn't if I tried,' step, 'Don't go breaking my heart,' step . . . I could continue fresh and oblivious to the strain for hours that way. The ascent became much easier, as it became governed and controlled by the song. It was not the first time that I had done this by any means; it had become a habit, in fact,—it was just the first time that I was conscious of the effect.

The descent looked tricky: steep snow and ice. A couple coming up the other side of the pass found it too cold to rest and came down at the same time as I did, slowly but safely, stopping to rest lower down.

'Would you like a sardine?'

'No, thank you very much. We will eat when we get back to the chalet.'

He was a lawyer from Zürich and very friendly, chatting about this and that, but his wife just listened as she didn't trust her English. What a relief it was to talk to someone. After ten minutes or so they left and headed on down.

I was happy to have crossed the range and to be heading south. It was warmer too, this side of the mountain. The wind and the rise in temperature made me very sleepy, so I took a snooze in a suntrap

190

behind a large boulder on the soft grass. The wind is called the Föhn. As it comes up from the valley it makes the weather warm and dry on the southern slopes but for some reason wet and cold the other side. It is known to give people headaches or make them restless and

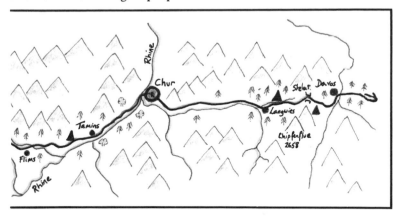

disagreeable, even unaccountable for their actions. In the law courts it is taken as extenuating circumstances if a crime of passion takes place on a day when the Föhn is blowly strong.

The houses in Flims were built of solid pine trunks from the forests above, the squares bright and full of the sound of fountains. I had crossed into the Grisons canton. Next day I would get to Chur.

Walking above the bubbling Rhine in the early hours was lovely. The skyline was edged with pink, the fields still wet with dew, the sun rising only as I passed through Tamins. Traffic on the road became heavy as the morning wore on and I had to be careful not to get sandwiched against the walls by passing lorries. The sun was well up and hot by the time I walked into Chur, a city busy with workers hurrying to the second shift, its air thick with ammonia, its factories belching smoke. They don't have strikes in Switzerland, or almost none: three in 1970, none in 1973 but 19 in 1976.

Chur was once *Curia Raetorum*, an important crossroads at the centre of a Roman province. I wandered round the remains of the mediaeval town and castle, preoccupied with finding a new washer for my stove which was beginning to play up after months of faithful service. It didn't like the pure *benzin* that I was obliged to buy. The thought nagged me that one night it wouldn't work. After half an hour and four attempts, I found a washer that would do and went to celebrate in a *Bierhalle*, a scruffy place where a tipsy old prostitute said things to me I was relieved not to understand.

191

I wanted to avoid the traffic on the way out, so I bought a ticket on the bright red train which passed through the centre of the town before winding up the ravine to Langwies through many a tunnel, screeching noisily round sharp corners as I hung out of the door of the guard's van watching the tumbling river below.

I chose a spot by the river just above the village and camped early. It was Friday, August 14th and I decided to rest till Sunday afternoon when I could stride over the Strela pass down to Davos. From there it would be two days' walking to the Italian frontier with a couple of long-haul passes in between. Frontier fever would ensure a cracking pace.

It was hot enough at midday on Sunday to strip off and sit in a shallow pool in the river. After letting the icy water scour my skin, I got out to sunbathe, slowly absorbing the heat as I lay listening to the boisterous water. Rivers have many voices; this one bubbled happily and ran, rushed and fell. I was enjoying being in one place long enough to make more detailed observations of a small area for a change. Here I particularly liked watching the colours change on the Chüpfenflue crag as night passed into day. During the night it had been a spectral shape caught in the bright light of the full moon. In the morning black shadow, then grey, turning a chalky white as the sun arrived late in the valley. By the time I started for the pass late that afternoon it was a faded yellow as it began to catch the sun's orange evening light.

A soldier in battledress with a machine gun slung over his shoulder was walking down. We met at a forest dustbin where we both threw

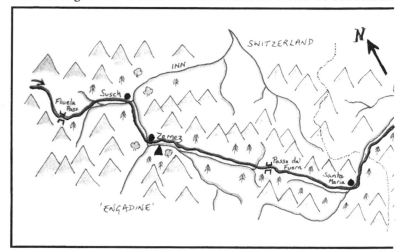

Danube. I was half an hour late for the shops at Zernez, but as I had only been going to buy a bar of chocolate to satisfy a craving, it wasn't too desperate. I camped by the river, the sky a clear purple tinted with shots of pink. There would be bright moonlight that night.

There was frost on the ground that last morning in Switzerland and the moon was still hanging in the clear sky, as I got up. My stomach rumbled fiercely on the way up to the Pass dal Fuorn. The P.T.T. bus honked by. The country post is often carried in these buses, so that two birds are killed with one stone, another example of in-built Swiss practicality. From the pass, the view opened out on the great white back of Mount Constainas. Italy was in sight.

In the woods the air smelt strongly of fox, a smell which only disappeared when I emerged into open farmland, where family groups were raking in the hay. An old woman walking up the path towards me stopped to pass the time of day.

'Isn't it lovely and warm today?'

My heart leapt; I had understood.

'*Si, Signora. Bellissimo!*' I beamed.

A man was in the process of helping his ancient mother from a field. She clung to the working end of her long, wooden rake as he hauled her up the bank. It came as a shock to see fields of dark, cool green wheat, of ripe barley beside green oats, cabbages and lush vegetable gardens. I noticed some graffiti on the wall of a house:

'*La Sort es L'Arade da L'Orma*'

A little shopping in Santa Maria, some food and then on to Müstair, where I spent my last coins on bread and pastries before walking down to the frontier and past a queue of cars. The border guards looked me over quizzically but became friendly at my first comic attempts to speak Italian. It was the 18th of August. I had come from Montreux in eighteen days (including four days of rest), a distance of some 350 straight kilometres (though the path had never been straight), and had crossed sixteen passes, twelve of which had been over 2000 metres. Three times I had climbed two passes in one day. I felt elated, carefree, almost light-headed as I followed a path through pine woods in the cool evening to camp beside the clear waters of the river Adige. I was in Italy at last.

195

Italy

A woman with three nanny goats went by.

'Buon giorno, Signora.'

'Guten Morgen,' she said.

She looked Italian enough in a headscarf, green jumper, black stockings and shoes, but the blue and white polka dot apron, the fair hair and the twinkling blue eyes didn't really fit. Perhaps she had mistaken me for a German. It was frustrating sometimes when people refused to believe that I could not understand what they were saying and talked on regardless.

Two men walked by with a calf, chatting to each other in German. It was a case of shocking ignorance on my part, which I hesitate to mention, but I had not realised that this part of Italy was the Southern Tyrol, home of the largest minority in the country, the 300,000 German-speaking Tyroleans. The Southern Tyrol only became a part of the young Italian Republic at the end of the First World War when it was ceded by Austria. I would have to wait a little longer before being able to communicate.

Prato was swarming with German-speaking tourists. I felt cheated. A funeral procession lumbered by, the cortège headed by a brass band, the bier followed by smartly-dressed men, women and children in that order. Feeling undressed, I retreated to the shadows before continuing down the Adige valley towards Merano.

My eyes had grown accustomed to following the line of mountains down to a river, with possibly a little pasture here and there. As I approached Merano, the new landscape caught me by surprise, a lush, broad valley of flat gold and green fields, maize and potatoes with patches of cauliflower, cabbage and beetroot.

A good path took me round the side of an escarpment above the old red tiles of Merano, churches with bulbous onion spires, castles and tiny chapels built on every surrounding hill and peak, the slopes dry and scrubby. Back again in the valley at Lana, I did some shopping and telephoned Anna to say I was in Italy, but that I would

196

not be in Padua for at least a week, since the Dolomites lay ahead. I would get maps in Bolzano. I sat on a wall having lunch in the neat suburbs of the town, watching a woman meticulously tending her garden, dreamily dead-heading faded yellow Dahlias.

'Where are you going?'

'Bolzano.'

'Are you German?'

'No, I'm Irish.'

'Oh, now there's a thing. Would you like a tomato with your cheese sandwich?'

She came over with four round, juicy, firm tomatoes from the greenhouse. *'Pomodoro'*, she said, pointing to a tomato. 'An apple of gold.' I would have to buy an elementary vocabulary book.

The valley between Merano and Bolzano was one vast, continuous orchard of crunchy, green apples, with miles of water pipes to irrigate and swell the fruit. The gurgling, rushing streams had gone, so I was happy to find an open canal to wash away the dust and dirt of the day. I camped in one of the orchards and here disaster struck. The stove started belching foul smoke and it was only after much patience that I managed to cook a pan of soggy, lukewarm pasta. Bad tempered and exhausted, I crawled into my sleeping bag, only to be woken less than an hour later by a loud clap of thunder and a burst of heavy rain. I forced myself out of my bag to put up the tent and then clambered back inside to finish my much needed sleep.

I was still tired in the morning and my morale was lower than it had ever been. The traffic on the way into Bolzano was unavoidable and did not help, keeping me on my toes dodging buses and heavy lorries, the filthy roar echoing in my head. The clocks stood at 10.30 when I arrived. It was a big town, bigger than any that I had seen since Grenoble. The people stared and made me feel uneasy. I bought some food and then went looking for maps, but I could find nothing suitable—it would soon be 12.30 and all the shops would shut until late afternoon, leaving me stranded. The crowds of people only made me feel more isolated and alone, a loneliness that gnawed at my stomach wall like a chronic ulcer. The walls began to close in, something inside was very close to snapping. I crouched exhausted, empty and drained in a telephone booth beside the station where I rang Anna, then Flavio, my brother-in-law in Padua.

'Flavio? I'm at Bolzano Station and on my way to Padua, so I'll be turning up some time this evening if that's all right.'

'Yes, of course, John, no problem at all. See you when you arrive then.'

From one of the spacious squares in town I could see the

Dolomites, but felt no desire to climb them. The mountain tamer was tamed. I was too tired, too near the edge of a gulf that I could feel yawning in front of me. The stove going wrong and the wet night had been the last straw; I yearned for company, to be able to talk to someone, to see a familiar face, to touch someone I loved. I had plenty of time to mull over my feelings as I waited for the train. It was the right decision. I could always return when I was rested.

My companions in the compartment were a middle-aged German couple and an opulent Italian businessman with a Zapata moustache, wearing a white suit. He had a shiny, black plastic handbag on his lap from which he drew a cigarette and lit up nonchalantly. The Germans objected and pointed to the 'No Smoking' sign, forcing him into the corridor to finish it. The countryside flashed by on the other side of the dirty glass, allowing no time to stoop and pick up a windfall. I changed trains, waiting on the platform for a connection.

'Verona, Ponte Nuova, dieci minuti di ritardo,' cackled the loud-speakers. It was a familiar scene, young lovers, nuns and soldiers. I felt calm and happy. I could always go back. I must be tired, time for a holiday. I was looking forward to seeing my sister Mary, Flavio and young Lucio.

Supper was served on a plate at a table covered with a cloth. I had a knife and fork to eat with, a shiny glass to drink from, an amazing variety of food spread in front of me. The happy chatter of my sister and Lucio filled the room as Flavio beamed at us all. My heart was full to bursting. Later, as I lay in the bath, I thought how lucky and privileged I was to be able to move freely from one world to another when so many kind people I had met remained trapped in theirs. While I could choose to go without the luxuries of life for a short period of time they did not have the choice or means to do the opposite.

The night was hot. I lay on my bed with just a sheet and coverlet, listening to the rumble of traffic in the city, drifting away to sleep, thinking the noise it made was no greater than that of a mountain stream.

A fortnight elapsed before I was back to tackle the Dolomites, one of the few mountain ranges named after a man, Gialet de Dolomieu, an eighteenth-century geologist.

It was September 4th, and 8.45 and according to the clock in the warm refuge at 2174 metres on the Passo di Gardena, where I sat downheartedly drinking a cup of coffee. Mother Nature was up to her old tricks again: the temperature only just above zero and a freezing fog curled round the rocks outside, reducing visibility to a few yards.

198

I had been lucky to find shelter the night before in a partly constructed house on the outskirts of Plan, where the bus from Bolzano had dropped me in a high street swept by heavy rain. It was a strange but not unhappy feeling to be alone again in the familiar empty silence of the mountains, that was so different from the comforts and noises of Padua and the hot crowded beaches of the Yugoslavian coast where Anna and I had spent a few days' holiday. I was fatter and well rested now, with decent maps, a new compass, a Camping Gas stove to replace the sadly defunct Optimus and most important, a new pair of boots. I had tried to persuade the local cobbler to patch the tattered, faithful Trickers that had put in such gallant service, but he told me it wasn't worth it. I felt they deserved a better grave than the dustbin outside my sister's flat.

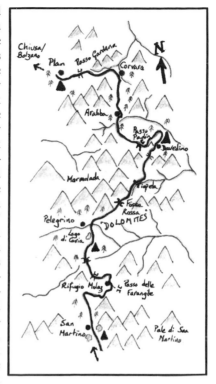

However, the new boots were comfortable, light and shaping well.

The only other additions to the pack were a small thermos flask and a Berlitz phrase book. Ever since that kindly woman had brought me coffee in a flask for the morning, I had wondered if it would not be a good idea to carry one. It would be the height of luxury to wake in the morning to a cup of hot coffee made the night before, without the bother of lighting the stove. It would start the day well.

I was carrying the Berlitz phrase book in the hope that I could learn a few useful expressions and words as I went along. The system worked well. When I was sure I had memorised the words and phrases of a particular page, I ripped it out. The booklet got steadily thinner and more tatty as I progressed through Italy, till the day arrived when I threw what was left of it away, confident that I could express myself sufficiently well to get along with those I met.

Mountaineers came and went around me, one in genuine *lederhosen*, cursing the weather under his breath. It was no good

199

going any higher. It would be horribly cold and the path probably dangerous. I studied my map sadly, deciding to head down to Corvara, keeping to the valleys while the mist hung around. It would take about a week to reach Padua, where I could rest briefly before continuing south through Italy. I would not go via Yugoslavia; I preferred to travel in a country where I had some chance of understanding the language. I set off reluctantly, wondering where I should be that night, something I normally did not worry about.

My shiny new boots were soon initiated into the hard, tough life destined for them when I slithered helplessly into a mass of soft, squelching mud a foot deep. Apologetically, I wiped them clean with a knot of grass, before continuing the descent to Corvara, the mist clearing briefly to allow a view of yellowing green pastures dotted with the occasional shrub or conifer, and woods on the higher slopes, the peaks as yet unseen. On the road to Arabba, a car pulled up ahead, a man jumped out and set his cine camera whirring as I strode along. He got back into his car and sped off before I could ask him what he was doing.

Encouraged by a shot of *Grappa,* the local spirit, I took the path for the Passo Padon which climbed steeply back into the mist. Fortunately I met a shepherd who told me the way and guided me over the soggy, barren moorland. I had been horribly spoilt in Switzerland where the paths were at all times clearly marked. Here there were no signs, arrows or markers of any sort, so I was compelled to use my compass. I took a path that led over what I thought to be the pass and clambered down through pine woods to a lovely track of ancient flagstones by a stream of cold, sweet, rejuvenating water.

I asked the way of the first person I encountered, a man in a blue apron with discoloured teeth. I was right off course, he told me, and I would have to make a lengthy detour with an extra climb for my pains.

The man walked with me a little of the way. He had once had a small farm with a few animals, he said, but sold them off when his mother died. Now he was working as a woodman in the summer and in the ski resorts in winter. He made more money now than when he was farming.

'It's no use working the land. *Non rende.*' The same old story—it doesn't pay.

My fitness was unaffected by the holiday, but by the time I had wound round the foot of the mountain to Davedino, I was very tired. It was here that I found shelter under the eaves of a barn, cooked supper and fell soundly into a deep sleep. The first day back on the road was over.

A cat chasing mice startled me awake in the morning. A little boy putting mud cakes into a miniature wheelbarrow looked up in surprise as I walked out of the village, his father glancing up from milking. He had a red moustache, I remember. A good breakfast an hour or so later gave me the energy to crest the Sasso di Roi, where I stood admiring the icy mass of the Marmolada across the valley, the glacier glinting in the first rays of weak sunshine. A man had warned that the path down was *bruto*, difficult, but I scrambled down without mishap past a flock of sheep with long, floppy ears like spaniels, and celebrated with a cup of tea in a restaurant at the base. This was where I should have come down the day before.

As it was Saturday, I was worried about finding provisions, but Ciapela had a small supermarket serving the skiers, so I needn't have worried. From Ciapela, I followed the river Pettorino upwards to the Focca Rossa, lunching in the shelter of one of the huge boulders that were scattered haphazardly over the valley, and probably left behind when the glaciers began to melt. The earth, which had been grey for so long, turned red at the pass where wide ledges of pasture land stepped down towards Pellegrino. I stopped for a shot of *Grappa* in a small hut cafe on the slopes.

'How far have you come today?' asked the proprietor.

'I'm not sure. I've been walking about eight hours now.'

'Eight hours! *Santa Madonna!*'

I bypassed Pellegrino, though the name, meaning 'Pilgrim', was attractive, and cut instead to the lake of Cavia, at 2100 metres, where I had planned to spend the night. The evening sky was clear but for a few pink-tinged clouds and the crescent moon that was reflected in the calm, unwelcoming waters of the lake. I decided it was too chilly to camp, so I kept going across the dam to the other side. Finding a group of barns lower down, I settled in a porch away from the bitter wind and the mist rising from the valley below, watching the shooting stars as supper cooked. With any luck, it would be sunny tomorrow.

The sun promised to be strong. Early in the morning, it was already turning the tips of the saw-toothed crags a creamy grey-pink. The Dolomites are marvellously striking mountains, somehow quite unreal and insubstantial, worthy of Grimm's *Fairy Tales*. I kept expecting them to melt away or topple over in enormous pieces. I kept to the ridges above the valleys, beginning the difficult climb to the Rifugio Mulaz, when I had to haul myself up the bare white rock, fresh snow covering the ice in places. The *rifugio* was a popular resting place situated in a basin beneath the Pale di San Martino, which I wanted to cross at the Passo delle Farangole, at 2969 metres the highest yet. Then the plan was to follow the path for a day or so before dropping down on Feltre with one more range of mountains to climb before reaching the Po valley at Bassano. I bought a glass of wine and some chocolate, then joined the other hikers and real climbers on the sunny terrace.

The Passo delle Farangole

I was within a hundred yards of the pass, a narrow gap between two jagged fingers of rock, with little more climbing to do, when I had to stop. In front of me the path edged along the rock face with a sheer, fatal drop to the right. The path was very narrow, iced and covered in the recent snow. I so much wanted to continue, but I was ill-equipped for such a path. Without an ice pick or spikes for my boots, I could not be sure that I would be able to cross those few yards. If in doubt, don't. I turned back sadly, muttering clichés to comfort myself. The only alternative seemed to be to go down to San Martino in the valley. I picked my way down for a rest and lunch by a stream where I washed away my sense of defeat. It was no use killing myself for a pass.

San Martino was a village of hotels. I headed straight through onto a path that led south along the valley through cool woods of beech and pine crossed by limpid streams in one of which I bathed, finally camping in a glade of luscious grass. The stars were out, all was quiet.

It took longer than expected to get to Primiero, walking from the woods onto close-cropped pastures, past houses built of whole logs on a raised stone foundation with wooden-tiled roofs. A deer suddenly appeared from behind one and bounced off across the fields. I was there in time to buy provisions before the shops shut, and ate a heavy breakfast by the side of the road out, drying dew from the sleeping bag.

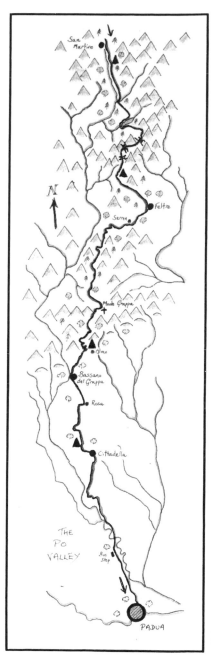

'Buon appetito, Signore.'
'Grazie tante.'
Berlitz was helping.

A deep ravine and the Levetti mountains lay between Primiero and Feltre. I would have to go like the wind if I were to cross both by evening. The road turned to a track, the track to a path and all signs disappeared. An Italian couple passed on their way down to the valley.

'We got lost.'

I pressed on regardless to the wooden village of San Giovanni, where three women sitting in a field knitting and chatting merrily in the afternoon sun, gave me directions on how to cross the ravine by the dam, thus saving all my energy for the Levetti. After lunch by a fountain, a large lorry carrying timber rolled by. The driver gave me a lift to a point we both agreed should be the right place for my ascent.

'Good luck'.

The new forest roads had played havoc with the old paths which were very difficult to follow. Obviously no one came this way anymore. I came across some blue stripes leading up the wild valley and followed these, hoping they marked the path. It petered out at the base of a wall of rock, not quite perpendicular, covered with scrubby trees. I decided to try storming it. Scratched and panting heavily, using the branches to lever myself up, I did eventually fight my way to the top, though I found later that I had lost my towel and torch as the branches tore at the pack.

Much to my relief, the signs continued. I laughed in the silent woods, made a cup of tea with the last of my water and ate some chocolate before continuing. A red sign said *Ciao*, which made me smile, but the word has two faces and the smile was soon wiped off my face when I realised it might mean good-bye rather than hello.

The path became very faint in the white waste of scree and barren rocks above the treeline. I still had about a hundred metres to climb to reach the crest of the Levetti. I tried a steep chimney but the stones began slipping and the handgrips gave way. I gave up on that one, slid down and rested a while before trying a tangent up, beginning to wonder if I was being foolish. Happily, signs of a path continued higher up, renewing my confidence. Again I lost it, scrabbling on till I was faced with a path that even a goat would have had second thoughts about taking: a line some six inches wide on a slope of 75 degrees with horribly frightening drops to the right. *Ciao!* Should I take it or turn back? I'd be all right so long as no rock or stone gave way and pitched me over the precipice. Very carefully I inched along the line to a small chimney that led up over the crest, low cloud beginning to threaten visibility. I absolutely had to get over before it closed in, a final battle with the Levetti. With loose rocks tumbling out of sight behind me, I scrambled up, fear giving me the strength I needed for that final push to safety.

I had come over the edge of a crater filled with low cloud, a pale moon hanging in the blue sky shot with the last rays of the sun. A little further down I came onto a good path of flagstones, at which point I sank down to ease my aching limbs and finish the flask of tea. I was very thirsty having lost so much liquid through sweating on the way up, but there was no sign of water. I would have to keep going whether I liked it or not. I paced along in the dusk, following the side of the crater round with no difficulty in the moonlight, over another pass and down to the doors of the Rifugio Diaz, my fears of not finding water at last dispelled.

Here there was company in the form of Enrico, his wife Gina and their daughter, the fair Stella, as well as two young Germans, Urs and Beatrix. It was good to have someone to talk to. They let me cook supper in the kitchen with much amusement while I bantered in atrocious Italian about the medicinal properties of garlic, with which I proceeded to stink out the ground floor. They didn't mind at all. We sat round the fire talking and joking in a mixture of Italian and English, drinking wine and smoking until bed called. I slept restlessly on a soft, squeaky bunk upstairs in a claustrophobic cubicle with only the smallest of windows to let in the outside world.

It was a cool, clear morning. I was up early, made a cup of coffee, paid and said goodbye to Gina, who was the only one up, before walking down into the valley from woods to vines to maize beside the road into Feltre, a pretty town with porticos round the square, fine churches and civic buildings, a rustic hint of glories to come further south.

I decided not to strain myself that day, but to relax, find somewhere to wash and do some clothes as well. The sun would dry them out in no time. I liked the square stooks of hay with their adjustable roofs, in the fields beside the quiet road to Serren del Grappa: they looked like small pagodas. A hazy line of mountains was just visible in the heat. The highest, Monte Grappa, was the last mountain between myself and the plain.

I asked the way of two old women waddling down the main street in Serren. They chewed the matter over thoughtfully without coming to any satisfactory conclusion. Then, as one, they hailed a passing 2CV and told the man to give me a lift.

'We can't have him walking all the way up to Monte Grappa, can we? It's much too far, and in this heat too . . .'

The driver shrugged and did as he was told. He had long, fair hair, a beard, two earrings, sandals and tatty jeans. He worked in a factory, making petrol tank tops, but said he couldn't stand it much longer. He hoped to be off to Brazil soon where he had a friend in Recife who said he'd find a job with little trouble. The conversation turned to travels in South America while we drank a beer in a bistro.

'I might as well take you all the way up now that I've come this far.'

'Thanks.'

He dropped me off at the top. So much for my plans of doing a little washing. They would just have to wait.

A sign pointed down, 'Bassano, 4 *ore*'. I was amazed that I could be in Bassano that very day. If my friends Sergio and Totti were there, I might even get a bed for the night. I took the path down through the woods, the leaves on the beech trees just beginning to turn brown.

As usual, the signs disappeared, I took the wrong turning somewhere and ended up on a road, but it didn't matter. Turning a corner, the mountains simply disappeared, to be replaced by a very flat plain of striped fields stretching away at my feet for 241 kilometres into the hazy distance; this was the valley of the Po, the industrial and agricultural heartland of Italy. Once a shallow sea, the level of the land rose as silt was washed down from the mountains. The delta advances some seventy yards every year. Ravenna, for example, which was once a Roman port, is now stranded more than five miles inland, like some of the villages in the Fens. The soil is naturally very fertile and productive. Sometimes it is still below sea level, but hundreds of years' work draining marshes, preventing floods and building canals has created the largest area of irrigated farmland in Europe.

There was no way of escaping from the road I was on, no way of cutting the corners either. For what seemed like an age it wound ever gently down and round, snaking to the valley floor, passing a monument to a labourer crushed by a boulder while building the road, inset with a photograph of the deceased, a small, mustachioed man of around forty smiling proudly in his Sunday suit, a southerner from the look of him. The inscription read simply 'From family, workmates and union.'

It was becoming slowly hotter, more humid and sticky as I dropped down to the plain. The sun was setting, its orange glow replaced by the lights of villages and roads as the music of a fairground drifted up in competition with the tuneless clang of a local church bell. I could imagine vividly the red-faced priest hanging on to the end of the bell rope, pulling with all his might to draw the faithful away from the wicked fairground entertainers.

Once down, I drank a celebratory and much needed cold beer in a cafe opposite the fairground, filled my water bottle and went to cook supper on a stone bench under a yellow street lamp in front of the now silent church. I was hungry, footsore and nearing exhaustion, but it was good to be able to sit out without getting cold. About the same time the day before, I had been more than two kilometres up in the sky where it was a lot colder and sweat froze nastily if you stopped to rest for too long.

The Alps now lay behind me. The plain would make a pleasant change for a day or so, though I knew that I would soon be longing to get back to the mountains.

The night was stiflingly stuffy, the air sultry. I slept fitfully on a football field, half aware of the fairground dodgems disco music throbbing through the night. When that was quiet, the frogs and crickets took over the shift while the mosquitoes arrived in the early morning for breakfast.

A bird-like old woman caught up with me as I was stooping to tie a bootlace and accompanied me as far as the main road to Bassano, giving me a lecture on taking care in the mountains as we walked, enjoying the sound of her own voice in the still, morning air.

'You didn't ought to go up in those mountains alone, young man. It's perilous. What would you do if you went and broke a leg or something?'

'I would hop, Signora.'

She didn't think that was funny and changed the subject. I was a willing victim for her lurid tales of drug abuse in this wicked present-day society. It seemed that heroin addicts were dropping like flies all over the streets of Bassano.

'You mean the ones with long hair and beards, earrings sometimes?'

'Yes, they're the ones.'

The towers of Bassano appeared on the horizon. 'An ancient town with monuments that are not sufficiently impressive to induce one to dally', says Eric Whelpton. He had not come straight from the mountain wilderness, though, nor had he thought the village of Feltre impressive the day before. For me, it was the first of the great Venetian fortress cities, a minor rival to Vicenza, Padua and Verona in mediaeval times. A dog barked as I passed through the arched

Bassano bridge

gateway in the battlemented walls of stone and red brick and headed for the bridge over the Brenta where I knew of a good cafe for a glass of wine.

The wooden bridge has often been destroyed, last time during the Second World War. In one of the squares, a row of trees has flower vases attached to the trunks, the flowers being for the partisans publicly hanged from those same trees by the Nazis. The centre, when I got there, was crowded with people and pigeons, the cafes under the porticos buzzing with the happy chatter of citizens, the air thick with petrol fumes.

My attempts to contact Sergio and Totti failed dismally, and then while relaxing with a glass of wine I was caught by Wednesday early closing. It was not my day. I was hoping it would be possible to follow the banks of the Brenta towards Padua, but it seemed unlikely from a cursory glance at the river and the map. Somewhat miffed at this, I took the main road to Padua, a distance of 32 very straight kilometres, hoping to find a shop that was open. I found nothing but petrol stations, minor industry, scrap yards, ceramic works, enormous supermarkets and car salesrooms.

Rosa was a pleasant roadside village but spoiled by the heavy traffic rumbling through and the fact that no shops were open. Pestered by a drunkard, I ate a couple of *panini* (rolls), downed a glass of wine and took a side road towards Cittadella. Fields of two-metre high maize alternated with strips of ploughed land intersected by small canals in which I soaked my sore feet. It was getting late, so I camped in a vineyard a few miles north of Cittadella. The air was oppressively heavy and strip lightning flashes lit up the sky as I prepared methodically for the storm which came rolling in. For some reason a huge puddle formed in my tent and that was that, one soggy, smelly sleeping bag. I slept on, indifferent to the water. It didn't seem to matter since that night I would be in a proper bed.

By dawn the rain had stopped, the air was clean and fresh, and mist was rising from the summer-warm earth. Cittadella was only just stirring when I walked in through the double gateway in the thirteenth-century walls. It is a lovely place, built by the Paduans as an outpost in their feuding with the neighbouring states of Vicenza and Treviso. The moated mediaeval walls are still intact, as is most of the old town, which has a gate at each of the cardinal points, the roads converging at the centre in the classical Roman way. I wandered round the familiar streets, drank a cup of good strong coffee and headed on, passing a seventeenth-century villa in a sad state of decay, the plaster and paint peeling from the façade, the stonework crumbling from the adjacent arched portico of its farmhouse.

A few miles further on, I caught the bus to Padua, old Patavium, founded by the Trojan hero Antenor, birthplace of Livy, the city where St. Anthony died in 1231, home of the oldest botanical gardens in Europe and a university founded in 1222 where Galileo Galilei once taught.

208

PART FOUR

Southbound

'Mezzo t'ho innanzi; omai per te ti ciba.'

(I have set it before you; now feed yourself.
(Dante Alighieri, 1265–1321)

ITALY - "SOUTHBOUND"

Sept. 15th — Nov. 3rd 1981

Italy

Five days later, I said goodbye to my sister and nephew at the door of the flat. Flavio then gave me a lift through heavy traffic to the northern edge of the Colli Euganei, rough mole hills on the flat surface of the plain. We embraced and I turned sadly away to walk on down an avenue of chestnut trees, holding back the tears. Before me lay the complete unknown. I had no addresses or contacts before Thessalonika in Northern Greece, and even then I could not be sure that my friend Liz would be there. I was back on my own again, left to my own resources. At least my pack was light and dry. According to a set of scales in the flat, it weighed fifteen kilos, the lightest it would ever be since this was without water or much food. I had left the mosquito net behind, but now carried the inner part of my tent which I had adapted to stand on its own without the fly sheet. It was not waterproof, but it would keep off the dew. If it rained, I would use the old plastic sheet. Otherwise, everything was much the same.

The weather could not have been better, the air had the sparkling clarity of an early autumn afternoon, as warm sunlight filtered through the trees, dappling the gravel. The feel of the staff in my right hand was familiar. Sadness lifted away as that old, well-loved rhythm returned to take over. I was on my way.

The Euganean hills were formerly used by the rich of Padua and the surrounding area during the summer months when the heat on the plain became unbearable. Petrarch had a house there, in the village named after him. It is a cold, sparsely furnished house, the walls lined with glass cases containing manuscripts and letters, as well as portraits of the man himself in reverend robes, crowned with poet's laurels, a fashionable bandaging around his jaws that makes him look as if he suffered from chronic toothache. I stopped to scrump ripe, bursting figs in the company of a peculiar woman in high-heeled shoes carrying a handbag, who said she was escaping from Padua for the day, though I thought it more likely that she had been dropped outside the city by the police. From the top of a hill

211

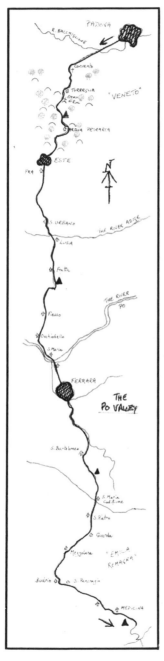

near Torreglia, I looked back over vineyards and fields of maize to the domes of the basilica of St. Anthony rising above the city of Padua. The Alps were hidden in haze, disappointingly.

The gates to the monastery above Torreglia were shut, so I followed the walls round and on, using my compass to head south cross-country. The sun was sinking, its last rays catching the underbelly of thin, fluffy clouds shot with orange and red. In a house nearby, an unhappy couple were screaming at each other behind locked doors, but declared a brief truce to fetch water for the passing stranger. The echoes of their quarrel were still ringing in the hills as I camped in a field of recently cropped lucerne.

Supper was bubbling on the stove when the owner of the field turned up in a baby Fiat, saying that I should move down the hill.

'It's dangerous up here, you know. There are mad dogs which might attack you during the night.'

I nodded, said that I'd just finish my supper first and he left. I stayed where I was, sleeping undisturbed till the sky began to lighten again.

The waning full moon still hung in the pale blue sky as I headed down towards Este beside the walls of a villa with a statue of Pan dancing to the tune of his pipes beside other, less familiar gods. The battlements of the castle came into view as the cool morning mist evaporated and the sun began to beat down hard. The shady porticos round the market beneath the clock tower in the centre of town were buzzing with activity. I stopped only to ask the way to Pra of a man sitting astride his

212

Lambretta, talking volubly to a friend.

'Hop on behind me and I'll take you to the road, if you want. It's much too complicated to explain, right, left, left, right, right . . .'

I clambered on behind, pack, staff and all, grabbing hold of his capacious stomach with my one free hand as off we went. His stomach was warm and wobbled madly as we cruised over the uneven surface of the road, but his sense of balance was happily excellent. On a corner stood a policeman. My heart sank, but he merely raised an eyebrow and smiled as we passed.

A minute later the man dropped me off, said good-bye and zoomed back to the centre with a toot. The Euganean hills gradually faded into the heat haze as I trudged across the silent plain, following a canal to Carmignano, where I stopped to watch ducks paddle among the reeds in the clear, still water, and listen to the occasional plop as a water rat made for cover.

In San Urbano, a group of cheeky children out to tease the stranger gathered round at the pump. I played along happily as I washed the crusted remains of porridge from my bowl until their mother appeared from a doorway.

'What are you doing?'

'Talking with the children, *Signora.*'

'Why?'

Her tone was menacing, hostile, suspicious, the aggressive instincts of a mother protecting her brood from molestation or kidnap. It caught me by surprise. I had been given my marching orders, and I took the hint.

A little while later, I crossed the river Adige for the second time. It seemed much more than a month since I had crossed the border from Switzerland and camped beside its clear, youthful waters. Now it was wide, slow moving, thick and sluggish with silt. Two crumbling brick towers guarded the opposite bank, the entrance into Lusia, a village asleep in the hot sun, seemingly abandoned, where I stopped for lunch and siesta in a shady grove, reading the book given me by Anna, *'Il Barone Rampante', (The Baron in the Trees)* by Italo Calvino. My reading comprehension was just good enough to understand about a quarter of it. I found I could follow the story if I ignored half the words and guessed another quarter.

It was time to move on. The maize and vines now alternated with orchards of huge, yellow apples and fields of cabbage, fennel, lettuce and onions as well as masses of parsley, aubergines and tomatoes. The earth was a rich, alluvial, creamy brown, the sky an immense bowl above. The farmers of such land are very lucky for they have a long, hot growing season. One told me that it was sometimes possible to cut the hay seven times in a year. The Po valley itself produces a third of Italy's wine, half its wheat, three quarters of its sugar beet and maize, and nine tenths of its rice and milk.

I camped that night beside one of the many canals, but sleep was difficult until the early hours. The figs I had eaten the day before were having a disastrous effect, the night was humid, the sleeping bag too hot, the mosquitoes out to kill. I lay there sweating in the moonlight, dreaming fitfully, hoping for a good wash and rest by the river Po the next day.

Ferrara castle

But one glance at the froth of muddy brown scum that swirled on the surface of the great river that had come all the way from the foot of Mont Blanc was enough to put paid to that idea. I caught up on sleep instead, before crossing the bridge and passing through the old city gates into Ferrara. The centre was dominated by the weathered rose brickwork of the castle, built in 1385 by the terrible Duke Niccolò d'Este. He had thought it prudent to defend himself from his subjects with a deep moat. The castle's evil reputation was further enhanced when Lucrezia Borgia came to live there after her marriage to the Duke of Ferrara in 1501. It was her third marriage. Her first was annulled and her second ended when her husband was murdered. She is rumoured to have commited incest with both her father, the Pope, and her brother Cesare. Legends abound. In one, she is said to have taken her revenge on the noble families of Venice

214

for ordering her out from a ball by serving a poisonous supper to a group of eighteen young Venetian nobles. The poison was calculated to take effect slowly, so that she would have the time to harangue them on their impudence as they died. As the poison took effect, she realised with horror that one of the young men present was one of her sons. She begged him to take the antidote before it was too late but he refused, so she killed him instantly with his own dagger.

The castle is now full of public offices, the latest in a long line of plagues that the people have had to suffer. I wandered the dark, narrow streets of the mediaeval part of town where the arches were decked with bright flowers and followed the river out. Marrows and pumpkins grew up against the walls of the houses and maize was sometimes spread out on the pavement to dry like a red-yellow carpet. In the shadows beyond an arched farm gateway sat a man turning the handle of a simple machine for scarifying the rock-hard cobs of maize that his wife would later make into *polenta*, a kind of solidified, sugarless custard that is far more delicious than such a description implies. A farmer passing on his tractor gave me a lift a few miles through endless orchards of apple and pear trees and set me down when he turned into one of the large co-operative warehouses. I spent the night near a row of tall blue cypress trees, the still air heavy with the mingling smells of hay, canals, ripe apples, strawberries, drains and roses.

Crowing cocks and the weird clickings of guinea fowl woke me. In the deserted streets of Santa Maria Codifiume beside the river Reno, a woman greeted me from the doorway of a jeweller's shop.

'I saw you yesterday on the road. Where have you come from?'
'Bolzano, *Signora.*'
'Walking all the way?'
'Most of it. Got a ride with a tractor yesterday, though.'
'*Porco Dio!* Are you carrying drugs?'
It was the same kind of reaction that I had had in Portugal and it made me smile. She was a stout woman with a kind mouth, her jet black hair streaked with grey. She asked if I should like a cup of coffee seeing it was so early, and brought one out to me on the pavement, an *espresso* in its traditional, tiny cup. We stood there talking of her first child who had died at the age of two. Her husband was in the cafe opposite, she said. They had had no more. In my turn, I told her of the journey and asked about the scene in San Urbano the day before.

'People are frightened of you, I expect, particularly the women. They probably think you're going to rob them or molest their children.'

215

She gave me her address and made me promise to send a postcard from Istanbul. The rest of the morning was spent walking towards Búdrio through an unchangingly flat landscape, alongside canals that were choked with weeds or on tarmac roads that were uncomfortably hot on the soles of my feet, a sensation I hadn't experienced since crossing the Carcassonne Gap in Southern France in June. Lorries loaded with sugar beet thundered by from time to time, but all else was quiet.

I arrived in Budrio at three in the afternoon. Peace reigned in the central square. Old men sat on benches in the shade of tall chestnut trees that were laden with conkers. Every so often one would plummet down and roll to a stop. One old man wearing a white panama hat and drainpipe trousers that were too short exposing his hairless, white legs, picked one up, looked at it for a moment, polished it gently, then launched it dexterously at the head of another old man sitting with his back to him some ten yards away. It flew direct to the target, knocking the man's hat off. He looked up into the thick foliage above and shrugged his shoulders, stooping to pick up his hat, dust it off and replace it. The culprit chortled gleefully behind his handkerchief.

The effete youth of the town were standing in groups around their Lambrettas, smoking. I got nothing but puzzled looks when I asked for the Palladian villa in the area.

'Palladio? Where's that?'

Nobody seemed to know. With lunch fortifying me, I headed on to Medicina, getting steadily more tired and thirsty. In search of water, I entered the yard of a farmhouse. Only women were around, wearing white scarves over their heads that made them look a little moorish. They said there was no water. I didn't press the point, remembering the words of the jeweller's wife. They were frightened of me, misopogonists like most Latin peoples. I found an old pump two kilometres further down the road where I quenched my thirst to the full. On the southern horizon, I could just make out shadowy bumps where the haze was tinted a darker blue. This was the beginning of the Apeninnes. I strode on.

The day had cooled and the sun was low when I stopped again beside an old well, determined to wash my feet for the first time since leaving Padua. I shall not go into details, but they felt better for a good scrub and clean socks. In the field opposite a caterpillar tractor was ploughing, pulling a single, wide share through the earth to a depth of more than a foot, turning the first dark, rich furrow in its wake. I stood up, stretched and took a swig from the flask. At that moment a woman across the road shouted a warning.

'Don't drink that water! It's not good. It'll make you ill.'

She hurried over, thinking that I had been drinking the stagnant green water from the well. I reassured her.

'Would you like a bowl of soup?' she asked suddenly. 'You look as if you could do with some food.'

I accepted with astonishment, soon tucking into minestrone, smoked ham, bread, cheese and plenty of wine. I would have no need of supper that night. She and her son talked a dialect that was not easy to understand, while they, in turn, had difficulty with my Italian, the son acting as interpreter. He was a student at Bologna University, studying engineering. As he had failed his last lot of exams, he would have to repeat the year, but it didn't seem to worry him all that much. His mother had been picking onions all day. There was no mention of a husband.

I thanked them sincerely and set off once more, the wine and clean socks helping greatly with the load. Dusk was falling at about seven thirty now. In the half light, I made my way through the porticos of Medicina with their hanging baskets of sweet smelling flowers, resisting the bars that beckoned with twinkling lights, camping on rough, humpy earth among some vines that rustled in the breeze, falling asleep the minute my head touched the ground.

I was on the road to Imola before sunrise, pacing along with renewed stamina as the eastern horizon turned pink, a single cloud illuminated gold. The morning was cool and crisp and the sweet smell of dew was rising from the fields as I entered the village of Castel Guelfo, a historic, pretty place, to buy food for breakfast. Imola, my next stopping place, was a fine fortress city with a squat castle that had great round towers of brick at the four corners, a dry moat and even a drawbridge. After touring the city, I chose a cafe near the centre that had tables outside under the portico to write up the diary and watch the world go by. A sweeper shuffled past, indifferent to the breeze that was blowing the rubbish back onto the parts that he had just cleaned. I concentrated on my writing.

'Where do you come from?'

I had not seen the two young women arrive at the table to my right. They were looking at me curiously.

'I'm English.'

They were called Luisa and Natascia. Almost immediately, they invited me to lunch, which we ate at a large table in their attic flat. Luisa was a professional basketball player. I thought her friend was a policewoman, but she was, in fact, a cleaner.

'No, no, not *polizia*, *pulizia*,' and they laughed at my confusion.

Over lunch they mentioned that a friend of theirs who kept a herb shop had done a lot of walking in the mountains himself and would

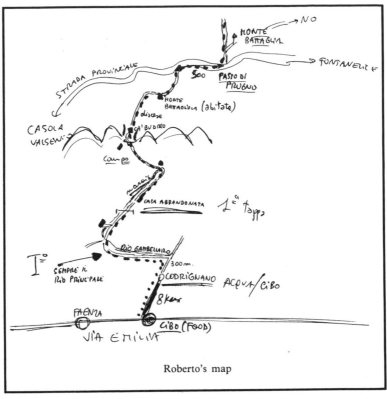

Roberto's map

perhaps be able to help. After lunch they offered me some cocaine, undoing a little packet and making three lines of fine white powder on the handbag mirror which they had placed on the table. One then rolled a crisp thousand lire note into a tube and we each took turns to sniff it up our noses. My right nostril went rather numb and I believe that we talked rather fast for a few minutes, but that was the only effect.

I was in luck. Roberto was one of a rare breed of Italians who had done a fair bit of walking, in the Himalayas as well as the Dolomites and Alps.

'Few Italians ever walk further than they need to,' he said, 'which is usually from the front door to the garage. There is, in fact, an Apennine Way which follows the crests and ridges of the chain nearly all the way to Naples. Parts of it are marked, even.'

He proceeded to keep all his customers waiting while he made me a map on four different pieces of shop stationery, showing how I was to get onto the pathway and the first two legs of the journey, kindly dotting out the path in red on my own maps when I went back later. He was very precise and knew what he was talking about, a pleasant change from the normal advice on how to get to the nearest road and 'catch the bus, lad, because it's much quicker.'

Over a cup of tea back at the flat, I was invited to stay the night. That evening we went out to the *Festa da L'Unità*, a festival organised and funded by the Italian Communist Party. They have great support in the Bologna region, which is often called the 'Red Belt'; most of the Partisans in the Second World War were Communist. Masses of people were milling around chatting to their friends, reading the mounted displays that explained the system of corrupt *sottogoverno* and patronage, 'the placing of trusted men in places where they can exert influence over government decisions'. Politically, Italy is represented by a tangled coalition of right and centre with a more than generous sprinkling of the left. The people have had to put up with more than thirty-eight successive governments since the end of the Second World War, a situation that is made use of by those in real power, for the ensuing inefficiency and confusion can be highly profitable. One of the most remarkable sources for political funds is the government agencies, or *Enti*. In 1972, the results of a four-year investigation by a Neapolitan professor were published. He found that there were 59,018 different agencies, of which 31,699 dealt with social health and welfare. Among the more classic examples were the 'Fund for victims of the 1901 Vesuvius earthquake', the 'National Assistance Board for War Orphans' and even one which allocated funds for the colonisation of Ethiopia, long since abandoned. The Communists, of course, pretend to be frightfully shocked and eager to expose this terrible corruption, though they are masters of the art themselves, spending almost as much on propaganda as the Christian Democrats.

I was dragged away from exposés of the secret P-2 freemason's lodge, complete with photographs of the men to watch out for, to eat at one of the long tables in the dining area, where we ordered *pasta fagioli* from a waiter who was being run off his feet by the crowd. Friends came and went, but I listened with only half an ear to the chatter and laughter, preferring to observe the throng milling around under the powerful spotlights, the hammer and sickle fluttering above their heads. I couldn't help wondering what a Russian Communist would think of his brother Italians, dressed in their smart shirts, jeans and elegant shoes. *'La Bella Figura'* might prove a difficult expression to translate into Russian.

We left late, motoring out to a park with an open air disco pumping heartbeat bop into the air beneath the trees. I had left my dancing shoes at home and went off for a walk to watch the moon

219

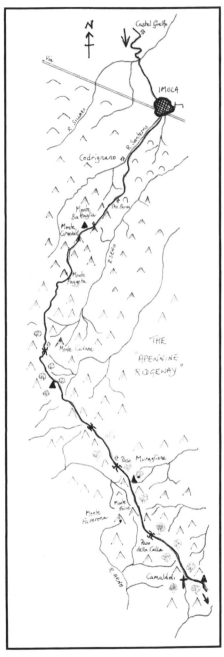

come up instead. It was after two when we got back, but we talked a while longer before going to bed.

Around nine, I quietly made myself breakfast. I didn't want to miss my porridge. Natascia insisted on taking me out as far as Codrignano, and here we parted. It was Sunday, 20th September, which meant that it had taken four days to cross the plain from Padua. I was glad that it was over. I would soon be in the hills again, away from the ultimately boring tarmac roads. My only worry was that I was not carrying much in the way of food, but I hoped to find a shop somewhere.

I perused Roberto's maps before setting off for the ridge, passing two disgruntled hunters on their way down to Sunday lunch. The catch had not been good, they muttered. The slopes were wild and dry, often sparsely forested and badly eroded, the naked white rock breaking through the scanty top soil, the lane soon a track of dusty white stone. I stopped early for lunch of bread, sardines, cheese and chocolate, the usual fare. The track I next took led straight into a farmyard with no exit. I would have to ask the way. A

220

woman appeared from the cool interior when I called through the open doorway.

'Excuse me, *Signora*, but I'm a little lost.'

I was not yet sure whether the Italian was *perso* or *perdido*, but she understood well enough.

'I'm looking for the path that follows the ridge towards Monte Battaglia.'

'I don't know. I'll ask my husband.'

I could see the family eating in the kitchen behind her. She turned, went down the steps back into the house where I heard a muted conversation with an invisible man.

'Hey, you! Come in!' the voice cried.

I ducked through the doorway into the cool shade of the kitchen. The man whose voice I had heard looked me up and down carefully while my eyes adjusted to the dim light. Then he smiled and asked if I should like something to eat. They had almost finished but I was welcome to help myself to anything I wanted. He asked my name, and introduced me to the people sitting round the table, two burly sons, unmarried, an old aunt, a sister and her husband.

'Maria,' he said to his wife, 'bring some water so that Giovanni can wash before he sits down.'

She brought a bowl of water with a clean towel to dry my hands, then the man motioned to me to sit on his right. He sat back at the head of the table, secure in his traditional paternal authority. *Capo di famiglia*, or absolute monarch. He commands, the family obeys. The mother does not command, only request, but her requests are not to be turned down either.

Maria was a traditional Bolognese cook. I don't think I shall ever again feast on such a Sunday lunch. I did not help myself. They served me, piling my plate with new delights at every opportunity. The lunch that I had already eaten was a modest snack in comparison. First, I tucked into two large helpings of *lasagna* with a glass of red wine, moved on to savour a dark, rich rabbit stew with white wine and bread for the gravy. When my plate was wiped clean, they suggested I try a slice or two of the grilled leg of mutton with more red wine, following this with salad, cheeses, fruit and small sweet cakes Maria said were called *ravioli*. To round things off nicely, the *capo* topped up my coffee with a generous shot of *grappa*, rightly impressed by my appetite. They quizzed me on the journey as I ate, politely waiting for me to finish a mouthful before asking a question. I felt instantly at home.

'What does your mother think of your travelling like this?' asked Maria. I was immediately reminded of Senhora Soares's look of sympathy six months before in the north of Portugal. They shared the same love of a large, happy family living together and found it sad, even unnatural, that a son should choose of his own free will to go wandering over the world far from the comforts of his home. We talked then of the Alps and mountain life. The old aunt left the room, coming back with a dried Edelweiss that she had found in the mountains many years ago.

'Take it,' she said. 'It will bring you luck and remind you of us.'

That made two. I would keep it with M. Poulot's. The *capo* gave his wife a look of tenderness and love.

'Shall we eat some of the cake you made this morning before he leaves?'

He turned to me while she disappeared into a corner and came back with a large ring tin.

'You just wait. This is her speciality, baked this morning in the wood oven. It melts in the mouth like butter in hell.'

Maria banged the tin on the stone flags of the floor to loosen it, then turned it onto a flat dish. It was heavenly, light and fluffy with just a tang of orange to balance the sweetness. The time was rapidly approaching when I would have to try and rise from the chair. Before I left, she insisted on giving me some further provisions, waving away my weak protestations by saying that I would certainly find no shops in the mountains. She loaded me up with a chunk of bread, three slices of cake, four apples, two boiled eggs, two tins of sardines and two cans of beer in case I got thirsty. I staggered out into the late afternoon sunshine speechless with gratitude, words of thanks sticking in my throat, powerless to put my feelings into words. They understood, bathing contentedly in their own hospitality.

'Go on, then, you'd better get moving if you can. Go up this road, take the first left and the track will take you up to the ridge where another will take you to Monte Battaglia. You'll see the way quite clearly when you get there. Good luck. Watch out for the snakes. God go with you. Remember us.'

I got lost immediately, but luckily one of the sons, a huge man with arms like hams, put me right and I tottered uphill to the ridge. The light golden track cut its way along the crest of the high hills, curling like a snake to the distant watchtower on Monte Battaglia, once one of a series of long, rocky islands before the land rose on either side to form what is now the boot of Italy. The watchtower was built in the thirteenth century to guard the frontier between Tuscany and the Pontificate, which at that time included the province of Emilia-Romagna. The track I was following was the former *Strada della Dogana*, the customs' road. It was pleasant walking with fine views into the carefully cultivated Tuscan valleys of corn, vines and orchards ceding to woods of scrub oak, beech, chestnut and pine below the bare ridge. At the base of the ruined tower was a plaque dedicated to the Brigata Garibaldi, September 1944. *Il loro sangue tinse di rosso l'erba*, (their blood has stained the grass red).

An hour or so later, I camped by a spring below the ruined church on Monte Carnevale, further evidence of heavy fighting on the Gothic Line a year after the 1st Allied landings in the south of Italy. To satisfy my curiosity, I walked up into the graveyard on a flat shelf overlooking the Santerno valley in the rapidly fading blue twilight. The chill wind was strengthening, causing the bells in the cracked tower to sway and creak in the darkness. The grave slab on my left had broken, leaving a large, gaping black hole. A sudden shiver ran up my spine and goosepimples broke out on my skin. I closed my eyes in an attempt to master such irrational terror. There was nothing I could do, after all, I had no home to run to where I could slam the door shut and turn on the radio. I had to walk out as calmly as I could and ignore the imagined dead that leered on all sides, who might at any minute creep up behind to tap me on the left shoulder with their skeletal fingers. Uneasily I watched the silhouette of the church as I ate my supper alone, checking the lighter area where the bells hung still, half expecting some fiendish, jesting goblin to spring out with a shriek and toll the bells.

I rose late, the night's fears allayed by the coming of dawn. The sky was thinly overcast, which meant the spell of bright, sunny weather might be coming to an end, but the temperature was ideal for walking and a single patch of blue was reassuring. A man out walking in the woods engaged me in conversation, a journalist from Bologna who had taken the day off to go mushroom picking. He said it was a pity he hadn't brought his camera or he could have taken a picture and written an article on the long-distance walker. As we sat chatting on the side of a worn ditch, he asked if I had seen the memorial to the partisans on Monte Battaglia, then pointed to the ditch.

'You'll see quite a lot of ditches like this on the mountainsides. They're really old trenches dug out by the troops during the War. Garibaldi himself took this route when he was on the run from the Austrians and priests after the retreat from Rome, in the summer of 1849, if I remember my history lessons.'

He was right. Garibaldi's wife, Annie, had died in his arms just a week before. Having disbanded the army, he was now trying to escape over the border into less hostile Tuscany, where the people would give him shelter and safe hiding. He had one companion, Leggiero, who was lame and had to be transported by cart or on Garibaldi's back. With the help of a sympathetic parish priest called

223

Verità, who had helped many others before him, he crossed the Apennine ridges, reached the coast and embarked for France on 2nd September, 1849. Ten and a half years later the intrepid adventurer was back again, this time in Sicily.

My friend went off in search of mushrooms while I continued along the crest which was slowly becoming more overgrown and difficult to follow. A spring on top of Monte Faggiola provided water for a much-needed breakfast before I moved on towards the Colla di Casaglia, which was where I would join the true spine of the Apennines, the Gothic Line, a position captured by the Eighth Indian Division. I arrived in the early evening, finding a cafe at the pass where I drank a coffee, downed a shot of *grappa* and bought chocolate for the next day. It was the only thing the man had to sell. I was grateful then for the provisions Maria had so generously given me at the farmhouse. One of the lumberjacks who was curiously interrogating me tried to persuade me that the path was much too difficult to follow, but I ignored his fat
pessimism.

'I can always turn back, *Signor.*'

The path was difficult. I made my way up through a barrier of felled trees and tangled branches to the ridge, found a spot behind a bluff out of the wind among some young pines and pitched camp. The sun had set, but a blue, misty light lingered on over the corrugations of the mountains, the Milky Way dazzlingly clear. I cooked supper happily, then slept deeply until morning.

It had been easy when the tops of the ridges were bare, but that next morning I lost my way three times, turning back and trying again, fighting my way through the tangled undergrowth that blocked the view completely. Things were made even worse because I was trespassing on the property of a colony of large, yellow spiders whose webs hung everywhere and soon covered my face, beard and hair with sticky strands that were impossible to remove. Water was another problem, since I was travelling above the springs. Luckily, I blundered into a herd of cows foraging through the woods and met the cowman, who told me where I could find water. That was breakfast solved.

I must have looked quite a sight when I arrived battlesore and weary at the Passo di Muraglione, 'The Great Wall', one place where my Apennine route coincided with that of J.M. Scott, who described it as 'a windswept ridge where a road goes over, and there is a barrack-like hotel, which however had cold beer'. I lumbered in myself for some refreshment. The proprietor introduced himself as Franco, waxing enthusiastic over the mushrooms that I had

224

collected. He was very pleased when I gave them to him, feeling it the least that I could do to return the kindness that others were always showing to me. He called his wife Carla to come and see, pouring a glass of wine and giving me a packet of cigarettes, proudly showing off a postcard of Vancouver by night sent to him by one of a group of cyclists who had passed by on a journey round Europe. I made myself a cheese sandwich as they chatted away, telling me of the high winds they experience in winter, that Franco called 'The Window Breaker'. Carla asked if I should like a shower and I jumped at the opportunity. It was Tuesday, 22nd September, eight days since the last time I had had a complete wash. She showed me to one of the rooms upstairs which had a private bathroom, gave me a clean towel and left me to peel off my filthy clothes and bask under the hot water. I scrubbed and soaped myself, washed the spider's webs from my hair and revelled in the water running deliciously down my spine. After drying myself with the large, lavender-scented white towel, my body was tingling, refreshed and renewed.

When I eventually came downstairs — even that seemed a novel experience — they made a cup of coffee, showed me the path on and presented me with a bottle of wine, a bottle of spring water, pears, apples, peaches, tomatoes, bread and a great hunk of local cheese. Carlo shook hands with a grin and Carla kissed me goodbye.

'Ciao, Giovanni. Bocca Lupo.' (Good Luck.)

I camped and feasted in the twilight, leaving most of the climb onto Monte Falterona for the next morning. Two deer came by cautiously upwind, but bounced off in alarm when they caught sight of me. Crickets chirruped and an owl screeched as the sound of the evening angelus drifted up from the valley below. Although the sky was clear and the stars were out, a great, forbidding cloudbank was forming to the west, the wind strengthening, growing brash and noisy. I could hear it approaching, bending the trees as tremendous gusts rushed over them, sweeping everything along, then receding, leaving the night quiet and still until it rushed in again. The 'Window Breaker', no doubt. Dry leaves rustled and fell, the plastic over the tent flapped madly as I wrote up my diary by torchlight.

It didn't rain, but Monte Falterona was hidden in low mist the next morning. I hoped I would not get lost again because it was so tiring. Istanbul seemed a long way away. Perhaps I would be there by Christmas, but I was wary about imposing deadlines and put it out of my mind. It had been a mistake to haul so much in the Alps and I had no desire for a repetition of the crack-up in Bolzano.

I need not have worried. An old road led up to the summit through wet, mossy, dripping beech woods, the mountainside running with streams, the source of the Arno on the opposite flank. An old couple passed carrying wicker baskets overflowing with cep mushrooms *(Boletus edulis)*, cramming their mouths with bread and ham as they walked home. I had my own breakfast in a tumble-down *rifugio* at the summit, out of the wind, by another monument to the partisans, 'Brigata Garibaldi, 13 April 1944'. Someone had scrawled *A MORTE I DROGATI* on the wall in red paint, 'Death to Drug Takers'.

It just happened to be midday when I next stopped to ask for information on the way ahead at the Rifugio Club Alpino which was marked on the last of Roberto's maps. Three men were sitting at the bar drinking aperitifs. I joined them, getting out my maps to ask their advice on the best way to get to the monastery of Camaldoli. They explained happily, asking if I should like to share their lunch with them. We sat down to eat spaghetti, followed by a dish of fried ceps which the older of them had picked that morning. He was the acknowledged mushroom expert, but said very little, leaving the conversation to Oscar and Paolo who were glad of their new audience.

'You never expected to be sitting down to lunch with three communists, did you? Have some more wine. Help yourself to the cheeses.'

I did my best to follow their rambling tales of the adventures of their friend 'The Bear' in Sardinia and Sicily. It appeared he was an enormous, hairy man who always went around dressed in a tunic. One day, he was passing the local army barracks when the soldiers started to wolf whistle, at which point the well endowed Bear exposed himself to public view and silenced their jeering instantly.

The conversation veered to politics. They told me of a poll that had been conducted some years before which asked whether it was possible to be a good Catholic and a Communist at the same time. Only twenty per cent of those questioned thought the two were mutually exclusive. It seemed a strange attitude, but then, as Oscar said, this was the Italian brand of Communism which 'had to be fulfilled within a pluralistic and democratic society'. It was only a name, after all. By the time I took my leave after coffee and *grappa,*they had persuaded me that their Communism was not as Russian as it was painted, though the shadow of Big Brother Kremlin still lurked uneasily behind in the shadows.

At the Passo della Calla the air was crackling with walkie talkies from patrol cars that had drawn up beside the road over the ridge. The policemen paid me no attention, so I continued unmolested on a fine track through the silent forest of Camaldoli where the trunks of the beeches were a smooth, glistening black, and the leafy floor was

226

strewn with large boulders. An eerie mist began drifting in, pierced by the occasional splash of sun, the muffled sound of my footsteps and thunder rolling in the distance the only sounds. I quickened my pace, resting briefly in a glade where a woman was calling forlornly to

The monastery 'cells'

her husband in the mountains, the wind carrying away her cries. The sky was getting progressively darker, the rumbling closer. A few drops of rain began to spatter down, but I did not heed the signs.

I had gone about a mile further when suddenly I saw a thick wall of rain coming straight at me across a clearing. I ran clumsily for cover, fumbling for the plastic sheet, but too late. Within seconds I was soaked and crouched helplessly beneath the inadequate shelter of a young pine. The worst was yet to come. The thunder rolled ever closer until the eye of the storm passed directly overhead, claps of thunder deafening me, the wind roaring angrily, lightning bolts cracking down on all sides. I crouched there for what seemed a long time, the damp and cold working its way into my bones, my legs turning numb, cowering like all the other animals in the forest and very frightened, knowing full well that under a tree was the last place I should be. The storm eventually passed, leaving the ground a mass of puddles and flowing rivulets. I had to walk fast and windmill my arms to bring the circulation back. Fifteen minutes later, I was at the monastery.

Once a simple hermitage in the forest, it had gradually expanded and was now an impressive place surrounded by high stone walls with an arched gateway into the courtyard in front of the church, a solid affair with two bell towers and a clock between. From the courtyard a path led through to a double row of stone huts used as cells or retreats, each with its own patch of garden around it. An old monk in a coarse, white woollen habit swabbing the floor of the church porch mumbled something incomprehensible when I asked permission to look around. I took it to mean 'Yes'. The interior was baroque, a style I find over-ornate, too rich in gold and bright white paint. In a side chapel lay the 'miraculously preserved' body of a

227

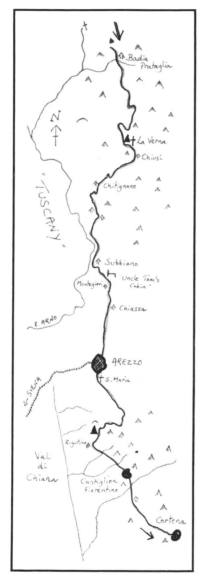

fifteenth century monk in a glass case. I spent a while observing the face, the dry, taut skin stretched like parchment over the cheek bones, an eagle nose, the mouth a stiff line of the greatest severity. My thoughts flew to the cathedral in Lima, where the decaying body of the great Francisco Pizarro who overthrew the Inca Empire is also housed in a glass coffin for all the world to see, though no miracle had preserved his remains from the worm. I was filled with an overpowering nausea as I contemplated the dead monk's mean face and left the church as quickly as possible, paying a visit to the tourist shop to buy three miniature bottles of Benedictine liqueur. I had thought I might find refuge at the monastery, for was this not one of their traditional roles? I was certainly in no mood to spend the night in the dripping woods or face another storm, yet the atmosphere of the place made me uneasy, the silent monks seemed as menacing as their brother in the glass coffin. It was obvious that we did not share the same God, ironic that the unbelieving communists could show more hospitality and kindness than monks whose lives were officially devoted to the God of Love.

I took the road wearily towards Badia Prataglia, wondering if my luck had run out, but to my relief found a wooden cabin with a veranda a few miles on. I tried the double door which was locked, but gave way with a slight push. On the table inside stood a bottle of wine, a small knapsack and a camera, though there was no one around. Not wishing to overstep the mark, I waited on the veranda, boiling up a strong brew to keep the chill off. Soon after, two young Italians turned up. They were in much the same predicament and introduced themselves as Roberto and Savio from Ravenna, saying they were out for a week's walking in the woods.

I moved my stuff inside, lit the fire and toasted some chestnuts while they made lentil soup. We whiled away the evening talking and drinking wine together and in the morning we strolled down into Badia. Here I was finally able to reprovision for the first time in four days. The only thing that I had bought was a bar of chocolate. The rest had been freely given to me by the people. It had happened too often to be a mere coincidence and simply meant that they were some of the kindest, most unreserved and hospitable people that I was ever to come across.

We parted after a coffee to go our separate ways, my destination the monastery of La Verna, perched high in the mountains between the Arno and the Tiber valleys. I was no longer following the ridges, for there were places that I wanted to see. I would follow the Arno Valley to Arezzo, the first of the old Etruscan towns, where I would buy a ticket to Siena, taking time to sightsee and relax. Then it would be back and on to Perugia and Assisi, which I was greatly looking forward to seeing. I felt of all the saints, Saint Francis was perhaps the one closest to my heart.

The countryside was more inhabited, there was pasture among the wooded hills, woodmills and masses of blackberries, the rosehips forming, the leaves on the walnut trees curling, turning brown, a tint of autumn creeping into the woods. An old farmer talked to me for a while as he kept an eye on his white cows and their offspring. He was complaining about his lazy son who never did any work and left it all for him to do, but other than that I understood little of what he had to say. It was not necessary, though, since I was content just to listen to his voice weaving patterns in the air with a wonderful lilting cadence, as near to a Welshman speaking Italian as can be imagined.

The sky had clouded over. I spent the rest of the day taking shelter from intermittent heavy rainshowers in barns, huts and even a pig sty, reading and escaping into Cosimo's world.

A shepherd went by on the road, herding his sodden flock from the comfort of a beaten up old Fiat. In the cafe at Rimbocchi, the blue-dressed workers sat at tables playing cards or simply staring. I made little effort to speak myself. The weather seemed to affect us all.

The village below La Verna monastery was pretty, shining and wet, the street lights on, the water from the fountain extremely good. Two modern houses being built on the outskirts offered their draughty skeletons as convenient shelter from the rain that had now set in for the night. Through the evening mist I could just make out the monastery, built atop a precipice, a large cross standing out above the roofs. There were just caves and woods there when it was given to St. Francis in 1213. His followers built a few rude huts around the openings of the caves and it was here, in September 1214, that he received the stigmata during one of his mystical ecstasies. In the sides of the sheer wall on which the monastery was built were two large, black holes like the eye sockets of a skull. My heart was heavy, but I had resigned myself to the rain. At least I was inside.

By morning the sky was a clean, well-washed blue, a single cloud basking in the rays of the rising sun. The towers and cross were now clearly visible among the trees, the face still there as well. I had been put off monasteries by Camaldoli and decided to give the place a miss, taking the road down into the valley which was dotted with the red roofs of tiny stone villages, flanked with ash and chestnut trees and oaks from which the acorns were tumbling in the strong wind that had swept the clouds away. Further down towards the Arno were olive groves and vineyards set on ancient Roman terraces. They grew the vines up the trunks of maples, a distinctive feature of Tuscany.

A straight avenue of cypress trees led into the village of Poggio, where I washed my feet and hair at the village pump, washed some clothes and put on clean socks. Two women sitting outside their front door in the shade watched the exercise with a faint smile. From there, after lunch in the warm sun overlooking a fine brick castle with battlemented turrets, I stepped on happily down to the Arno, treating myself to an ice cream on the way. A lost dummy hung from a nail in one of the trees at the roadside leading into the long main street of Subbiano. I must have been happy, for I treated myself to a doughnut from a passing vendor, soberly studying the list of war dead above the main doors of the city hall as I ate, shocked by the number of women and civilians on the list.

I was beginning to wonder where I would spend the night when, on coming over a hill on a white gravel road a few miles out of town, I caught sight of a sign proclaiming boldly *La Capanna dello Zio Tom*, Uncle Tom's Cabin. Two elderly men were wandering round the garden of an obviously self-built house. I leaned over the gate to check that the road went to Montegiovi.

'Yes it does,' said one. 'Why are you going there? Got friends?'

'No, Sir, just another place along the road, I suppose.'

'Where are you going to spend the night?'

'I don't know. I'll find somewhere.'

'You can stay the night here if you wish. At least come and have a drink.'

'Lady Luck, thank you' I mumbled. 'Yes, I will.'

Uncle Tom was wearing dirty black trousers and a broad brimmed canvas hat, and had a good day's stubble on his cheeks. His friendly smile revealed chrome-plated teeth and deepened the furrows that lined his face. He showed me round: he had a fifteen year old Shetland pony in an overgrown field and a lovely trap in which he took his grandchildren for rides around the lanes.

'I used to be a keen horseman, but I can't ride any more 'cos I'm ill, dying actually, but don't let that worry you, it's just a part of getting old.'

His teeth flashed. There were various shacks around, housing piles of timber, pigeons, doves, rabbits and dogs. Inside his cabin, he had a bathroom with a splendid tub of the type that you sit in upright. He didn't have to ask if I would like a bath—one look at me was enough. He heated up the water with fast-burning, resinous pine cones and poured me out a drink of Campari on the veranda, reminiscing about his time in the Army of Africa. He was not complimentary about his officers, a load of incompetent fools by the sound of it, concerned mainly with saving their skins.

I went to have my bath and slipped into the warm, deep water up to my neck, soaking sleepily in a world very close to paradise. I was brought back to reality by a shout.

'Have you fallen asleep?'

I reappeared scrubbed, fresh and relaxed. He had shaved, put on a clean shirt, pressed trousers and black shoes, a different man altogether.

'Come, I have to rejoin my family in Subbiano, but first I must show you where everything is. Here is a bed to sleep in. In here is the kitchen. The cooker works on gas. You'll find everything that you need for supper in this cupboard—pasta, stock cubes, cheese, tomatoes, onions. Have it outside on the terrace and help yourself to as much wine as you want. I can't drink it myself. Look after the place for me, will you? If anyone turns up, you just tell them I told you *you* were the boss.'

We shook hands and he set off in his car. There were olives soaking in a tub on the veranda, chestnuts, walnuts and mushrooms in baskets, while from the ceiling hung an old yoke on which I kept banging my head. I made supper and sat outside watching the sky grow dark, the stars coming out, the twinkling lights of Arezzo and the villages of the Val di Chiana below, as I drank the sharp, slightly fizzy wine stopping only to sing softly. With an electric light, I would be able to sit up in bed and read for a change, but I fell asleep too soon on the soft feather mattress.

In the morning I made a cup of tea, had a leisurely breakfast, swept the place out, tidied up and pushed on down through the hills towards Arezzo. Like all Etruscan towns it is built on a hill, and dominates the valley bowl around it, the spire of the cathedral rising gracefully above everything else. The land is cultivated right up to the base of the mediaeval walls; you only have to close your eyes a fraction to drift back in time to the Middle Ages.

Getting to Siena involved taking a train, a bus and then another train, with a fair amount of waiting in between. A little man with most of his front teeth missing sidled up to me on the platform, asked if I were English, then launched into an account of his war experiences—how he had been taken prisoner in Sicily, transferred to a camp outside Birmingham and set to work as a farm labourer. He hadn't liked the food very much, but otherwise he had a good time, obviously, secretly bicycling round the countryside looking for English women to seduce. It was a mistake to prompt him on the subject: his eyes sparkled lasciviously as he started on a series of crude fantasies, with rude gestures to illustrate, chortling at the looks of disapproval he was thrown by two middle-aged women who had been eaves-dropping on the conversation. An older man joined in with his experiences, melancholically telling how he had made friends with an English Lieutenant, then thirty-five years later received a letter from him. He was going to reply but found that he had lost the address. He looked around mournfully to gauge the effect of this tragi-comedy.

In Siena I went to a camping site with good facilities, set on an extraneous hill. There were plenty of people in campers and tents littered around under the trees, but I found it difficult to make contact: they all seemed to be Swiss or German, perfectly paired off, happy with their own company. I got rather lonely and spent much of the time wandering the old town, writing letters and reading. I was there three days in the end, mainly because of the weather which was foul for most of the time, but also because it is one of the most beautiful cities in Europe.

Tobias Smollett, travelling through the city in the eighteenth century, stopped for only one night, writing: 'Of Siena I can say nothing from my own observation, but that we were indifferently lodged in a house that stunk like a privy and fared wretchedly at supper. The city is large and well built . . .' There was little to interest a classical scholar like Smollett, except perhaps the symbol of the city which you see everywhere, the she-wolf suckling Romulus and Remus. According to legend the city was founded by Senius and Ascius, the sons of Remus.

The Sienese were Ghibellines, granted the right of self government by the Emperor Frederick Barbarossa in 1186, at roughly the same time as the Swiss Cantons were granted theirs. Siena swiftly became a powerful commercial and banking centre, her biggest rival being Guelph-supporting Florence, whose armies they defeated at the battle of Montaperti in 1260.

The new city-state was an oligarchy, ruled by magistrates known as 'The Nine', who confined the nobility to building towers to boast their social status; the higher the towers, the greater the status. Most of these towers have since fallen or been pulled down, and the skyline is not what it was in the Middle Ages, when it looked more like New York. The system was worked wisely and efficiently under 'The Nine'. A 'Water Authority' looked after water supplies and the fountains, a 'Judge of the Streets' was brought in from outside so as to be able to make objective decisions on street widening and the removal of steps and obstructions from the way. Trade and the arts flourished. In 1309 a law was passed that required all new houses to be built of the local red clay, the famous 'burnt Siena', and this gave a unity to the city that others don't have. Then, in 1348, the Black Death arrived, wiping out almost a third of the population. The city declined, the magistrates lost their hold, and the nobility began, once more, to take control. In 1555 the city lost its independence and the French King Henry II gave it to his son Philip, who sold it in July 1557 to Cosimo di Medici, Grand Duke of Tuscany, Master of Florence, which now had its revenge and ascendancy secure. Siena was relegated to the second division. To this day a certain rivalry exists: Sienese football fans, for example, will taunt the Florentines with cries of 'Remember Montaperti', and the Florentines, in their turn, insult the Sienese with cries of 'Lupa Puttaneggia', which translates badly as 'She-wolf Whore'.

The city itself is built on three hills around the cup of an old volcanic crater, the famous *Campo*, dominated by the Palazzo Publico on one side and the Mangia Tower on the other, which acts like an enormous sundial on the fan-shaped *Campo*. Originally a sports arena, it then became a market place – there are still a few stalls there in the morning, selling fruit and vegetables—and today it is a spacious square with cafes and shops, a general meeting place. The two main streets of the city run parallel to each other, and sweep through the traffic-free centre between imposing ranks of four- or five-storey brick houses in curves 'which accord precisely to the needs of those riding on horseback at high speeds', thus good for the prompt defence of the city.

The civil life of Siena may have decayed, but the religious establishment flourished. When Smollett visited the city there were at

233

least two thousand priests and their acolytes under the bishop, representing one eighth of the population. The Cathedral, which dominates the town from outside, but which is invisible from the Campo, is an impressive building with a facade of dark green, light brown, pink and white marble. I loved the floor inside with its mosaics of the Sibyls, and there is a narrow doorway leading to the room where the illustrated manuscripts done by the monks are on show. The blues are heavenly and no one is quite sure how they were made. The Cathedral also contains thirty-one sacred relics, including the Veil of the Madonna. The Virgin Mary is the patron saint of Siena, *'Maria Advocata, Mediatrix Optimum inter Christum et Senam Tuam'*, and she is often depicted protecting the city and her children with her mantle.

When Henry James visited the city, he found everything 'cracking, peeling, fading, crumbling, rotting . . . a world battered and befouled with long use'. Revenue from tourism has since given the Sienese people the money to take care of their inheritance, of which they are justly proud. I found the place clean, quiet, well kept and somehow haunting.

I arrived back in Arezzo on Tuesday, 29th September and ate lunch under the airy porticos of the cloisters of the church of Santa Maria, outside the town, watching two boys play football on the grass in front. In the church a Madonna stretched out her hands, beckoning to the faithful and weary from above the altar, her veil falling low on either side to protect her children. The painting behind the altar was quite unique. Everyone is used to seeing Christ with long, normally fair hair and a wispy beard, but here he was with short, cropped black hair and no trace of beard, more like a sullen convict than the Saviour of Mankind. Just the idea seemed to turn the world upside down. He was not a hippy then, after all.

The plan was to cut across the hills to Cortona, then on to Perugia, but it proved difficult to put into effect. The path, marked so clearly on the map, was overgrown, choked with brambles and unused. An old man pushing a wheelbarrow of earth down the hill recommended I take the new road. Everybody else did. It would take me too far east and involve walking sixteen kilometres on the main road, but there was no alternative. After a steep climb, I didn't dally at the top because of the cold wind. I found shelter that night in the doorway of a farmhouse being converted into a restaurant, eating supper at one of the tables outside as the sun set behind the mountains on the other side of the Val di Chiana.

Imagine a hot summer's day in the same valley, along which is tramping a column of four thousand tired, desperate, ill-equipped soldiers, some dressed in ponchos, others wearing grimy red shirts, flanked by groups of scouting cavalry with plumes in their hats, riding fine horses. They were led by a thick-set, bearded man who rode between a woman and a friar in a red shirt with a crucifix round his neck. They were Giuseppe Garibaldi, Annie and Ugo Bassi on the retreat from Rome. Bringing up the rear above the dust churned up by the wagons and the one small cannon, rode the bizarre figure of Colonel Hugh Forbes, dressed in a summer suit and wearing a white top hat, the commander of what was left of the Provincial Army of the Republic. 'A most courageous and honourable soldier', according to Garibaldi.

The odds against their reaching Venice were considerable. It was 1849. Rome had fallen on the 2nd July, two days before Garibaldi's thirty-second birthday. Four armies were now in hot pursuit of the rebels, the French threatening from the west with 30,000 men, the Neapolitans from the south and east with 12,000, the Spaniards from the south with 6000, while the Austrians waited in the north and east in 15,000 freshly laundered white coats. It took a great man to slip through the net, deceiving them with feigned marches and clever use of the cavalry to lead them astray. The time he had spent in South America had taught him a great deal about basic guerrilla tactics and proved invaluable. His words to those who came with him from Rome were simple: 'I offer neither pay, nor quarters, nor provisions; I offer hunger, thirst, forced marches, battles and death. Let him who loves his country in his heart and not just with his lips, follow me.'

Half of the 4000 were really on their way home, so plenty deserted along the way. Garibaldi had hopes that the people of Umbria and Tuscany would rise against their overlords, but the priests in black had done a good job. It was a disillusioned man who stood at the gates of Arezzo on the 23rd, parleying in vain with the governors of the town who had closed the gates firmly in his face, afraid that the Austrians would take reprisals if they helped him. His army spent the day camped around the church of Santa Maria and retreated during the night, but the rearguard went astray, clashing with some Austrian forces, while bands of peasants led by the priests combed the hills cutting down stragglers.

The main body escaped over the pass and on to reach the haven of San Marino eight days later, where what was left of the army was disbanded. Garibaldi escaped down to the coast with about two hundred men and his ever faithful wife, who refused to leave him despite the fact that she was not well. At the coast, they found boats and set sail. His was the only boat that was not captured. He was back again for the Sicilian Campaign in May, 1860, at the start of

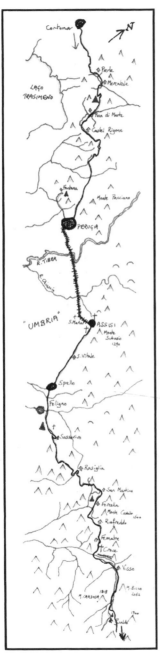

the 'March of the Thousand.' For centuries Italy had been a convenient term for the separate kingdoms in the peninsular. By the end of that year, it was almost a country united.

The light faded from the plain, leaving just the faintest silhouette of the Chianti mountains. I made up a bed of straw and hay under the arched entrance to the yard and lay back. I would have to get up before dawn if I wanted to avoid the traffic on the main road into Cortona.

By eleven o'clock the next morning I was in sight of the town, walking cautiously in the face of the oncoming traffic, keeping an eye out for cars overtaking from behind. They were the real danger. Cortona sits on a hill overlooking the valley, a jumble of faded red roofs and towers surrounded by ramparts of grey stone, like Castiglion Fiorentino but larger. I took one of the steep, cobbled streets up to the main square, bought food and rested. As the Etruscan Museum was open, I climbed the twenty steps to the entrance and wandered round.

Quite where the Etruscans came from nobody knows. Herodotus said Asia Minor. They first appeared in the twelfth century B.C., founding the Twelve Cities and responsible for the introduction of the idea of the City State. They eventually succumbed to the Latins and other Italic tribes, but left much of their art behind to be kept in glass cases in the museum. I particularly like their figurines. They have a delicacy, fluidity and appealing simplicity. If one traces the outline of one of these figurines, it is remarkably similar to the figures in Egyptian hiero

236

glyphs. Their language, which had a Greek script, has no affinities with any others and is thus unintelligible.

From Cortona I turned east for Perugia, wishing to follow the road bordering Lake Trasimeno, beside which Flaminius Consul had come in hot pursuit of Hannibal in 217 B.C., but I chose the quieter lanes that ran parallel on the other side of the hills in the end. It was a real pleasure to walk along in the warm sunshine, watching the clouds frisk by overhead, the hillsides woolly green above dripping olive groves, the white undersides of the leaves flickering in the breeze.

Every scooter enthusiast will know the Vespa, or 'Wasp', but few know the Ape or 'Busy Bee'. It is a peculiar, three-wheeled, motorised barrow. The driver sits above the front wheel in a steel and glass bubble, while behind, on two wheels, there is room for all manner of things. If you are a builder, it's your spades, bricks and cement, if you are a farmer, a sack or two of corn, the goat, your wife and mother-in-law. Domenico was a builder, a happy man with a big laugh for such a small body, his teeth long since gone, a flat nose and a tweed cap. He gave me a lift along the road a mile to a cafe at the base of the hill up to Perle and bought me a glass of wine.

'I can't take you any further, I'm afraid. She won't make it up the hill with you *and* the cement.'

He sputtered away on the road that twisted up to a formidable ruined castle overlooking the bright green valley of Mercatale. At first I didn't recognise the crop. The murmur of voices drifted out from somewhere in the field of head-high plants with large, fleshy leaves and flowers like pink bells. The sound of a murmured conversation came from a group of women working their way through the field, choosing and picking the best leaves. Tobacco, of course. In the drying houses beside the road hung row upon row of brown leaves. Dusk fell, whole families came out onto the road, walking home for supper. I bought liver at a brightly lit butcher's and sat at a table outside a cafe under the street lights, sad to have dusk fall so swiftly now. It was the last day of September, the days were getting shorter and I had become accustomed to long hours of walking. I would have to adapt, making sure that I rose with or before the sun. I did not mind walking at night if there was a moon but it was tiresome finding a place to sleep and very irritating to see a much more comfortable site a few yards away in the morning. I groped around in an olive grove that night, cooking liver and noodles by the light of the torch, wondering how cold winter was going to be.

The birds woke me and a short climb brought me to a crossroads where I turned left for Perugia. The road to the right wound down

237

to Lake Trasimeno past the site where Hannibal had camped on a summer's night in 217 B.C., the year after he had come across the Alps. His Spanish and African infantry, light troops, the mercenary Gauls and his cavalry were strung out across the hill to the west, overlooking the lake, waiting for the Roman Consul Flaminius to take the bait and fall into their perfect ambush. All but one of the thirty-seven elephants had died, while Hannibal himself had lost an eye. He wandered through the camp unrecognised by his men, for he was terrified of assassination and would disguise himself in one of the many wigs he carried with him.

Flaminius was rash and greedy for glory. He didn't wait to join forces with his fellow Consul, Servilius, but set off in pursuit from Arretium dreaming of the triumphal entry into Rome that would be his alone. His intelligence told him that Hannibal was bound for Perusia and he thought to take him from the rear.

The morning was cold, causing a thick mist to rise from the surface of the swampy lake. The Carthaginians could see each other and their signals clearly, but the Romans could not see them poised above, ready to fall on the thin column of men marching along the edge of the lake. The Romans were taken completely by surprise and had no time to take up battle order, being caught in a perfect pincer movement. The battle lasted for three hours, at the end of which 15,000 Romans lay dead, Flaminius among them, his body never found, unrecognisable among all the other looted bodies. Hannibal lost 1500 men, mostly Gauls whom he did not trust. The Praetor's announcement to the Commons in Rome was brief and to the point: 'There has been a great battle. We have been defeated.' Cannae was yet to come.

The shop in Castel Rigone had everything necessary for a good breakfast, which I ate in an abandoned grove of ancient, twisted olive trees. When not deserted, the farmhouses were guarded by really vicious dogs that set up a nerve jangling barking that followed me for miles over the high, smooth, desolate pasture land north-east of Perugia. It was a long, tiring day and late afternoon before I reached the city walls, the outskirts of the town a sprawling mass of recently constructed flats, or *edilizie* as they were called. A hassled *carabiniere* told me how to get to the camping site, which was a long way and involved taking a bus before a five kilometre walk uphill. In fact, I had almost come full circle. It was dark by the time I arrived. I checked in and had a shower. The water was cold, the site completely empty, the holiday season over. I slept, exhausted, until morning, made a silent breakfast and went into Perugia for the day.

I arrived about eleven and went straight to the post office. There was no post for me. Dispirited, I wandered the old town, past the square, grimly beautiful, blackened palaces and down the alleyways of steep steps with mediaeval ghosts at every corner. The weather did not help. It had turned wet, cold and thundery. The clocks began to strike twelve, lunchtime. It did not take long for me to eat mine. The shutters and grilles rattled down over shop windows, the whole city closed, leaving the streets deserted until three or four that afternoon. Morale sank very low. I wished then that I had taken a room in some cheap hostelry to which I could retire peacefully, but as it was, I had absolutely nowhere to go and my budget did not really stretch to having a good time in a city. What I needed was some kind soul to stop and say hello, talk a while, but it never happened. It was no fault of the Perugian people. Making contact in a city is simply much more difficult than it is in the countryside. People seem so busy, so accustomed to the presence of strangers that one more is of no note. I would have given everything at that moment to be with an old friend or just see a face I knew and loved. Loneliness produces such an empty, gnawing pain. I returned sadly to the campsite to read away the rest of the day.

The storms blew over during the night, allowing me to dry my things on the platform at Perugia station while waiting for the train to Santa Maria degli Angeli, below Assisi. It was a pity to cross the Tiber in this way, but some concessions had to be made to twentieth-century traffic conditions and the President of Italy himself would be there to open the Feast of Saint James. Santa Maria is a tiny village with a vast church, modelled on Saint Peter's in Rome, built to enclose a hovel that was once in the middle of the Forest of Porziuncola where Saint Francis died. He is one of the Patron Saints of Italy. I had always been drawn towards this simple figure who married poverty, talked to the birds and tamed wolves. I had been anticipating this moment, the Basilica on the rocky crag above, strongly buttressed to prevent its crashing down into the Tiber valley, its thick stone walls and towers white in the harsh sunlight. The time had come to investigate the myth.

Twenty-six coach loads of tourists were milling around the streets of Assisi, that were lined with souvenir shops and stalls. The Basilica echoed to the click of high heels on marble, a confused and general hubbub underlying the cries and loud explanations of the official guides, who carried numbered placards above their heads so their flock would not get lost in among the others. There are two churches, one above the other, both imposing and sombre, the walls covered in lovely, faded blue and red frescoes depicting scenes from the Bible and the life of Francis.

Christened Giovanni Bernadone sometime in 1182, his father, a rich merchant of the town, called him Francesco, or 'Little Frenchman', as a sign of affection for his mother, who was French. His childhood and youth follow the usual pattern. If he was to rise on the social ladder, he would have to join the army, for this gave him the chance of being dubbed a knight. At the age of twenty, however, he was taken prisoner in a battle with Perugia and spent a year shut away in a dank hole underground before being released. In 1204, he set off to war once again, this time to fight with the Papal troops in Apulia, but he didn't get far, turning back at Spoleto, 45 kilometres south of Assisi. The chroniclers tell of visionary dreams. His own words were *'Uscii dal Mondo'* or 'I left Society', which would be translated today as 'I dropped out'. Exchanging his clothes with those of a beggar, kissing a leper, preaching, his reputation slowly spread. The first fresco is from this time, a man paying homage to him while two others look on askance. The fourth shows him praying in the half-ruined church of San Damiano where, in 1206, the crucified Christ spoke to him, saying: 'Francis, go and repair my house which is falling in ruins'. He obeyed, selling bales of his father's cloth to raise the money needed, which did not help a relationship that was already strained. The next panel shows him renouncing all worldly comforts, standing naked before the crowd, his halo glowing, his father holding the clothes he has just taken off, looking very angry, perplexed, no doubt, by his son's madness.

Further down the wall, he and twelve disciples have gone to Rome to ask the Pope for recognition of the First Rule, to live strictly in accordance with the Gospels. 'Wherefore, if God so clothe the grass of the field, which today is, and tomorrow is cast into the oven, shall he not much more clothe you. O ye of little faith?' It was a prudent move, for the Albigensian Crusade had just started and he would do well not to be branded a heretic. Mathiew Paris, an Englishman with a slight chip on his shoulder, was there at the time and recorded Pope Innocent III as saying, 'Listen, Brother, find a herd of swine, because you would do better to mix with swine than men. Roll in the mud with them and give them the rules you have drawn up here.'

Undeterred, Francis duly went and rolled in the mud with some pigs as his master the Pope had ordered, came back and addressed his Holiness: 'Lord, I have carried out your command. Now I expect you to grant me my request.' Recognition of the First Rule of the Franciscan Order of Friars was granted.

The devils being driven out of Arezzo, Francis talking to the birds, the stigmata on Monte Verna and his death were clear enough, though many of the frescoes have faded away with time. Towards the end of his life, his eyesight and health deteriorated badly, so he was taken in to the church at San Damiano where he was nursed by the aristocratic Chiara d'Offreducci, his great love, the founder of the Order of the Poor Clares. It was here that he wrote his 'Canticle of The Creatures': Brother Sun, Sister Moon, Brother Wind and Sister Water, Brother Fire and Mother Earth, lastly Brother Bodily Death, 'from whom no living man can ever escape'. He asked to be carried down to the hut in the forest of Porziuncola to die, telling his followers to strip him naked and lay him out on the bare earth. He died on October 3rd, 1226, at the age of forty-four. Exactly 755 years had passed since that day.

He was canonised two years later. A subtle reinterpretation of the passage in the Rules about the renunciation of property by the Order allowed work to start on the building of the Basilica. The size and magnificence of the churches and the wealth of the Order were direct contradictions of Francis' ideals.

His tomb, like that of Saint James in Compostela, was conveniently rediscovered in the nineteenth century hidden in the crypt under the lower Basilica. The crypt was tightly packed with worshippers, candles had burnt up most of the spare oxygen, the air was close, the atmosphere hot and oppressive, priests in white vestments were intoning mass and murmuring canticles around the altar. I fled to the air and sky of the cloisters. As I was leaving the Basilica, I noticed a group of people crowding round a shallow glass case on the wall. It was the reliquary, containing a patched grey habit, a belt of camel hair and thorns, some sandals and a stamp sized piece of parchment, said to be the skin of the Saint. I went looking for the other market place. It was Saturday, which meant stocking up for the weekend.

After shopping, I leaned the now heavy pack against the base of the fountain opposite the temple of Minerva and waited with the slowly growing crowd behind barriers that the police had set up. The President was late, but the crowd accepted this with good-humoured resignation, laughing and joking in the sunshine. The news that he was on his way spread quickly, necks craned eagerly, children were hoisted onto shoulders, fingers pointed. A long cortège of sleek black limousines swept down the road, flanked by motorcycle police in gleaming boots astride their powerful Moto Guzzi, travelling fast, accelerating past and away to more pressing affairs of state in Rome. We just caught sight of Pertini's balding head bobbing in the back seat of one of the cars and that was it. He didn't even wave. The crowd clapped and dispersed quickly. I had expected something a little more regal.

I took the road out, past the church of San Damiano, the slopes of the hills terraced with olive trees all the way to Spello, a hill village built of pinkish white stone, the blocks carefully cut to size. Steep, stepped streets snaked up to the church, the view from which was lovely, of traffic throbbing on the main road below, which cut across the fields of short strips of tobacco, maize and ploughed land. There was minor industry on the outskirts of Foligno, to the south, and a warm, tiring wind blowing up the valley, perhaps the Scirocco. Visible beyond the terraced hills were the rounded backs of the Sibillini Mountains, the main Apennine ridge in sight again. My heart lifted. Foligno I bypassed, content to drink a litre bottle of mineral water to quench my thirst before camping on the slopes of an olive grove, too tired to look around for a place that was suitable and flat.

First stop in the morning was the gates of the Sassovivo mineral water bottling plant, which blocked the track that I was following up into the mountains. The gates were made of wrought iron about two metres high, tipped with nasty spikes and barbed wire, an obstacle that I got over without many problems, throwing my pack over first, thus burning my boats. As it was Sunday, everything was locked and the source itself imprisoned in the bottling factory, the outlet choked with rubbish and plastic cups. On Sunday, women go to church and men follow their own ritual in the woods, hunting down and shooting anything that moves, from sparrow to hare, sometimes even each other. Above the woods the mountain tops were bare: it was good to see where I was going. I cut across country, over the close-cropped pasture, towards the downy, rounded flanks of Monte San Stefano dotted with juniper bushes, passing a little chapel surrounded by the cars of hunters, dedicated to the memory of Brigata Garibaldi V, 3rd. February 1944.

The countryside was more inhabited that I had thought from looking at the map and supported a mass of tiny villages. In Morro three old men gathered round on the wall overlooking the valley and pointed out the best way to reach Visso, hidden behind Monte Cavallo where a distant flock of sheep was grazing peacefully. Rasiglia was a lovely place nestling in the valley beside the river Menadre, which flows down to Foligno and on to the Tuscan Sea. I drank a little too much wine on a bench in the sun and floated off to Verchiano. Here, I bought an ice-cream to sweeten the aftertaste of the wine while half the village men gathered round to discuss ways and means of getting to Visso, curious to gaze at the maps, saying surely such maps were top secret? The women kept away, peeping from doorways and windows. It was decided by general consensus that I should go via the Piano Grande. I liked the name: it is a former volcanic crater, the eastern side forming the backbone of the

Apennine ridge, Monte Vettore rising to 2476 metres, the plain itself at about 1400 metres.

I took the dirt road out, past peasants collecting acorns for their pigs. In Civitella they were holding a village fete, the people all in their best suits and printed cotton dresses, standing around the streets that were decorated with strings of coloured lights and flags. A brass band passed in dark blue uniforms and peaked caps, playing a solid marching tune. The man next to me said there would be a candlelit parade later from the church, but I did not stay, moving on to San Martino, Forcella, just names along the road. The countryside was well husbanded in the traditional way, a mixture of oak trees, pasture, orchards and the smooth curve of ploughed fields. Black and white cows were being brought in to the village, their udders full and swaying gently, hoofs ringing on the concrete as they headed for the water trough where I was busy with domestic chores. The cowman had lost an arm in a combine four years before, on 2nd August, he told me.

'Really! That's my birthday. I was in Bolivia at the time.'

'Mine's on 7th March, you know.'

It had been a good day, full of contact with the people, the walking interesting, tiring but worthwhile. I camped. The sun set, the sky a warm pink brushed with pastel blue, the clouds golden, the crescent moon up, the stars twinkling, I was asleep in seconds.

My back felt stiff in the morning: so much sleeping on the ground was giving me rheumatism, the ground cooling down after the summer, the sun often not hot enough during the day to dry the sweat from my back when I stopped to rest. I remember Femature for a beautiful eleventh-century church of white stone and the smell that pervaded the village: a healthy aroma of farm and cow. Villages of this type have nearly all been abandoned in France and Spain. The atmosphere was one I hadn't sensed since the north of Portugal. There it was very much a way of life, but here I sensed the beginning of decay, the gradual abandoning of the village. The empty, shuttered houses and tumbled walls were not there but were, perhaps, lurking in the near future. A large white cow suddenly came out onto the road in front, just fitting through the low, arched doorway under the farmhouse.

At Croce I found a shop, interrupting an angry exchange between the owner and the local representative from the Electricity Board. They glared sullenly at each other as I bought provisions, their voices joining battle again as I worked my way down into the gorge that would take me to Visso. The sun beat down directly overhead, the river classified 'Category A', was called the Nera and ran west to Spoleto. The avenue leading into Visso was tree lined, reminiscent of similar scenes in the south of France. The crumbly white crags hung above the little town grimly. Everything was shut. I had a look around and rested on a wall beside the madly rushing mountain river, listening to its different voices. Birds twittered in the branches of a willow nearby, the ground was alive with tiny red and blue grasshoppers. I decided I would walk the last few miles up river to Castelsantangelo and camp the other side. There were willows, ash, alder and walnuts and clouds of gnats dancing in the twilight as the valley cooled. It was dark when I left the cafe in Castelsantangelo, but as I was well fortified with wine, the hill up to Glauco was no great effort. Here I stopped, cocking my ears for the sound of water, following the sound in the pale moonlight to a fountain and roofed washing house, settling down happily on the grass away from the wind. This would do nicely.

I was pottering around in the dark making myself comfortable when a shadowy figure appeared at the fountain, carrying a bucket. The figure froze.

'Buona sera,' I said.

'What are you doing here?' a gruff voice replied.

'Making supper.'

'There's a restaurant up the road.'

'Is there? I don't have enough money to eat in restaurants.'

'You can sleep there, too.'

'I don't have enough money to sleep in hotels either. Anyway, I'm quite happy here: I have water, it's out of the wind and there's a roof if it rains.'

'You'll get cold.'

'No, I have a good sleeping bag.'

'It's very humid in the mornings, you know.'

Neither of us had moved. We argued stubbornly for another few minutes, going round in circles, covering the same ground.

'Look', he said at last, 'as Christian to Christian, I invite you to my house.'

It was a strange expression to use, but the rural Italians seem to divide the world into Christians, meaning Catholics, and Pagans or Saracens if you want to be rude, which embraces all others. When they say 'We poor Christians' they mean simply 'We poor people'. After all, to be a person is to be Catholic.

I accepted his invitation, packed up hurriedly and followed him up a little alley to his house, where we went through a dark, arched doorway into a room lit by a single naked bulb. The unboarded ceiling was blackened by smoke from the wide chimney place, the walls of paint once white were now peeling and brown. Various plastic bags were hanging from hooks in the beams. The floor was

244

tiled and clean swept, and a gas cooker stood over against a wall in the corner. Next to it was a table with two chairs and a washbasin. It was his kitchen.

He put his bucket down. We looked at each other for a moment, then shook hands and introduced ourselves. His name was Gian Battista. He had grizzly white hair, black eyebrows arched above heavy, rather bloodshot eyes, a scar on his broad nose and a Laurel moustache beneath. In stature he was short and thick-set, coming up to my chest. He motioned me to a chair and set about preparing a steaming hot soup. We sat at a table facing each other, breaking bread into the soup, which was peppered and full of onion and garlic. He made an incredible noise slurping it which made me feel positively genteel as I just puffed and blew. This was followed by a slice or two of cold mutton and some cheese, which he took out of one of the bags hanging from the beams. Then we talked.

He was a shepherd and had lived most of his life alone. He would be off to the Roman Campagna soon with the sheep. They had walked when he was a boy, but now they were all taken in cattle trucks. He said that no one stayed there during the winter, it was much too cold and thick with snow. His boss let him have a cottage on the plains and they returned in June.

He lit a cigarette, inhaled deeply, then shook the walls with his coughing, hawking and spitting on the floor, rubbing it in with the leather soles of his boots. He had been alone too long. He had a habit of getting up, walking around and talking with his arms outstretched for emphasis, his body bent forward slightly. He kept repeating himself unknowingly, chasing his tail in an argument over the relative values of the pound and the lira. He made a cup of coffee after we had been for a walk under the stars, into which he tipped an inch or so of sugar.

'Is it sweet enough?' he asked.

On the mantelpiece was a photograph of him as a young boy soldier during the Second World War. He had been an A.A. gunner, stationed in Sardinia.

'I never did understand what was happening. First the Germans were friends and then we were told they were the enemy.'

He made a mattress of greatcoats on the floor and after seeing me into the sleeping bag, turned out the light and left the room. It was a late night for both of us.

I was surprised at the speed with which I reached the lip of the Piano Grande, the bare Sibillini rising to the left, Monte Vettore squatting on its stomach like a huge, tired grey elephant, its sides covered with a patchy moss of trees. The plain is famous for the production of lentils, which had long been harvested, leaving the

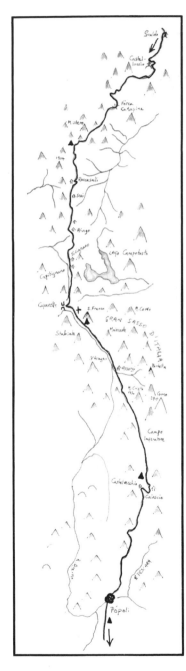

sheep and cows to graze the parched grass. The village of Castelluccio overlooked the plain from a crag beneath the western edge of the crater. It was a sad place: everyone seemed short-tempered, aware of another harsh winter on the way when those who stayed behind would be isolated from the rest of the world for months. Dogs wandered the streets uncared for, the buildings were never quite finished off, the whole place breathed an air of hopelessly tired third world dilapidation. I was crossing the line between Northern and Southern Italy, entering what is really another country, the *Mezzogiorno*, the *Midi* in France. There had been signs already in the attitudes of the people, their way of life, the questions they asked, their inability to understand why anyone should wish to walk when they could go by public transport.

The differences between the two Italies are marked, though there has been substantial progress in some areas. A glance at some statistics bears this out: in 1951 only 28 per cent of houses in the south had inside drinking water, whereas 43 per cent did in the north. By 1971, the figures were 82 and 87 per cent respectively. In 1951 only 19 per cent of the south had inside lavatories, while by 1971 it was 83 per cent, a higher figure than the north. The figures for literacy are interesting: in the south, in 1951, 48 per cent of the population was illiterate or at least lacked the elementary certificate of education, whereas the north had a figure of 20 per cent. By 1971 the south had improved: only 35 per cent

246

were illiterate, but the figures in the north had increased to almost 30 per cent—the southerners had been emigrating to the large industrial towns in the north, like Milan and Turin. The overall reduction in illiteracy was thus quite small. Net income over the same period increased twofold, but it also doubled in the north, making sure that a worker there continues to earn up to six times as much as his fellows in the south.

I left Castellucio after a glass of wine in a cafe, cutting across the grassland, up out of the bowl, arriving exhausted at Forca Canapine, where there was a water trough next to which I rested and ate lunch. I had grown to distrust my maps, for the paths marked were often non-existent, so I was happy to find the one along the next ridge actually did exist, for it marked the watershed between the Tyrrhenian Sea and the Adriatic. The views on both sides were magnificent, the track perfect for walking, sometimes through scrubby woods, at others over grass, the sun warm and bright. At heights over 1600 metres autumn had arrived. It is my favourite season when the weather is kind, a time for reflection, for looking back on the things one has done during the year. It seemed incredible that I had walked all the way, or nearly all of it, from the south of Portugal. The walking was often hard, an endurance test, but the life was so simple, the cares so few and the taste of complete freedom that it gave so sweet I was certain now of the value of the journey. The soft evening light was crystal clear, the multiple autumn colours sharp, lemon yellow, lime green, orange, brown, red and russet playing one against the other. Time seemed meaningless. I felt a surge of spontaneous joy and exhilaration, happy as I had not been happy for many years, a bubble of contentment floating lightly over the mountains. It was all the compensation that I needed. The villages on either side of the divide were scattered among forest, the peaks of the Gran Sasso d'Italia, the highest in the Apennine range at almost 3000 metres, were clearly visible to the south. The setting sun rose again as I climbed the flanks of Monte Utero, finding a hollow at the summit where I curled up away from the wind, disturbing the birds who had already gone to roost.

I was winding down from the ridge before the birds had woken. If there were worms to catch they would be mine. The first person I met was a shepherd, who told me that the President of Egypt had been assassinated, gunned down in full view of the world. He had heard the news on the radio that morning. It seemed light years away.

The countryside was fertile and well watered, the cross-country walking pleasant and easy. Cobs of corn were strung up around the farmyards to dry in the sun, and the vintage had started, a family working together to unload the first half-barrels of grapes from a truck. At Capitignano they were up ladders picking apples in the orchards. The blackberries were ripe, warm and juicy. A woman passed, leading a mule and cart on her way home to cook supper; a man touched my arm gently and pointed out the direction that I should take to round the western neck of the Gran Sasso at the Capannelle Pass.

Night had fallen by the time I arrived there, to find there was no water, so I walked on in the bright moonlight under the stars over Campo Imperatore, a flat shelf beneath the light grey, smooth hump of Monte Corvo, alert for the sound of running water. I heard horses instead, which cantered away into the shadows as I approached. They had been drinking from a trough of clean fresh water. I made supper, slipped into my sleeping bag and slid away into the land of dreams.

The range of the Gran Sasso runs from west to east before curving south. The morning was chilly but the day turned out as bright, blue and hot as ever. I sat in the midday sun in Assergi, soaking up the warmth, letting it ease the tired muscles of my back. In winter the mountains are used for skiing and there is a funicular to take skiers up to the heights. In Mussolini's day the cables were ropes and he was loath to undertake the journey up to the isolated hotel where he was to be kept in captivity, safe from the rescue attempts of the Nazis. It was a blow to Hitler's pride to have such a man in enemy hands. His spies found out quickly enough where he was, eating little more than grapes, suffering from delusions, drawing parallels between his betrayal and that of Christ. A spotter plane was sent to take photographs of the area round the hotel: one relatively flat space some two hundred yards away would do. On 12th September, 1943, four out of twelve gliders carrying 120 commandos under Colonel Skorzeny managed to land, taking the hotel without bloodshed, the garrison running away into the mountains or simply giving up without a fight. The haggard, bristly-headed Mussolini was then escorted to a Storch aircraft standing by in which he and the Colonel were flown to safety, though they had their doubts as to whether or not the plane would take off. A few days later he was with Hitler in Vienna.

The rest of the day was spent crossing the hills to Santo Stefano, a grey village nestling round the tower of a castle above the plain, merging with the backdrop of parched grey mountains.

Castelvecchio was another hilltop village where I breakfasted the next day, buying provisions at the local stores, which contrasted sharply with the stores that I had been seeing: dusty affairs, sombre, selling little more than tins and dry biscuits. This shop was bright, clean and packed with tempting delights. The southern Italian faces a choice: to stay where he is and live in poverty, or emigrate, work long and hard in some foreign country sustained by the dream of saving money before returning to his native country a richer man. The poverty and consequent lack of opportunity in the Mezzogiorno led to mass emigration after the war. In thirty years more than four million people, a quarter of the population, emigrated to the industrial north or further, to Germany, Switzerland or other Western European countries, to become despised 'Guest Workers'. The owners of this shop had been in Australia for thirteen years saving the money to return to the wife's village and set up a shop and bakery. The husband told me he would have preferred to stay down under, but his wife was homesick. The bread they sold me they called *Pizza al Olio*. It was salty, flat, oily and very crisp. I cooked up four rashers of bacon and a couple of fried eggs, split the bread lengthways to make an enormous sandwich and downed it with the help of a cup of strong, milky tea. In fact the bread was so delicious that I went back and bought another loaf. Chickens clucked around in the alleys, a mule was driven past with wide wicker baskets of grapes on either side, picking its way cautiously down into the valley where furrows of ploughed earth alternated with pasture and grazing sheep.

It gave me great security to see where I was going. I was full of a new spirit of courage and adventure as I slithered down the rocky hillside, slipping frequently, muttering to myself: 'Careful, you don't want to break your neck', before making it to the track that I had seen from above. Now I walked along under tall walnuts by the side of vineyards, olive and almond groves, scrumping as I went for the figs which were dark red inside and succulent. A man, cultivating on an old red Ford tractor while his wife burnt the scrub and weeds, called out to me, fetching a bottle of white wine from the shade as he did so. He took a swig and handed it to me.

'Here, have a drink. Where are you from?'

'England'.

'I like the way you travel. Good luck!'

He hopped back on the tractor to work.

I believe that many people think walking allows you time to gaze at the scenery as you would from the comfort of the back seat of a car, the only difference being that things pass more slowly. They do not realise that on any surface other than tarmac or light, compacted, sandy soil, it is necessary to concentrate most of the time on the prosaic business of where you are putting your feet. I took a bad tumble that afternoon, a second's inattention being all that was necessary to pitch me down a stony embankment. Luckily the slope was short and I was only lightly bruised, but instinctively I had put out my hand to break the fall. A sharp stone the size of a large pea lodged itself in the palm of my hand, on the life line, I noticed, before easing it out with the knife and walking to the nearest farmstead to wash away the blood and clean the wound thoroughly. Here, I was greeted by seven frantic dogs which barked and snapped at my ankles unrestrained by their owner, an inebriated farmer who talked happily despite the noise and the obvious fact that I could hear nothing of what he said.

I was still cutting across country, hoping to reach Pòpoli before dark. At Collepietro I received the time-honoured reply to my inquiry after the track to Pòpoli—

'No, there's no track anymore. You'll have to take the road. It's a good surface and if you're lucky there'll be a bus . . .'

I was not put off. I had heard it all before. It was hard stone-hopping down into a wild, abandoned valley and past a sad, neglected olive grove and the remains of a hamlet, before I had to fight my way up to the hill above Pòpoli. The blood was pounding in my ears as I crashed through the undergrowth like a wild boar, gasping for air, enjoying every second of the battle. Then down again, the knees weakening, shoulders tired, to arrive at nightfall. On the outskirts, I found a very special washhouse, basically a roofed section of a fast-running mountain river that swept through the building and out, filling various washing basins beside it on the way. The water was icy cold. It was completely dark inside so I hoped no one would see me taking a bath in the washtubs.

The *passeggiata* was in full swing in the centre of the town. I sat on a bench and watched the people out for this ritual evening stroll, before getting up to look in the shop windows at the smart new clothes that I would like to buy some day. The road to Sulmona was a straight eighteen kilometres. I thought I would take advantage of the moon to cut into the distance and make the morning easier, but soon huge double trailer lorries were blinding me with flashing lights, their message clear: get off the road. A side road led to a recently constructed house with a shining blue marble terrace open to the skies on the second floor—a home for the night, where I would be above the dew, I thought happily.

At the very first hint of the grey morning I was off, while there were still no maniac lorries around. The mist gradually lifted to reveal maize and vineyards, the high peaks of Morcone to the east, the fetlock of the Gran Sasso. The road was lined with walnut trees

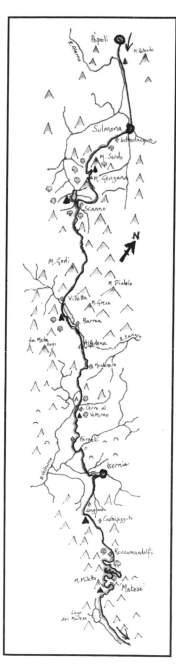

that had dropped their fruit, which lay untouched at the sides of the ditches. I arrived in the town at nine, my pockets bulging with nature's loot. My next set of maps should be waiting for me at the post office, where I had sent them from Padua. Perhaps I should have registered them, I thought, but they'd had as much time to arrive as I had to walk, so there should be no problem. I went through the doors.

'Good Morning, *Signor*. I've come to collect a parcel of maps that should be waiting for me. John Waite is my name.'

The man eased himself from his stool and went to look, coming back empty handed.

'I'm sorry, but there's no parcel for you.'

'There must be. I sent it almost a month ago.'

'Look, if it hasn't arrived in a week you can apply for a refund.'

My heart sank into my boots but I wasn't going to be fobbed off so easily. It was not possible that the maps had taken longer to arrive by Italian post than I had on foot. I described the package carefully, kinetically, patiently. There was only one clerk and a queue was forming. The Italians have no patience for standing in line and they were getting restless, muttering, craning their necks to see what was going on. It was my sole advantage. I stood and waited for something to happen, starting again from the beginning. Another man appeared behind the glass. He listened, went off and came back bearing the roll of precious maps.

251

'Thank you very much indeed. *Addio.*'

It was a major victory. I sat at an outdoor cafe table, spread out the crisp new maps and studied them avidly, sipping a *cappuccino* and trying not to lick the sugar from my lips, left there by a feathery-light jam doughnut.

I had originally planned to walk down to Naples before heading East for Brindisi where I would take a boat to Greece, but I thought there would be too much traffic on the Neapolitan roads to make it in any way more than a nightmare. Instead, I decided to take a train from the Benevento area to Pompei, rest up somewhere cheap, look around the ruins and the city of Naples, climb Vesuvius, then return to Benevento and the road to Brindisi.

I did not stay long in Sulmona. It is an old Roman town, the birth-place of Publius Scipio Naso, with an ancient but still serviceable aqueduct above the main square named, like a thousand others, Piazza Garibaldi. The streets are narrow, the houses on either side tall and austere, the ground floors lined with the windows of top quality grocers. I was particularly happy to find they sold Quaker Porridge Oats.

Introdaqua was a pretty village built into the foothills south-west of the town. The locals were friendly and informative, giving directions on how to reach a *rifugio* up in the mountains where I could spend the night. There were women in the street braising chillies as I took the road out. The trees in the valley were green, turning to russet and gold as I climbed, while higher still I walked through a winter landscape of bare branches, the wind cold and penetrating.

I was not expecting such a long, steep climb and it was dark when I arrived. The *rifugio* was a haven: protected in a thick wood, quiet and isolated, yet equipped with a gas cooker, cutlery, pots and pans, a table and chairs, and a side room with four bunks. Outside there was a bench beside the spring of fresh water. I was looking forward to a good night's sleep.

I never saw Nino, Lino and Pino by day. They arrived shortly after I had finished cooking an excellent supper and I was too tired to stay up listening to their stories. They were from Rome, escaping, so they said, from their wives, and would be getting up early in the morning to go hunting. They had gone when I woke.

The smooth summit of Monte Genzana was over 2000 metres, well above the heads of the hunters. To the south lay the surly mass of the Abruzzo, to the west the cultivated bed of Lago Fucino. Like Trasimeno, it was once a volcanic crater lake, marshy and partly dried up, with 46,300 acres of fertile soil beneath the waters. Julius

Caesar was the first to think of having it drained, but it was Claudius who had it done with a workforce of 30,000 slaves. They worked for eleven years, digging a tunnel more than five kilometres long to take the waters to the river Liri. Claudius celebrated the completion of the work with a mock battle: two fleets of galleys manned by 19,000 slaves. When they had all killed each other, the flood gates were opened. Unfortunately only about a quarter of the water drained away. They started again, this time on a smaller budget with only a gladiatorial contest, but it worked better: the land was, indeed, very fertile, and before long, the rich moved in and built their houses there, to begin farming the land.

With the Barbarian invasions it reverted to its former state, and it wasn't until 1854 that Duke Alessandro Torlonia pledged his massive fortune to draining the lake once more, employing four thousand men for twenty-four years. The project was a success, the Duke was made Prince of Fucino and given 35,000 acres as a reward. In 1931 this was expropriated as part of the Agrarian Reforms.

I was unwilling to continue along the crest of the Genzana because of the strong, tiring, cold wind that was piercing my eardrums and freezing my hands, so cut straight down to the lake I could see near Scanno in the valley below. It would be good to have a rest; perhaps there would be a campsite. My knees were aching after much sliding over white, shaly rock, and it was a relief when I came out onto a dirt road and a couple in a flashy Japanese Jeep gave me a lift, playing Pink Floyd at full volume all the way down the twisting road, the sun for a minute obscured by clouds, the lake a dark ruffled blue. I tottered a couple of miles to a camping site, where I was the only tent among the many caravans. All the cares of the day vanished under the hot shower. I washed some clothes, hung them out to dry and sat cross-legged on the ground in front of my tent cracking open the walnuts I had collected on the way into Sulmona, banging them with a stone, which was effective and nicely primitive.

A gypsy tried to sell me a blanket on the way into Scanno, trying to persuade me that it would soon be so cold that I would bless him for selling me such warmth as his blankets would afford. I escaped into the dark, hillside town of narrow streets, steps, old fountains gushing clean, sweet water and shadowy arches where women, their billowing skirts tucked in severely at the waist, came and went on their domestic business, their eyes on the ground, their heads wrapped in black headscarves. On the way out, a farmer and his wife kindly offered me a lift in the trailer behind their tractor. They were off to collect hay. Speech was impossible over the thundering of the engine. At the pass I stood and took in the view, noticing how autumn was creeping slowly down the slopes of the Abruzzi mountains, the sky clear above, but black and menacing behind their jagged silhouettes.

It didn't rain: the wind that kept the crows cawing restlessly the whole night blew the clouds away. The lake was turquoise in the morning sun, the mountains lit up, La Meta rising to 2241 metres above. Although I was tempted to climb up there, the paths marked over the Abruzzo would take me the wrong way, and so instead, I hacked along beside the lake to Barrea, a miniature Scanno, the clock striking half past eleven as I arrived. From there, I took the path out to Alfedena. It was narrow and rough. I had to pick my way carefully over the white rocks between crumbling stone walls, in the shade of which an old, deaf shepherd sat looking at the world through rheumy red eyes. He seemed somehow symbolic of the south; an old man left behind.

The path died, so I had to beat my way through to the pass, then down through clean, prosperous Alfedena, the enticing, lunchtime smell of beef stew wafting in the empty streets. I followed a compass bearing to get myself out again, but lost my way in thick tangles of overgrown woods and brambles. I crashed through regardless and uncaring to Montenero, pounding along the road, before turning off on a track through oak woods, thinking it was time I had my own lunch.

I sat and rested, listening to the sound of a herder's cries and the barking of his dog drifting up from the valley of bright green pasture below, and watching the cows and horses grazing. Some mushroom pickers went by.

The earth had changed colour from yellowy white to milk chocolate brown. I walked some of the way to the next valley with a man who was leading a mule laden with firewood, and who told me how he lost his arm in a grenade explosion before his four years in prison camp in England. He said he was surprised that they had given him so much food. He showed me a short-cut down through ancient oak woods, the trees sometimes a metre across at the base, a glimpse of what the south was like two thousand years ago. A large grey castle loomed over the head of the Volturno valley, the river flowing down towards Naples. The main street of Cerro al Volturno snaked down past the houses below the castle to a washing place beside the infant river. I was busily engaged in ablutions in the dark when two boys appeared.

'Where are you going to sleep tonight?' they asked.

'I don't know. Anywhere will do.'

'They're building a new school just up the hill. No one will mind if you sleep there.'

It sounded as good a place as any. When I had finished, they took me through the moonlight to the half-built school. They were called Mauro and Antonio, the former very much the spokesman, excited by this unexpected adventure. He sent Antonio racing up the hill on his bicycle to fetch some wine for me; he returned with a beer bottle of red wine which he had stolen from his father's cellar. They sat down watching as I prepared dinner, plaguing me with questions about the cooker, my equipment, how much it had cost, trying the pack on, strutting around in the shadows. When I said that I was going to Brindisi, Mauro told me how to get there, pointing west towards Naples. I did not argue, but when the conversation drifted to the man Mauro had known who went up Everest on a bicycle, I called it a day. They watched curiously as I brushed my teeth and slipped into my sleeping bag. We shook hands solemnly.

'Good-night. Thanks for the wine and showing me this place.'

They disappeared into the night, arguing about whether or not there was any air at the top of Everest. The moon was full; I had been on the road for a month.

The morning brought warm sunshine. The villages reeked of freshly picked grapes. Everywhere I went barrels were being washed out ready for the next load and whole families were working in the trellised vineyards. I wanted to join them and help with the vintage but the harvest was nearly over, the plots small, yielding just enough for the year's consumption. I was not needed. Two roadsweepers waved cheerily, asking me where my 'woman' was. A black-haired bandit pulled up in a beaten Fiat 500, just to talk, showing me proudly the fat trout he had just caught, before launching into a tirade against his government. For him it was synonymous with corruption, a puppet show controlled by the Mafia in which anyone honest was bound to lose. He said he sympathised with the Red Brigade: at least they made people aware. I wondered if this were true, if the man in the field above us ploughing with a team of oxen knew much about them or cared at all. It was the first time I had seen oxen ploughing since Galicia.

Women were sitting alone in doorways or in groups in the straight, cool, cobbled high streets of Isernia, making lace on fat cylindrical cushions, their fingers moving the bobbins and threads with unconscious skill. A teenager called Mario made friends, bought me a drink and took me to talk to his aunt, who was making lace in the square, chatting to her friends as her fingers played. She was keen to explain the details of her art, showing me intricate examples of her work, teasing me gently to buy a shawl for my girlfriend. We said

255

good-bye and went to look at the church, where they were excavating the foundations. The vaulted, baroque interior contrasted sharply with the ancient stones of the pagan temple that had originally stood there. The workmen told us to clear off and we parted after another drink. The road out led past piles of buckets, barrels and marc to the spaghetti junction that was being created in the valley below for the road from Naples to Pescara. The roadworkers idled away a few minutes with me, laughing and joking over the differences between Italian and British women. They wanted to know why they were allowed to travel unaccompanied, when it was much safer for them to stay at home where they belonged. I walked on towards Longano, a village in the northern foothills of the Matese mountains, which marked the border between Molise and Campania. They were the last high mountains I would cross in the Apennine chain.

Triptolemus' plough

A young woman wearing a bright green printed cotton dress and flowery headscarf was working in an olive grove, breaking up the clods of earth with a mattock while her husband ploughed with two tired oxen. To plough an acre a man must walk ten miles. A gaunt-looking old man led two donkeys past while a sunken-cheeked old woman sat guarding three goats with glossy, long black coats below. A loudspeaker crackled in the square, broadcasting the evening mass to the people. Four white oxen were being driven home, a man, wife and elder son chivvying them from donkeys with long wooden ploughs strapped to their flanks, the kind of plough you see in Egyptian hieroglyphs, the kind Demeter taught Triptolemus to use when she gave him the very first grain of corn.

Many billions of lire have been poured into Southern Italy since the formation of the *'Cassa per il Mezzogiorno'*, but more than half of this investment has gone to the petrochemical industries on the coast. The remoter areas of the interior have been largely unaffected, in the same way that they were unaffected by land reforms. Certain areas have been haphazardly developed, but the high agricultural interior has been abandoned. In 1951 there were 3.8 million people working the land; this had fallen to 1.8 million by 1971. The E.E.C. would have it lower still at about one million. The Campobasso area is one of the poorest in the whole of Italy: 216,100 people emigrated between 1955 and 1971, which was thirty-five per cent of the population (the average for the southern spine is 30 per cent). The outlook for such places is grim. Their culture is against them, for being a peasant in Italy is to be the lowest form of human life, contemptible. There are no Heidis in Italian literature. 'Peasants are not civilised people, and making them restless for something they can't have, couldn't do if they had the chance . . . why, it would be silly.' —the words of a young primary school teacher. For a peasant, to survive is to win, but most have admitted defeat and left to live in exile in some northern country where there is a chance of success, however slim. This means that in some areas only women, children and senile old men like the rheumy-eyed shepherd outside Barrea are left to look after the land.

I lay that night beneath a giant oak, away from the maddening beams of moonlight, thinking of those people I had seen, of their plight. In one sense they are lucky for, though they live on the edge of poverty and have no opportunities other than emigration, they do at least have just enough to see them through the year. They are resigned to their lot and their ignorance, content to react against events, but never initiating them. In international terms they are the tip of an enormous iceberg: 'Half of the 2,000,000,000 people in the world who live in under-developed countries suffer from hunger or malnutrition. Twenty to twenty-five per cent of their children die before the age of five. Of those that survive, thousands live an impoverished life because of brain damage, arrested growth or low vitality due to an inadequate diet. There are 800,000,000 who are illiterate. One third of the world's population, the industrialised nations, has seven eighths of the world's revenue, while the remaining two thirds have to make do with the other eighth.' (Robert Macnamara at the I.M.F. Conference in Nairobi in September 1973.).

To the east the sky was a rosy pink, the silver-blue moon still hanging above the horizon. A woodpecker started work as I packed up to take the road to Castelpizzuto. A brisk wind was bringing clouds in low over the valley of Isernia below, giving me the sensation of being underwater, the sunshine dispersing oddly beneath the surface of the clouds. The road petered out shortly after, but a passable footpath led on between two hills to Roccamandolfi, the bracken brown and crackling, the last of the high mountains ahead.

The map was inadequate to the task, my compass reading poor and the afternoon was spent chasing wild geese in the beech woods where freshly fallen leaves had formed a soft pile carpet to walk on. I had water, provisions, blackberries to keep me going and being off-course didn't worry me much for I was overawed by the beauty of the place, feeling privileged to be there. An hour or so later I was well and truly lost. There were two things that I could do: retrace my steps or climb above the tree line where the view would allow me to see where I was. It is when you are tired that you take risks. Too tired to retrace my steps, I decided to risk new ground and climb above the tree line. My blind determination to get to the Rifugio Campitello marked on the map nearly cost me dear.

It started easily enough. The first crest was still tree lined. I followed it right, working up and along. The trees were thinning. The next crest was in sight and the pitch of the rock did not seem too steep. I started to climb straight up. I had been climbing for sixty feet when things began to get difficult. I had to get round an obstruction before I could reach a little gully that would lead me further up with ease. A few minutes later I found myself flattened against the outcrop, groping for footholds, unable to move up or down or sideways without losing my balance, the weight of my pack threatening to tip me over backwards into a drop of seventy feet. I stayed exactly where I was, petrified, trying to catch my breath, relax and clear my mind, kicking myself for such stupidity, muttering insults at myself: 'Think you're a bloody goat do you, *pendejo . . .*'

The solution, when it came to mind, was simple: I undid my pack belt with one hand, holding on to a knot of what I hoped was well-rooted grass with the other, taking the full weight on the shoulders. Then slowly I eased the straps loose, slipped my left arm out and let the pack go, peering round to watch it bounce four times before it crashed into a knot of undergrowth. My stave sailed down behind it. Released of the weight, I scrambled easily down to examine the wreckage, but found, to my utter amazement, that the frame was unbent. Nothing, not even the thermos flask, was broken. My tin cup that hung outside all the time was badly dented, but that was all. My admiration for the Karrimor pack increased even more.

I tried again, this time more carefully. The ascent brought me over 2000 metres to the high, broken white rocks of Monte Miletto itself, a strong wind gusting through the bare crags, threatening to blow me sideways over the precipice. At last the *rifugio* was visible, the evening drawing in as I made a difficult but not particularly dangerous descent to Campitello. Campitello turned out to be a grotty skiing resort, which workers were patching up in preparation for the onset of the first snows. I downed a litre of mineral water and a coffee in a bar, the only one that was open. The workers, who had knocked off, thought I was completely mad to walk to Brindisi. I kept quiet about my point of departure and entertained them instead by putting on my trousers in a corner. Another hour's walk was all that I could manage. Seeing the outline of a shed to my right I stumbled over to the doorway, cleaned the muck from a patch of floor, cooked supper and went to sleep exhausted. I had been walking most of the day with only short rests, which was about fourteen hours, and had covered six kilometres as the crow flies.

Mist hung in dense folds over the Matese Lake below, like clouds seen from the window of an aeroplane. I had eaten all my food the day before so my stomach was rumbling furiously by the time I reached Guardiarègia, just in time to catch the shops before they closed for lunch. On the way out, as I was salivating at the thought of a slice of fried liver, bacon and two fresh eggs with bread, cheese and half a litre of milk, a school bus braked to a halt, and the driver offered me a lift to the turning for Sepino. Curious children watched with their mouths open as their teachers questioned me. One of the children lived up the road and accompanied me as far as his house, trotting along beside me in his blue uniform with a white collar, talking about his school, which he liked very much. He was going to be an engineer, he said. His sister came out to meet him and invited me into the house. Her father had just come in from work, his clothes covered in purple stains from the wine making. They were a poor family but naturally kind, inviting me to share their lunch with them, setting a bowl of pasta before me at the kitchen table, a hunk of bread, some cheese and wine, apologising for the humble fare.

'You could do with a good wash, you know,' said the girl. I apologised for my appearance and she told me I should visit the ruins nearby, fetching a booklet that outlined the history of a Samnite settlement of the first century A.D.

The land began to open out into flatter, rolling hills as I followed a perfect path through oak woods in the cool afternoon sun, stopping in Sepino for water at the triple-headed fountain, a drink in the cafe and information on how to get to the ruins. It appeared that I had walked straight by them, so I doubled back in the company of a stooped old man with wise blue eyes that looked up at me from beneath the brim of his soft felt hat. For some reason he liked bright red woollen checked shirts. He pointed out the way through a tiny village built in and around the ruins, the dogs welcoming me with a chorus of shrill barking. I settled down in the remains of a temple beside the forum, happy to camp with Samnite ghosts for company. The dogs eventually quietened down, I rested my back on the ancient walls and tried to picture the place as it once was, the columns standing out against the pale pink, evening sky, the scent of wild mint heavy in the air, the only light that of the stars and the cooker hissing blue. How different from the night before!

259

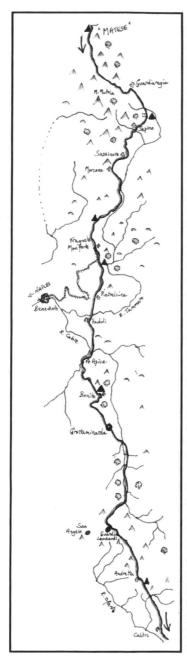

I walked through the ruins at first light, admiring the walls that were still standing, a fine network of cobbles like a narrow street turned on its side. They were fourth century, like the towers and gates, built at the expense of Tiberius, the future Emperor of Rome, and his brother Drusus. One fine arch was still complete and stood over the west gate leading to Bovianum and Isernia, the face of Tiberius looking down impassively towards the paved forum and the Ionic columns of a temple to Minerva.

In mediaeval times the peasants had built houses that followed the curve of the amphitheatre outside the walls. It was clean and well preserved, easy to imagine Aristophanes' Chorus of Frogs croaking across the stage behind their masks, or a tragedy unfolding as Fate sat by and smiled. The old man had said it was different when he was a boy: the porticos under the seats of the theatre had been used as chicken runs, while sheep and cattle were conveniently enclosed within the city walls, grazing around the columns of the forum. It was still unsullied.

The rest of the day, after such a start, was humdrum, spent making my way towards the station at Fragnelo Monforte, where I would take the train to Naples and Pompei. I did have one interesting conversation with Michele, who had travelled extensively, trading in cloth in Venezuela and Germany and Greece, which he recommended heartily for good, hospitable people. He explained how the land was distributed.

260

'When a man dies, his property is divided equally between his sons and daughters, even when he has only a little land.' He pointed to a small garden plot on our right. 'That's mine, that bit, but the vines next to it are my neighbour's, the orchard there belongs to my aunt, while those olives on the left belong to another woman who lives in the village with her mother.'

He picked a bunch of grapes from his neighbour's vine and handed it to me with a grin.

'That's the sort of thing that might start a vendetta.'

At Campolattaro I was instantly surrounded by children eager to show me to the shop, I left with an escort of bicycles, mopeds and shouts of *'Auguri, Giovanni, Auguri'*.

The evening stars were winking when I knocked at the door of an isolated farmhouse to ask for water. An old man leaning on a stick answered the door.

'What do you want?'

'Can you give me some water, please?'

He stared up at me. Candlelight flickered inside the kitchen.

'Where are you from?'

'England, sir, I'm English.'

'How can you be English when you speak Italian?'

His wife arrived at the door.

'It's all right dear, young people these days speak all sorts of languages.'

They gave me a large bunch of white grapes with the water and watched me leave. I hung the grapes up where I camped as a special treat for the morning. It was always good to start the day with a little fruit.

I just caught the train to Naples in time, then another to Pompei, which is little more than a suburb of Naples, Vesuvius not visible from the campsite where I stayed. There were washing machines and showers: I stripped down to my shorts and washed everything I could. The difference to the colours was astonishing. I had forgotten that my trousers were light grey-green, for instance. I slept badly under a dusty, soot-coated orange tree, unaccustomed to the constant rumble of trains, the swish of the traffic on the road the other side of the wall, the click of a pinball machine, the occasional shout of hilarity from night revellers. The vibrant rumble increased at dawn as the city stretched and woke.

Naples itself was incredibly noisy and dirty, the drivers fond of hooting and revving their engines. There were no letters for me at the post office and sadness killed off the day. Since I no longer trusted

261

anyone in an official position, I would have been happier if I had been sure the clerk had really looked. I was half way through a pizza when a small, ugly man approached and asked if he could sit down. He was carrying a sleeping bag in a roll tied to a small knapsack. His hair and beard were red, unkempt, his forehead and bulbous nose pitted with the marks of a pox, yet he was not old. He ordered a pizza and half a litre of white wine.

He was Austrian, formerly a teacher of German, now down and out. He had not been happy in his work or private life so left in search of adventure. All his documents and luggage were stolen in Rome, leaving him with nothing but the clothes he was wearing. Hunger drove him to ask for food in shops, in the streets, anywhere he thought the people might take pity on his plight. The life was easier than he had imagined. He swallowed his pride and quickly adapted to the way of professional beggary. He fumbled in his bag, bringing out a mangy strip of cardboard on which was written in Italian:

'I am Austrian. All my possessions were stolen in Rome. I have no money. I must eat. Please give generously.'

With this he would sit and wait for charity in the street, or hustle shopkeepers until they lost patience and gave him something to get rid of him. He grinned a yellow smile.

'Rome is definitely the best place to beg: every beggar has his place and we change every fortnight so the clientele don't get to know us too well. I made fifty pounds once in a day.'

I asked if the police didn't try to move them on, but it seemed they didn't mind so long as they weren't drunk, drugged or thieves. They had even given him money sometimes, as a gesture of sympathy. What *were* dangerous, he said, were the gangs of 'fascists' who always seemed to come in groups of six or ten. He had been beaten up six times, ending up in hospital on two occasions. The first time he was in for three months. He had been sleeping in a park when they poured petrol on his sleeping bag and set it alight. Two days after being discharged he was attacked again, this time with exhaust pipes filled with wet sand.

He was on his way to Sicily, where he thought a friend might help him get a job looking after the villas of the rich while they were away. Then he was going to India. He said he would never go back to Austria now. There was nothing to go back for as he would only have to support his wife. He was called Petre. I wished him luck and escaped.

The shift had changed at the post office: a different man handed over three letters. I was learning slowly.

More than enough has been written about Pompei. I enjoyed

walking the streets, imagining charioteers swearing impatiently at the drivers of slow carts blocking the rutted stone ways, ladies carefully picking their way from pavement to pavement over the stepping stones that kept them above the muck, the cry of merchants selling wine and oil in their shops, urchins in rags, the nobles in their beautifully frescoed houses. I had often seen photographs of the plaster casts of those who died in agony as the town was buried, but they did not lose their power for all that. I gazed, fascinated, at the cast of a dog lying on his back in the position of total surrender, his head thrown back, his legs out wide. The ruins were certainly worth a complete day of investigation. Sadly, there was no way of spending the night there, as I had at Sepino.

Naples, in the sixteenth century, was the largest city in Europe, the capital of the Kingdom of the Two Sicilies. Its history is sadly negative. Like Lisbon, it has left a legacy of neglect and oppression, remaining a bureaucratic and aristocratic parasite on all the lands it controlled, allowing the church and feudal landlords to sap the rural vitality of the South, taking relentlessly without ever giving anything in

The Porta di Nola at Pompei

return, content to collect the taxes but unwilling to plough anything back. The woods were deforested in attempts to make the land arable. Wheat, which is unsuitably hard on the soil, was planted. The grazing of goats rendered the pastures barren. Over the centuries floods and erosion have washed away the top soil from many places, leaving a poor earth and a wretched people.

It is now the third city of Italy with a population of over a million, many of whom live in conditions that are more like Calcutta than Europe. One evening I went for a walk in the more dangerous areas, making sure I left my money behind, not knowing quite what to expect. The city boasts the greatest traffic density, the largest number of rats, the highest concentration of sub-standard housing, the highest levels of atmospheric and noise pollution, infant mortality and infectious diseases of all the Italian cities. Unemployment officially stands at 25 per cent of the working population while 50,000 people live from contraband, the little men dealing in cigarettes, watches, cameras, hi-fi systems and televisions, the big

263

fish dealing in drugs, all overseen by the Camorra, the Neopolitan equivalent of the Mafia.

The steep, serpentine streets that run between the five-storey houses are like narrow gorges. It was surprisingly quiet, the lines of washing taken in, the families in the *bassi* settling down to their food or watching television, their doors open to the street. It looks a romantic sight, but these '*bassi*' are damp and badly lit. The families count themselves lucky if they have two rooms in which to live, with an average two to three people per room. Privacy is not something they have the chance ever to find out about. Feeling that I was prying, I returned to the campsite where I had now spent four nights. I would be off again in the morning, heading for the sea on the last leg of the Italian journey. It was an exciting thought.

A drizzling mist greeted me back in Fragnelo Monforte. I camped a little way out in a boggy field and woke with a sore back, wondering if it was just the cold earth or something more serious. I was happy to be back in the countryside, following the river Tammaro to Pietrelcina, relaxing in the shade of a willow now that the sun had started to get hot, watching a man ploughing in readiness for winter drilling. I remember Pietrelcina for the dogs: at some point on the way south dogs had become annoying, distrustful and aggressive and I longed for a special gun that would turn them into pillars of salt until I had passed by. The way dogs behave says much about the people who are their masters. These were simple curs, uncared for, ill-fed, often mangy. Perhaps the way people treat their dogs is a reflection of the way they are treated by their own superiors.

An old man in a dark blue suit wearing a felt hat was sitting on a wall in the ruined village of Paduli, looking out over the hills. He turned at the sound of approaching footsteps and looked me up and down. He had an incredible face, the wrinkles and deep furrows in the leathery brown skin seeming all to guide the onlooker to his deep-set, piercing blue eyes. Most of the houses in the village had collapsed during the earthquake almost exactly a year before. A fat woman sitting on a stool in the sun outside her front door told me all about it, but I hardly understood a word of her dialect. A boy shouted down from a balcony as I left. '*Razza bastarda!*'

I had never been so clearly and unequivocally insulted. My first reaction was to retaliate with one of the phrases that I had inevitably picked up on the way south, but I bit my tongue and waved instead, giving the lad a cheery smile, which must have been most annoying.

Fat drops of rain were falling when I arrived in Apice, beside the river Calore, so I took shelter in the nearest shop while the shower passed. News of the arrival of a stranger travelled like lightning, inquisitive men, women and children pouring in to listen to his tales. A child was sent off to get eggs from his mother, a man disappeared for a minute and returned with a bottle of wine. The shopkeeper talked authoritatively about the earthquake in a language that I could understand. Many houses had collapsed, many people had been killed. He himself had lost his house and had to move in with his cousins. He led me through the throng to the door, pointing out over the river to a complex of incongruous, modern flats on the other side.

'That's Apice Nuova. Half the people are living over there now, but I'm damned if I want to live in a flat. I don't see why the government doesn't give us the money to rebuild our houses instead of spoiling the view with these monstrosities and lining the pockets of the Camorra with building developments. They're all going to fall apart the next time there's an earthquake, anyway.'

He laid out my provisions neatly on the counter, adding a bag of nuts, two chocolate-coated eskimos, a packet of chewing gum and some chocolate, letting me pay for only a fraction of the goods. When he offered me a lift out of town, I readily accepted.

'Why don't you go home? It's getting cold, even here in the south, the winter will soon be here, there are bad people around, you are not safe.'

'I don't want to go home yet.' (At least there was no mention of snakes or wolves in the mountains.)

'Look, I have an idea. Go to the *Carabinieri*, tell them that you've lost all your money—tell them it's been stolen or something and that you want to go home. Don't tell them you're a teacher, though, say you're a student. They're bound to help, put you on a train to the north.'

He obviously had my safety and happiness at heart, but we were talking at cross-purposes.

'It's kind of you to think about me, but I'm all right, really. I have enough money, my bank manager's not too tough and I'm perfectly happy to be travelling.'

I just wanted to get out and walk on through the evening light now but he was taking full advantage of my helplessness and his previous hospitality.

'You see how many kilometres I'm saving you? I think you should go home. It's getting cold. There are bad men around. It's dangerous. Look, I'll take you to the station if you want, or the road to Bari. I'll stop a car and get the driver to give you a lift.'

'No, thank you, it's O.K., really, I'm quite happy. I don't want to go home.'

He brought out his trump card:

'Your mother will be missing you, worrying for you, sad, frightened that something terrible has happened to you. Go home, Giovanni. It's too cold to travel now. Come back for a holiday in the summer, when there are plenty of pretty girls around. You've travelled enough; forget about Greece and Istanbul. It's a pity, you know, I had a friend who left for Milan in his Mercedes just before you arrived. He would have been happy to give you a lift.'

He did drop me off eventually. I was not sad to see the last of his tired, black-rimmed eyes and baggy jowls. That night I camped among the ruins of a deserted hamlet called Bonito, the air thick with the smell of wild mint, wondering if I really was crazy to be contemplating crossing Greece and Turkey in November and December.

There were heavy dews in the morning now which made me appreciate the additional weight of the tent. The stubble crackled as it dried in the sun, the earth steamed gently. In Grottaminarda the church bells were ringing, and I listened to the piped service as I walked through and past a long line of sleeping lorries. It was Sunday, 25th October. The Fiat factory on the outskirts was deserted, with newly finished bright blue and orange buses standing outside waiting for their future passengers. It was built in the early seventies and caused an uproar in Eboli to the south-west, for the government had promised to build it there. The reason was simple: De Mita, the minister in charge, happened to have Grottaminarda in his constituency, so naturally favoured them. The workers of Eboli went on strike, blocking the motorway to Salerno and the main railway line in protest, putting up barriers of old cars and telegraph poles, digging the road up with mechanical diggers. The decision was final.

It was easy walking so I made good progress, bowling along in the sun by the river Ufita, the sky dabbed with fluffy white clouds. A battered mauve Escort Estate pulled up, the driver offering a lift up the hill to Guardia Lombardi. His wife climbed out of the front seat into the back with the three children and I clambered in. He was in the building trade, making prefabs for the victims of the earthquake. They had built more than 12,000 so far, some of which came from as far as California, but many more were still needed, and many of those that had been built lacked running water, electricity and proper drains. The epicentre had been around Eboli and had registered 6.8 on the Richter scale, he said, which made it the worst this century. It came in thirty waves, devastating buildings in more than a hundred towns and villages. The weather had been vile, the temperature dropping below freezing point with snow and sleet.

When the tremors subsided, the government was left with 400,000 homeless to take care of, 100,000 of those in Naples. Relief only started to arrive on the 28th, by which time many had spent three or four days in the open. More than half the dead showed no signs of serious injury or asphyxiation. One old pensioner somehow survived six nights buried under the rubble. When we arrived on the outskirts of Guardia Lombardi, he pointed up the slightly sloping high street:

'They had the coffins lined up there; people looking for their relatives had to open them and look inside until they found the one they wanted.'

He told me I should visit the sister village of San Angelo in the valley below. Almost half the population had died, most of the buildings had collapsed, including six churches and the recently built hospital. Despite the fact that it was a well known earthquake area, no precautions had been taken to make it quakeproof. In fact they found that the tallest building, the Panorama, in which twenty people had died, had 392 beams instead of the 568 specified in the architect's plans. He said most building contracts were at least indirectly controlled by the Camorra, who certainly got their fair share of the £8.5 million allocated by the government for aid to the area.

I got out of the car, his wife climbed in the front once more and they rattled off. I did not go down to San Angelo, but followed the tops of the hills, which were bare and rocky, the soil poor and eroded, reaching Andretta as the sun sank behind a wall of threatening black clouds. A house would appear perfectly normal from one angle, but another would reveal a great crack down the wall or a collapsed roof. The barmaid said there had been 10,000 victims, eight of them in Andretta. The epicentre had been in Cenza, she said, a few miles away. I had somehow lost the top of my water bottle, so she kindly tried all the bottle tops she had until she came to one that fitted and handed it back to me with a smile. I was being very lucky with the weather, she told me. It was an exceptionally fine autumn. The clouds that had looked so menacing never arrived, the night turned clear and starry.

I walked into Calitri the next morning through a sea of prefabs. The worst damage had been done at the top of the village, where I wandered round looking at the rubble, the gutted houses and collapsed archways, thinking the people must have the patience of Job to put up with this life. An elderly woman leaned out of her window:

'Are you a reporter?' she asked.

'No, *Signora*, I was just looking around. Were you here when it

267

happened?'

'Yes. I was in my house when suddenly everything started to shake like a jelly, it did. I tried to stand up and run out but I lost my balance immediately and fell to the floor. I was terrified, I tell you, the walls bouncing, everything wobbling, glasses crashing from the tables, the pictures smashing on the floor, my neighbour screaming across the road ... *Santa Maria!*' She crossed herself. Her eyes were sparkling with the tale. I asked her why she was still living among the ruins, when she could have moved in to a new house.

'Hah! No one wants to live in those tin boxes. They prefer to go and stay with their family somewhere else.'

As I was leaving a woman beckoned me into her house, built into the rock, carved from the soft *tufa*, troglodytic but with a high ceiling, well whitewashed, cool. She apologised for her husband, who sat in the corner of the room on a wooden chair, his face and hands covered in sores, a rag stuffed into his mouth to stop him crying or dribbling.

'He's ill.'

'I'm sorry.'

She made me a cup of tea, chatting away happily, after which we set off into the valley together, working our way down through the complex network of alleyways that often ran over the tops of the houses below, the arching buttresses so solid no earthquake could shift them. She was on her way to plant garlic. Before we parted she gave me two heads of garlic and a bunch of grapes.

'Take them. Go on with you now. *Buone cose.*'

'Good things': it was a nice way of saying goodbye.

The yellow, barren, treeless land became more fertile by the banks of the Ofanto. I followed a shallow tributary through the woods beneath Monte Volture, the sound of a chain saw carrying in the silence, white cows blundering through the undergrowth, my boots thudding on the packed earth track as I paced along towards Atella. On the road leading in stood a wiry, broad-shouldered man in a beret and blue overalls, about to start up the motor of his barrow that was loaded with grapes.

'Would you like a bunch to quench the thirst, mate? Have a drink while you're at it. Where are you from?'

'England.'

'Oh, pity, I thought you might be German. I worked in Germany for twenty years, in a bottle factory, saved enough money to buy a house in town, some vineyards, an olive grove and three cows, which was a lot better than working in the mines in Sardinia, I can tell you. Sit on the back there and I'll give you a lift into town. Tonight you are my guest.'

He put great emphasis on the last word. The light faded as we talked and unloaded the grapes which would be taken away to the co-operative in the morning. His son was going to be a doctor and he was paying him through his studies at Bari. All his ambitions were centred round this one desire: that his son should not grow up in the same stifling surroundings as he had.

'Come. I will show you my fine house.'

It was a large stone house on the corner of one of the main streets, whitewashed, well proportioned. Half the house had fallen in during the earthquake though, and the walls of what remained were propped up with wooden struts. He grinned.

'God punishes those who work. We live in a new flat now, but come and see the cellars first, I have to get some wine.'

The cellars were cavernous, our voices echoing as we went down into the murky depths hidden form the candlelight. It was cold and dank, the air reeked of wine. *'Piano, Piano'* he kept saying. (Slowly, Slowly.)

After filling two litre bottles from one of the enormous barrels we drove out to the flat. His wife opened the door. Her face fell. I would have understood the meaning of what she said simply by the tone of her voice and the way she looked at me.

'What have you brought this tramp home for?'

'I have invited him to stay the night, dear. He can use Paolo's room. What's for supper?'

The look of disgust that crossed her face affected him no more than water on a duck's back. Throughout the evening he blithely ignored her displeasure, remaining good-humoured despite her sourness.

He plied me with questions and wine over supper, noisily sucking the meat and juices from a bit of chicken neck while I ate a piece of veal that was probably to have been his. Mother and daughter looked on, but we did not eat together. The wine was having its effect on both of us. His favourite theme was that the young didn't want to work any more. He also had a strange idea that a pound sterling was a gold coin and so worth much than 2000 lire. My eyes were dropping. I had come a long way, it seemed. He showed me to the bedroom. There were plastic flowers in an ornate vase, a few gewgaws scattered around and a lovely hard double bed in the centre of the room. I washed carefully in the bathroom before slipping gently between the white starched sheets. It seemed like an age had passed since I last had a bed to sleep in, back at Uncle Tom's Cabin above Arezzo.

He appeared for breakfast in a woollen vest, a little red-eyed, hungover, but raring to go after coffee and a slice of cake. He pointed out the track that would take me to Scalera and I thanked him sincerely for his hospitality, before setting off across the bare, ploughed fields into the wind. I would have offered to help him finish the vintage, but the shadow of his wife was too forbidding: I was obviously not in the least bit welcome so far as she was concerned.

The fattest of four road workers slapped me across the shoulders jovially in the cafe at Scalera, bought me a drink and introduced me to his work mates. They talked and joked together in a dialect I had trouble understanding, but it was contact of a kind, enough to keep me from getting lonely.

It rained on and off all day, though the sun kindly came out between showers to dry things off. I kept up a good pace, enjoying the last oak woods I would see in Italy, an isolated blotch of green on the map, protecting the source of the Bràdano flowing to the Gulf of Taranto. The wind on the ridge road to Acerenza was cold and biting, the town visible for some time perched on a rocky crag overlooking Basilicata, so named after the Greek King Basil, who kicked out the Saracens. Darkness fell when I was still some distance from the town: I would have to find water and camp. A sign by the road side said: *Ristorante Casone*. I made my way up the drive to ask for water.

It was a large building, but only a single light lit up the gloom. The doors were open, a young man was sitting by the fire watching television. I held up my bottle:

'I'm sorry to interrupt. Could I have some water?'

'Yes, of course, I'll go and fill the bottle. Sit down, warm yourself up, you look cold. Don't worry about the dog, he's friendly.'

He was keen to show me over the restaurant, the spacious kitchen, the discotheque upstairs, where he proudly played some reggae on the costly Pioneer equipment.

'Nothing much happens here during the week, but things really buzz at the weekend, I can tell you.'

He fetched a bottle of wine to drink with the large sandwich he made me, explaining there were three partners, himself and two friends. They were doing well now that the place had got a name for itself. The two friends came in a little while later.

'Hey, Giorgio, did you know there's been one and a half metres of water over Venice?'

'No, really?'

'Yep, I'm not kidding, and a half a metre of snow at the Brenner Pass.'

They invited me to dinner. Later I fell asleep in front of the television, waking the next morning to find that I was in a bed in the

270

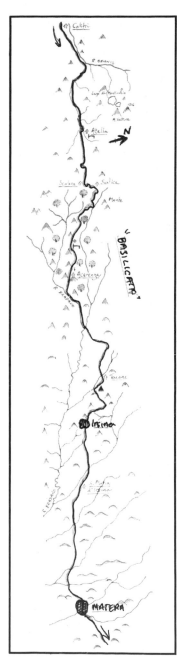

same room as five others. I left for Acerenza by mid morning to catch the shops before the curfew came down. It was cold in the irregular streets and the people kept asking why I didn't put my trousers on, saying *'Fa freddo'* (It's cold) in an uncomprehending way, much as the Portuguese in the Alentejo had done, though there they had asked 'Are you hot?', which is perhaps a clue to their cultural differences.

For centuries the south has been a spectator to events in the north, but in classical times the south was culturally more advanced, a part of Magna Graecia. Acerenza was a colony of the Greeks, who lived in towns on easily defended hilltops a day's march from each other. It was called Acherontia then; Horace refers to it in his Odes as 'the nest of lofty Acherontia' *(celsae nidum Acherontiae)*. It is a peculiar name to give a town, Acheron being the river of sadness in Greek mythology, the entry to the underworld.

Acerenza lies at a very strategic point as it controls the watershed of rivers draining to the Adriatic, Ionian and Tyrrhenian Seas. Charlemagne wanted the walls razed, but his orders were ignored; it was one of the first towns occupied by the Normans, who set up the feudal state that continued until the agrarian reforms were introduced. The Cathedral is simple and severe, similar to that at Rouen built by William the Conqueror. The remains of the fortified battlements are still there, but one of the towers collapsed in an earthquake. There is the bust of what looks like a saint in the façade, but if

271

you take a ladder and inspect it, as François Lenormant did in 1883, you will find that it is engraved with the name of Claudius J. Aug. Imp., or Julian the Apostate, the man who attempted to revive paganism in the Roman Empire. It may be simply a coincidence, but in the porch, built in the twelfth century, there are two stone carvings of a man and an ape and a woman and an ape, both of a startling obscenity, which must have come from an earlier temple dedicated to a completely different god. The Bishop had them taken away but the town council forced him to put them back.

From Acerenza I could see the countryside slowly flattening out towards the east, the hills rolling in smooth, bare curves towards the Murge, a high, limestone plateau that covers most of Apulia. The day was uneventful, spent walking cross-country towards Irsina, stopping for water in the evening with the sun setting behind the smooth horizon at Tacone, a dusty, dry village of interest only for the eucalyptus trees that grew there. I found shelter for the night in a barn not far off, that was used for housing combines and other machinery. To my delight there was a heap of rusting bed frames in a corner; three nights off the ground seemed like a record. I woke with a start during the night to hear snuffling and the pad of paws on the concrete floor. The dog barked furiously when it heard me move, backing away to the door, a black shadow against the lighter night sky. I threw a metal bolt in its direction and it turned tail and fled with a yelp.

A light frost covered the ground. In Irsina there were stares and muttered exclamations of 'Tedesco'. I did not like being taken for a German, though it was natural enough, and walked quickly through the town and on over the ploughed land to Santa Maria d'Irsi. In certain lights the land became a rolling yellow desert, not a tree or bush in sight, with only an occasional sharp line of eroded sandstone to show it was not dunes. Swifts dashed about in the air hunting insects while way above in the wide, pale blue sky two buzzards floated gracefully on the current before two fighter planes broke the silence as they thundered overhead.

A motorway was being built from Santa Maria to Matera, but it seemed to have been abandoned, probably due to lack of funds, for these take up to two years to arrive from the government. It was certainly what they call a 'cathedral in the desert', serving no real purpose. I followed it through tunnels, over half-built bridges, the road crumbling in places, amused to have a whole motorway to myself. It took me within a few miles of Matera, past a large white farm where I was given two fresh pomegranates and a bunch of grapes with my water. The earth had changed colour again to a

272

rocky white limestone. There were orange trees and vines which were trained up the trunks and branches of the olive trees. The stars blazed that night, a tall industrial chimney belching smoke in the face of the moon.

I took a certain masochistic pleasure in walking the dusty, unfinished pavements into Matera next day, passing new and half-finished buildings, cranes, diggers and workmen. Once at the centre, I climbed the tower of the twelfth century basilica to look down over the town, the roofs of the Palaeolithic troglodyte quarter below set against an intricate maze of interconnecting alleyways. The houses were built into the rock face on the steps above the gorge, the doorways and small windows gaping black holes, staring bleakly out, condemned, abandoned and left to crumble.

These *Sassi* have been inhabited for thousands of years. Not so long ago there were 15,000 people living there, seven to a cave with the animals and no sewers. The stench was horrific and little sun or fresh air could penetrate the inside of the cave where the walls oozed damp and the fireplace smoked. A table, chairs and a single bed for the family constituted the furniture, while chickens clucked around on the dirt floor and rabbits nibbled in hutches beneath the bed. Little wonder that they were abandoned for the modern flats to the west, but it seems a pity that an inheritance of such historical value should be left to crumble away so completely.

After wandering the maze, I went down into the gorge with the idea of having a wash in the river, but it stank, of course, and some heathen had tipped a load of rubbish, including plastic and broken glass, down the sides. I ate my lunch on the other side, outside a cave, lizards skittering between the hot stones, the sheep bells tinkling on the hillside, looking north to the hazy white walls of Altamura, east to Gióia where I would be heading.

It was in the area round Altamura that a young man called Michele Colonna once lived. He came from a poor family with four children, the mother a housewife, the father caretaker at a local school. The father sold his son to a local landowner in return for 40,000 lire per month and some cheeses on condition that he proved tough enough for the job he was to do. His day started at about four in the morning when he had to milk the flock of 200 sheep before taking them out onto the hills to graze. For lunch he was given a hunk of bread. In the evening, when he returned, he was given a bowl of pasta and locked in the cowshed where he slept. In summer it meant that he was working a fifteen hour day. His only day off came once a month when he was allowed home to change his clothes. He survived, then after two years he was resold for 70,000 lire, an

273

annual eight kilos of cheese and an Easter lamb, the increase in his price due simply to inflation. The work was the same, the conditions unchanged. A year later he was up for sale again, fetching a price of 125,000 lire this time, with ten kilos of cheese, fifteen quintals of wood, twelve kilos of oil and twelve of salt thrown in. The money went to his mother.

One day in early winter he didn't come back from the fields. It was two days before they found him. He had taken his master's shotgun, steadied the gun against a stone, tied a string to the trigger, a stone to the string and shot himself ineptly, bleeding to death in the middle of nowhere, at the age of fourteen. At the trial of the four men involved, the council for the defence praised the way of life, extolling the virtues of a life led far from the drugs and vice of the city, saying the boy had no intention of killing himself. He was only playing with the gun. Two of the accused were sentenced to a year in prison, the other two got eight and six months respectively. His mother said that he was happy in his way of life. He had chosen it after all. Somebody must have murdered him. He died on the 6th November, 1975.

I headed down over the scrubby pasture land to a minor road that would take me to Gióia, crossing the ancient Appian Way, which the locals called the 'New Road' because it has only recently been paved. When it was built the Romans had to hack their way through great oak forests. Even in the thirteenth century Apulia was an evergreen countryside covered with woods, flowing with natural springs that guaranteed a good harvest. Dante called it the *'fortunata terra di Puglia'*, but today the trees have all gone, along with the good earth and the water.

I needed a drink badly and approached

an isolated farmhouse where a highly suspicious woman fetched some in a bucket from the well, glancing over her shoulder to make sure that I was keeping on the other side of the fence. I camped a little further on among the stony pastures on a knoll. Light faded, a dog barked in the distance.

The last day of October broke clear and fresh and I made good progress to reach the slopes of the Murge before the sun was fully up. Because it is a limestone plateau, it has no lakes, ponds, streams or rivers on its surface. It is flat but broken up by walls dividing olive groves from almonds and vineyards where the grapes had long since been picked, the veiny leaves now clotting red. It was lovely walking, ploughed land alternating with pasture, cows crossing the road whipped along by two herdsmen, the towers of the church at Gióia on the horizon.

I stopped to buy the famous Mozarella cheese and glance at the Norman castle, but the sea was calling. Imagine the thought of a day at the seaside after a week's hard work, then multiply the pleasurable sensations of anticipation tenfold and you will understand how I longed to reach the coast. I had seen the sea only once on the walk since leaving the Atlantic at Lagos on 28th February, a distant cup of blue water glimpsed from the hills above Mas Bas. More than that, it marked the beginning of new adventures in Greece and Turkey, a whole new culture to adapt to and try to understand.

'Could I have some water?'

'No, we don't have any.'

I was very thirsty.

'*Signora*, I am not a thief or a robber, but a thirsty traveller. If you could just fill this bottle with water from your well over there, I will leave you in peace instantly.'

She did fetch water, but suspiciously, warily, avoiding all eye contact. The evil eye must be avoided at all costs. The glance of a stranger becomes a threat. Life is a dangerous affair. The danger hangs in the air, waiting to catch you unawares.

Later, I bumped into a man wheeling a bicycle down the lane, looking for some kind of thistle that his wife would make up in an omelette. He said it was natural for the women to be scared of strangers. Why, only the other day two lovers in their car in the quiet of the woods had been attacked. They killed the man, raped the woman and stole everything they could lay their hands on. Such a thing would never have happened if Mussolini were still around, he assured me. When he was young, he had earned five lire a day as a game keeper, a hard life, but healthy, with just enough money to make ends meet. Mussolini was a good man, helping the people of

The *Trullo*

Italy. It was a sad day when they had to abandon Libya and Turkey. Now the young didn't know what work meant, a bunch of layabouts and thieves the lot of them, went to school, came out with a piece of paper at the end which meant nothing, couldn't find a job, so took to stealing.

We walked the road together. He would stop and shade his eyes from the sun when he had something particularly important to say. He had been a travelling salesman for forty years but had just retired. On his upper lip he sported a little white bristle to show whose side he was on.

Late that afternoon I saw the first *Trullo*, a small, primitive shelter built without mortar from blocks of limestone, the conical, vaulted roofs sitting on a square base like beehives, with a decorative bobble on top. It seemed like something out of a fairy story, the sort of thing that you might expect to see in Egypt or Mesopotamia in the third millenium B.C., but not in the south of Italy. No one could tell me anything about them. They were scattered all over the countryside, which was unusual for a start, because the people tend to live in towns even when they work the fields an hour's walk away. They feel safer there, secure from the skirmishing bandits and murderers that used to roam the countryside. I counted one settlement with seven of these beehives all joined together, some with steps up the side to get at the figs and tomatoes left out to dry. The better-kept ones had plaster over the capstones and were whitewashed, sometimes decorated with signs or crosses in red, a colour to ward off the devil.

The word *Trullo* comes from the Greek *'troulos'*, which means cupola or dome. Most of the shelters were built in the sixteenth century, at a time when the Duke of Nardó, Gian Giralomo II, the 'One-Eyed of Apulia', as he was known, wanted to develop the area as his own personal monarchy. His primary concern was to eliminate the hiding places of outlaws. His subjects were required to live on the land they worked, thus making it far more difficult for bandits to keep their hideouts secret. The plan worked, and he created incentives for further settlement.

The King of Spain had issued an edict to all his Barons, the

276

Prammatica de Baronibus, requiring permission to be granted for all new buildings. This was calculated to ensure the Barons paid their just share of taxes in proportion to the number and value of the buildings on their territory. The wily Gian Giralomo had no intention of sharing his income with the King of Spain: if, he reasoned, he had all new buildings made from stone without mortar the people could live quite adequately in shelters and, at the first sign of the King's taxman on the horizon, the entire village could be reduced to innocent-looking piles of rubble such as there were already all over the Murge. The villagers could then build them up again when the taxman had left.

His logic was sound. The Duke of Martina Franca was greatly annoyed that he was evading his taxes and reported him to the court in Spain. In 1644 an investigator was sent to find out if the allegations were true. Gian Giralomo was warned of his approach and had all the new *trulli* levelled in one night of frenzied activity. The inspector arrived, found everything in order and went home satisfied. The peasants then turned to the work of rebuilding their villages.

The first modern house I saw of rectangular design with a flat roof seemed oddly angular after the *trulli,* and appeared to float like a brilliant white ship on a green sea. It was easy, pleasant walking on the old road to Noci where I approached a house for water. It was dark by then and the women panicked, trying to shut the gate in my face, but I jammed a boot in to stop them, called for the head of the house and got my water. I headed on, looking for a place to rest my weary bones, the yellow lights of a factory dwarfing a group of *trulli* beside the main road to Alberobello. An abandoned shelter by the level crossing looked promising, but the place was used as a public lavatory, and the remains of a pornographic magazine lay scattered on the filthy floor, so I moved on.

I had better luck the second time, climbing a wall to reach a group of four *trulli* knitted together to form a house with four rooms, each with a tiny window, the ceilings blackened by smoke from the fireplace. The floor was paved with stone and clean, so I settled in, happy that I would not get touched by the heavy morning dew.

It was All Saints' Day, the first of November. In Alberobello mass was in full swing; I attended briefly, listening to the mumbling voice of an old, stooping, white-haired priest over the p.a. system. He kept forgetting his lines but a young woman was there to prompt him. Outside, the sun was shining, the roses, geraniums and chrysanthemums were still in flower in the gardens and there was little traffic on the road. Lines of hunters combed the countryside in

277

the ritual Sunday morning massacre.

I took a side road to Martina Franca, a large fortress town built by the crusaders, with very narrow, whitewashed alleyways, thick buttresses and outside steps leading up to the doors of the houses. The place seemed more Arabic than Italian, but there was the usual scene in the main square: mahogany-faced men in tight blue and brown suits with dented felt hats standing around on the corners waiting to see their friends, plotting against their enemies, dealing and building castles in the air. They were understandably shocked at my pretence that it was Midsummer's Day. I walked out past the largest monument in town, the cemetery, where two flower sellers were doing good business. Water was a problem. I was tired of begging for it from suspicious women, though my faith in human nature returned a little when I was hospitably received at a house on the outskirts, and given both water and a glass of wine to send me on my way. That evening I managed to find a tap outside a country railway station and strip-washed in the twilight, much to the amusement of the station master and his family. I spent the night in another *trullo*, the scent of ripe quinces drifting through the open door, as I dreamt of the sea.

I woke with a nasty pain in my back. I thought I had slept on a rock or lump, but there was nothing under the Karrimat. A young girl waiting for the school bus saw me coming up the road and bolted back to the safety of her house, while her mother came out to sweep the courtyard innocently, broom in hand. At Ostuni I finally caught sight of the sea below. It was a moment of rare happiness. I marched along with a song in my heart, exhaustion tapping at my shoulder. I felt an overwhelming craving for chocolate and waited an hour in Carovigno for the shop to open. There were palm trees now, prickly pear, which I left well alone, agave, almonds and an ancient olive tree propped up by a stone pillar.

The chocolate gave me energy for the last push down an avenue of cypress trees, past a 'Private, no entry' sign into another long avenue of trees that seemed vaguely familiar, but which I couldn't recognise. A man came by in a car, stopped and got out.

'This is private property. Didn't you see the sign?'

'Yes, I did.'

I pulled out the map and showed it to him.

'I was just trying to follow this path here past the little chapel to the sea.'

His attitude softened and he became friendly, telling me the trees were carobs, rummaging around in the thick foliage to find one, giving it to me.

278

'We make cattle fodder from them.'

'You can make chocolate from them too, I believe.'

'Really? All I know is that *cornuto* Mussolini tried to make us eat them during the war against you lot. Full of vitamins, he said. Men like that are best dead anyway. We don't need maniacs like him to dominate the world. It's better that we all be friends.'

We shook hands and I set off again. *'Tante belle cose'*, he said as we parted. 'Many beautiful things'. It was a lovely way to say good-bye.

I could smell the sea now, then I could hear it. A cluster of buildings loomed ahead in the dark. I had stumbled on some sort of summer work camp, though there wasn't a soul about. The buildings were open, so I chose a small, whitewashed cell with a bench and table with *Altomare* scratched onto it with a knife. 'High tide'.

After supper, I took the steps down to the beach, took off my boots and waded into the lightly phosphorescent water, feeling the contentment of a job well done slowly spreading through every inch of my body, the bubble of happiness growing, bursting out in a great shout of triumph as I realised just how far I had come since last I saw the sea at Lagos. I sat on a rock listening to the regular breathing of the sea, the swish of lapping waves, taking deep draughts of the salty, humid air, digging my toes into the sand. A light breeze was blowing, the new moon hung in the night sky. The next day I would take the boat to Greece.

My back was very stiff in the morning. I was in no hurry. I made breakfast and sat gazing out over the Adriatic with visions of Odysseus flitting through my mind. Was it not he who said 'There is nothing worse for men than wandering'? I tidied things away, lifted my pack as I had done so many times before, then dropped it with a scream as a searing pain ripped up my back, leaving me gasping, breathless, broken.

Epilogue

I had pulled a muscle in my back, the *Sacrospinalis* my doctor tells me. I could not stay where I was. A little dazed and numbed by shock, I cautiously eased on the pack and walked gently the last fifteen kilometres to Brindisi. Two hours later I was aboard ship, bound for Patras on a Greek cargo boat. I made for the washrooms and let hot water from a shower pummel my back, hoping that I had not done irreparable damage to my spine. At Patras, I took a train to Athens, where I found cheap accommodation sharing a hostel room with Bertold, from Stuttgart. He had taken LSD ninety times and had finally seen the 'Shirt of God'. They were his words. His eyes were glassy, almost brittle.

In the next few days I found good maps, got my boots resoled and started to learn modern Greek. I would wait until my back was well rested, then head north in a curve to Thessalonika, within striking distance of Istanbul. It would be foolish to start off again before I was sure that my back was going to take the strain. I was having to wait too long, though. My thoughts kept turning to Cosimo up his tree on a cold winter night, watching the festivities in his father's hall, the warm lights twinkling, the sound of happy laughter carrying from the comfortable world he had shunned. Was he thinking how short the step was that separated him from a return to their world, how short and easy?

Outside in the street it had begun to rain. Winter was very close and it would be cold in the mountains, the nights long and lonely. I was spending money that I didn't have and making little progress in conversational Greek. My dreams slowly faded away, a great weariness took their place. Perhaps my body was telling me what my mind refused to accept, that it was time to go home.

I have waited until this moment to work out with a length of string roughly how far I walked. It didn't matter at the time, but too many people have enquired for me to leave the question unanswered. About 4500 kilometres or 2812 miles. London to Mecca, as the crow flies.

Ickleton, June 1984.

Bibliography

PORTUGAL

AITCHISON John, *Letters of an Ensign in the Peninsular War* (Ed. W.F.K. Thompson), Michael Joseph, 1981.

BRADFORD Sarah, *Portugal*, Thames & Hudson, 1973.

GIBBONS John, *Afoot in Portugal*, Methuen, 1933.

GRATTAN William, *Adventures with the Connaught Rangers* 1809-1814, Arnold, 1902.

KEEFE E.K., *Area Handbook for Portugal*, Am. Univ, 1976.

LIVERMORE Harold, *A New History of Portugal*, Cambridge University Press, 1969.

MARBOT Baron de, *Memorias*, Castalín, 1965.

MYHILL Henry, *Portugal*, Faber & Faber, 1972.

NAPIER William, *History of the War in the Peninsular* (abridged), Chicago University, 1979.

PELET J.J. *The French Campaign in Portugal* (Ed. Horward), Minnesota, 1973.

ROBINSON Richard, *Contemporary Portugal, A History*, Allen & Unwin, 1979.

SALTER Cedric, *Portugal*, Batsford, 1970.

SCHAUMANN August, *On the road with Wellington*, Heinemann, 1924.

WUERPEL Charles, *The Algarve*, David & Charles, 1974.

SPAIN

BEEVOR Antony, *The Spanish Civil War*, Orbis, 1982.

BOTTINEAU Yves, *Les Chemins de Saint Jacques*, Paris, 1984.

CANICIO Victor, *Vida de un Emigrante Español*, Gedesa, 1979.

CLARK R.P. *The Basques – The Franco Years & Beyond*, Nevada, 1979.

CLISSOLD Stephen, *In Search of the Cid*, Hodder & Stoughton, 1965

de CHASCA Edmond, *The Poem of the Cid,* Twayne, 1976.
DELIBES Miguel, *Castilla, lo Castellano y los Castellanos,* Planeta, 1979.
FORD Richard, *Gatherings from Spain,* Murray, 1846.
GAVELA M.J.A., *Gaudi en Astorga,* Fray Bernadino, 1972.
HINDE Thomas, *The Great Donkey Walk,* Hodder & Stoughton, 1977.
KEEFE E.K., *Area Handbook for Spain,* Am. Univ, 1976.
LIVERMORE Harold, *A History of Spain* (2nd Ed), Allen & Unwin, 1966.
LORCA F.G., *Romancero Gitano,* Madrid 1935.
MENDIZABAL Isaac, *La lengua Vasca,* Buenos Aires, 1943.
THOMAS Hugh, *The Spanish Civil War,* Pelican, 1961.
da UNAMUNO Miguel, *Andanzas, Visiones Españolus,* Renacimiento 1922.
The Chanson de Roland, (Ed. F. Whitehead), Oxford University Press, 1946.
The True Description of the Voyage of Sir Francis Drake, 1587.
The Codex Calixtinus, (Liber Sancti Jacobi), Santiago, 1944.

FRANCE

ADLER Stephen, *International Migration and Dependence,* Saxon House, 1977.
ARDAGH John, *France in the 1980s,* Secker & Warburg, 1982.
BELLOC Hilaire, *The Pyrénées,* Methuen, 1909.
DANK Milton, *The French against the French,* Cassell, 1974.
DUPUY André, *Histoire Chronologique de la Civilisation Occitane,* Butterworth, 1980.
EHRLICH Blake, *The French Resistance,* Chapman and Hall, 1966.
GIONO Jean, *Regain,* Livres de Poche, Paris, 1942.
HUNTER Rob, *Walking in France,* Oxford Illustrated Press, 1982.
JOLAS Tina, *Gens du Finage, Gens du Bois.*
LANDS Neil, *The French Pyrénées,* Spurbooks, 1980.
LANDS Neil, *Languedoc Rousillon,* Spurbooks, 1976.
LAZENBY J.F., *Hannibal's War,* Aris & Phillips, 1978.
LEVRAULT, *L'Architecture Rurale en France,* Berger, 1977.
MARION Elias, *A Cry from the Desert or Testimonials of the Miraculous Things Lately Come to Pass in the Cévennes,* 1707.
PEYRAT Napoleon, *Pasteurs du Désert,* Paris, 1842.
RANUM E.L., *The Deserted Villages of France,* Hopkins, 1979.
SAVAGE George, *The Languedoc,* Barrie & Jenkins, 1975.
SCOTT J.M., *From Sea to Ocean (Walking the Pyrénées),* Bles, 1969.
STEVENSON R.L. *The Cévennes Journal,* Mainstream, 1978.

THOMPSON I.B., *Modern France, A Social & Economic Geography,* Butterworth, 1970.
WHITE Freda, *West of the Rhône,* Faber, 1964.
WILLINGS Heather, *A Village in the Cévennes,* Gollancz, 1979.

SWITZERLAND

BELLOC Hilaire, *The Path to Rome,* Allen, 1902.
BLEASE W. Lyon, *Suvorof,* Constable, 1920.
BUNTING James, *Switzerland,* Batsford, 1973.
BYRON Lord, *Letters & Journals* (Ed. I.A. Marchand), Murray, 1976.
BYRON Lord, *Prisoner of Chillon,* Oxford, 1976.
COOPER James F., *Switzerland,* NY Press, 1980.
COWIE Donald, *Switzerland, The Land and People,* Barnes N.Y, 1971.
COXE William, *Sketches of Switzerland,* London 1779.
DE BEER, G.R., *Alps & Men,* Arnold, 1932.
POWYS Llewelyn, *Swiss Essays,* Bodley Head, 1947.
LOCKETT W.G., *R.L. Stevenson at Davos,* Hurst & Blackett, 1934.
LUCK J.M., *Modern Switzerland,* Sposs Inc, 1978.
LUNN Sir Arnold, *The Bernese Oberland,* Eyre Spottiswood, 1958.
LUNN Sir Arnold, *Switzerland and the English,* Eyre & Spottiswood, 1944.
MILLER Douglas, *The Swiss at War 1300-1500,* 1979.
MULLER, *Swiss Alpine Folk Tales.*
RUSSELL John, *Switzerland,* Batsford, 1950.
SCHMID C.L., *Conflict & Consensus in Switzerland,* California Press, 1981.
THURTER George, *Free and Swiss,* O. Wolff, 1970.
ZIEGLER Jean, *Switzerland Exposed,* Allison & Busby, 1976.

ITALY

ALLEN Edward, *Stone Shelters,* Massachusetts, 1969.
BANFIELD E.C., *The Moral Basis of a Backward Society,* Chicago University, 1958.
BELLONCI Maria, *Lucrezia Borgia – Her Life and Times,* Weidenfeld & Nicolson, 1939.
BELMONTE Thomas, *The Broken Fountain,* Colorado University, 1979.
BRADFORD Ernle, *Hannibal,* Macmillan, 1981.
CAVEN Brian, *Hannibal's War,* Aris & Phillips, 1978.
CHUBB Judith, *Patronage, Power and Poverty in Southern Italy,* C.U.P., 1982.

CORNELISEN Ann, *Torregreca*, Macmillan, 1969.
CORNELISEN Ann, *Flight from Torregreca*, Macmillan, 1980.
CRONIN Vincent, *A Concise History of Italy*, Cassell, 1972.
GIBBONS John, *To Italy at Last*, Methuen, 1933.
HEARDER H. and WALEY D.P., *A Short History of Italy*, C.U.P., 1963.
HOOK Judith, *Siena*, Hamilton, 1979.
HOWELLS W.D., *Italian Journeys*, D. Douglas, 1883.
JAMES Henry, *Italian Hours*, Murray.
KEATES Jonathan, *The Love of Italy*, Octopus, 1980.
KEEFE E.K., *Area Handbook for Italy*, Am. Univ., 1977.
LENORMANT François, *A Travers l'Apulie et la Lucanie*, 1883.
LINKLATER Eric, *The Campaign in Italy 1943-1945*, H.M.S.O., 1951.
ORGILL Douglas, *The Gothic Line – The Autumn Campaign in Italy 1944*, Heinemann, 1967.
PEREIRA Anthony, *Pompeii, Naples and South Italy*, Batsford, 1977.
RODGERS Allan, *Economic Development in Retrospect*, Winston, 1979.
RUSSO Giovanni, *Baroni e Contadini*, Un. Laterza, 1955.
SCOTT J.M., *A Walk Along the Apennines*, Bles, 1973.
SMOLLETT Tobias, *Travels through France and Italy 1721-71*, O.U.P., 1981.
TREVELYAN G.M., *Garibaldi's Defence of the Roman Republic*, Longman, 1907.

Index

Aare Valley 182
Abedim 49
Abrantes 26-7
Abrejoeira 23
Abruzzi Mountains 252
Acebo 67, 69
Acerenza 270-72
Adige River 195
Afonso III of Portugal 1
Aigoual, Mont 135
Aiguebelle, Monastery 141
Albergaria das Cabras 44
Alberobello 277
Alcácer do Sal 20
Alentejo 3, 10-26
Alfedena 254
Alfonso II of León 52
Alfonso VI of Spain 52
Algarve 1, 7-9
Algerians 119
Allo 88
Allobroges 147
Altamura 273
Altdorf 187, 171
Altefage Woods 137
Alvalade 16
Amarela 10
Andalucía 1
Andretta 267
Antoñán del Valle 72
Apice 264
Apulia (Puglia) 274
Arcos de Valdevez 48
Ardagh, John 93, 121
Ardèche Valley 139
Arezzo 232
Ariège 112-14
Arno 229
Arouca 45
Arrens 106-7
Assergi 248
Assissi 239
Astorga 69-70
Atella 268-9
Aulas 133
Autrans 149-50, 159
Avèze 133

Badia Prataglia 228
Bagnères de Bigorre 108
Banios 108
Barre des Cévennes 136
Barrea 254
Basil, King of Greece 270
Basque Country 82-95
Bassano 202, 206, 207
Bassi 264
Bastille Day 142
Baudelaire, Charles 93
Bédarieux 122
Bedous 102

Beira Province 30-43
Belledone Mountains 154
Bellefond, Cabane de 155
Belloc, Hilaire 86, 182
Beresford, Viscount William
   Carr,
Bielle 103
Boi 36
Bolzano 197, 199
Bonderalp Oschinensee 173, 174
Bonito 226
Bonivard, François 167
Bardou 121
Borgia, Lucrezia 214
Borrajeiros 56
Bourdeaux 142
Brejeira, Serra da 9, 14
Brenta River 207, 208
Brigate Garibaldi 223, 226, 242
Briteiros, Citania de 47
Brixton Riots 144
Broa 43
Buçaco, Battle of 32-3
Budrio 216
Burgos 78-80
Byron, Lord 167-8. 169, 177

Cabarcos 65
Caetano, Marcello J. das Neves
   A. 23, 40
Caldelas 45
Calitri 267
Camaldoli 226-8
Cambridgeshire 73
Camisard Revolt 136-8
Camorra 264, 267
Campo Imperatore 248
Campolattaro 261
Canal du Midi 114
Capitignano 248
Caramulo, Serra do 33-5
Carapeçoes 23
Carovigno 278
Casais 7
Castel Guelfo 217
Castellucio 246
Castelnaudary 114
Castel Rigone 238
Castelvecchio 248
Castile 74, 76-81
Castro 57
Castropetre 64
Catraia 64
Caurel, Sierra del 61
Causse du Larzac 132
Cavia, Lake 201
Celts 47, 167
Cerro al Volturno 254
Cévennes, National Park 133-9
Ciapela 201

Cid, The (Rodrigo Díaz de Vivar)
   80
Cittadella 208
Civil Guards, Spanish 2, 81
Civitella 243
Civil War, Spanish 2, 60, 71,
   78-9, 86
Charlemagne 92
Charles the Bold of Burgundy
   167
Chassezac, River 140
Chianti 236
Chiara d'Offreducci 241
Chirrido, El 58
Chocolate, Swiss 175
Chouto 26
Christian Democrats, Italian 219
Chüpfenflue Crag 192
Chur, 189, 191
Claudius, Emperor 253
Cluses 163
Codex Calixtinus 53, 86
Codrignano 220
Col D'Aubisque 104
Col de Bougès 137
Col de Chésery 165
Col de Coux 163
Col de la Séreyrède 134
Col de Marie Blanque 102
Col de Soulor 105-6
Col des Nantes 160
Col du Coq 155
Col les Annes 161
Colla di Casaglia 224
Collipietro 250
Colli Euganei 211-2
Comminges 110
Communism, Italian 219, 226
Conrad, Joseph 62
Cork Trees 16
Cortes 62
Cortona 236
Coruche 24
Coruña (Corunna) 60, 67
Corvara 200
Coxe, Willian 186
Croce 243

Dante Alighieri, 274
Davedino 200
Davos 192, 193
Dent du Volan 165
Dents du Midi 163
Deslys, Gabi 34
D'Estaing, Giscard 115, 139
Dias, Bartolomeu 1
Dieulefit 142
Djibuti 119
Dolomites 197, 201
Dolomieu, Gialet de 198

Drake, Sir Francis 53
Du Chayla, Archpriest 137
Duke Alessandro Torlonia 253
Duke Gian Giralomo II 276
Duke Niccolò d'Este 214

Earthquake, Italy 264-9
Eaux Bonnes 103
Eboli 266
Ebro, River 82, 85, 87
E.E.C. 84, 256
Eiger Mountain 176, 179
Eleanor of Aquitaine 108
Elm 189
Engadine Valley 194
Engins 151
Engleberg 186
Equipment 2-3, 211, 258
Ermidas Sado 16
Este 212
Estérençuby 97
Estragiz 59
Estela, Serra da 29
E.T.A. 92, 98-9
Etruria 236
Ezcaray 82

Fátima 38
Feltre 202, 205, 207
Fematre 243
Ferrara 214
Flaminius Consul 237
Flaubert, Gustave
Flims 189
Flüela Pass 194
Foligno 242
Fontemanha 34
Footpaths 96, 218
Forbes, Colonel Hugh 235
Forca Canapine 247
Ford, Richard 5, 72, 185
Frades 22
Franco, General Francico F.
  Bahamonde 60, 73, 78
Freiberg Mountain 188

Gaea 178
Galicia 49, 61-5, 100, 255
Garibaldi, Giuseppe 223, 235
Gaudí, Antonio 70
Gessler, Hermann 187
Gibbons, John 93
Gioia 273, 275
Giono, Jean (Regain) 135, 136,
  148, 157-8, 164
Glauco 244
Glion 168, 169
Glosas Emilianenses – Codex 84
Gorge d'Héric 121
Gorges de la Bourne 147-8
Gran Sasso d'Italia 247-8
Grand Bornand 161
Grappa 205
Grenoble 149-51, 154
Griesalp 175
Grindelwald 180

Grisons, Canton 191
Grosse Scheidegg Pass 180
Grottaminarda 266
Grotte du Mas d'Azil 112
Gstaad 170, 172, 173
Guardão 38-40
Guardia Lombardi 266
Guardarègia 259
Guernica 81
Guimarães 46

Hannibal, son of Hamilcar 147,
  237
Henry the Navigator, Prince 1
Hérault, River 136
Hercules 91
Herodotus 236
Hillaby, John 45
Hitler, Adolf 248
Holmes, Sherlock
Horn, Fritz 153
Huguenots 167

Imola 217-8
Inácio Paulino 24
Innocent III, Pope 240
Introdaqua 252
Iraty Forest 97-9
Iraukotuturo Mountain 97
Isère, River 147, 151, 154
Isernia 255

James, Henry 186, 234
João VI of Portugal 33
Jochpass 186
Juan Carlos de Borbón y Borbón
  60
Julian the Apostate 272
Jungfrau Mountain 176, 178,
  179
Junqueira 34

Kandersteg 174
Khomeini, Ayatollah 86
Klausenpass 188
Kleine Scheidegg Pass 177, 178
Knights Templar 66
Knights of Santiago 52

Labastide-Rouairoux 119
Lac d'Annecy 154, 160
Lac Leman 154, 166, 169
Lac d'Hongrin 169
La Chapelle d'Abondance 165
La Garde Guérin 139
Lago Fucino 252
Lagos 1-2
Lake Trasimene 237
Lamalou-les-Bains 122
Lana 196
Languedoc, National Park 114
Langwies 192
Lantadilla 78
Lardero 85

Larrau 100
Latifundios 15
Lauterbrunnen 177
La Vaquerie 132
La Verna, Monastery 229
Lazagurría 87
Lenin, Vladimir Ilyich 183
Lenk 173
Lenormant, François 272
León 73-4, 76
Leopold I of Habsburg 167
Le Puech 131
Les Montagnès 116
Les Vans 140
L'Etivaz 171
Le Vernet 114
Le Vigan 133
Lodève 130-31
Logroño 85
Longano 256
Lorca, Federico García 87
Lortet 109
Louis XIV of France 136
Lousã, Serra da 29
Lózara Gorge 61-2
Lozère 134, 138-9
Lusitania 43, 47

Machado, Antonio 5, 90
Macnamara, Robert 257
Madreñas 64
Madrid 56, 67, 83
Mafia 255
Manhouce 43
Mann, Thomas 193
Mansilla de las Mulas 75
Manuel II of Portugal 34
Maps 3, 53, 95
Maquis 150
Maragatos 71
Marley, Bob 110
Marmolada Glacier 201
Martina Franca 278
Mas Bas 122-130
Masséna, General André 32-3,
  189
Massif Central 115, 141
Matera 272
Matese 259
Medicina 217
Meiringen 171, 182
Merano 196
Mercatale 237
Meseta, Spanish 69-75
Mezzogiorno 246, 256
Migration 12, 27, 42, 55, 83-4,
  185, 247, 249
Milice 117
Mimente Valley 137
Minerva, Temple of 241, 260
Minho (Miño) 49, 58
Minifundios 30
Mira Basin 10
Mitterand, François 115, 154
Modronho 11, 13
Mola, General Emilio Vidal 78
Monchique 7-8

Mondego, River 31
Montagne Noire 115-19
Montaperti, Battle of 233
Mont Blanc 163
Monte Battaglia 222
Monte Carnevale 223
Monte Cavallo 242
Monte Fagiola 224
Monte Falterona 225
Monte Genzana 252
Monte Grappa 205
Monte Miletto 258
Monte San Stefano 242
Montes de León 69
Monte Utero 247
Monte Vettore 243, 245
Monte Volture 268
Montjoie 110-11
Montremont 161
Montreux 167, 168, 195
Moore, Sir John 67-8
Moors 16, 27, 52, 76
Murge Plateau 272, 275, 279
Mussolini, Benito 248, 275
Müstair 195

Naples 261-2
Napoleon Bonaparte 32-3, 67-8,
  167, 189
Nancy-sur-Cluses 162
Navacelles 132
Nelson, Admiral Lord
Noci 277

Occitania 134
Odysseus 279
Oja, River 82
Orb, River 122
Oribio, Sierra del 59-61
Oschinensee 174
Ostuni 278
Oteiza 89
Oui 114

Padua 197, 200, 208
Paduli 264
Pamplona 89
Paris, Mathiew 240
Pas de Bellecombe 151
Pas des Prés 160
Passo dal Fuorn 195
Passo della Calla 226
Passo delle Farangole 201
Passo di Gardena 198
Passo di Muraglione 224
Pazuengos 83
Pego da Curva 26
Peninsular Wars 27, 32-3
Pertini, Alessandro 241
Perugia 237-8
Petrarch 211
Piano Grande 242, 245
Pia Pájaro 61-3
Pic d'Annie 100
Pic d'Arlas 101
Pic de Nore 117-18

Pietrelcina 264
Pizarro, Francisco 228
Plan de Baix 145
Plateau des Gras 140
Pliny 194
Poggio 230
Pompei 262
Po Valley 202, 205, 220
Ponferrada 65-6
Pont-en-Royans 147
Pòpoli 250
Porto 45-6
Porziuncola 241
Pradoluengo 82
Prato 196
Prester John 1
Primiero 202, 203
Puertomarín 58
Pyrene 91

Quixote, Don 76

Rasiglia 242
Reagan, Ronald 46
Rebocho 23
Revolution, Portuguese 16-17,
  23, 45
Rhine, River 191
Rhône, River 141, 167
Richelieu, Cardinal 123
Riego 67
Rifugio Campitello 258
Rifugio Club Alpino 226
Rifugio Diaz 204
Rifugio Mulaz 201
Rimbocchi 229
Riquet de Bonreposs, Paul 115-16
Rolà 29
Roland, Chanson de 92
Roman Roads 44, 139, 274
Roman Bridges 47, 78
Romansch 194
Roncesvalles 91
Rosa 208

Sadat, President Anwar 247
Sahagún 75
Saillans 143
Saint Anthony 2, 208
Ste. Engrâce 100
Saint Francis 230, 239-41
St. Gingolph 167
Saint James 52, 90
St. Jean-Pied-de-Port 95-6
St. Martin du Froid 121
St. Michel 158
St. Montant 141
St. Nizier 150
St. Papoul Abbey 115
Salazar, Antonio de Oliveira 39
Samoëns 163
Samos Monastery 60
Samnites 259
San Angelo 267
San Damiano 241

Sands, Bobby 90
San Giovanni 203
San Martino 202
San Millán 84/85
San Román 70
Santa Clara-a-Velha 10-12
Santa Luzia 14
Santa Maria, Church of 234
Santa Maria Codifiume 215
Santa Maria degli Angeli 239
Santa Maria d'Irsi 272
Santiago de Compostela 52-4
Santo Domingo de la Calzada 90
Santo Stefano 248
San Urbano 213
São João do Monte 36, 38
São Martinho 13-14
Sarria 59
Sassi 273
Sassovivo 242
Scalera 270
Scanno 253
Schaumann, August 27, 68
Schwanden 188, 189
Sefinenfurke Pass 175
Segnas Pass 189
Séguier, Pierre 'Spirit' 137
Sejães 41-3
Sepino (Saepinium) 259
Serren del Grappa 205
Shelley, Percy Bisshe 167
Siena 232-4
Skorzeny, Colonel Fritz 248
Smollett, Tobias 232
Soares, Mario 40
Soult, General Nicolas 68
Spello 241
Strela pass 192
Stevenson, Robert Louis 134,
  137, 139, 193
Subbiano 230
Sulmona 250
Suso Monastery 85
Suvorof, General Alexander 189
Swabians 44

Tacone 272
Tagus 26-7
Teixo 36, 38
Tejero, Lieut. Colonel Antonio 2,
  60
Tell, William 187
Teodomiro, Bishop 52
Thatcher, Margaret 90
Thônes 161
Tiberius, Emperor 260
Torquines 10
Torreglia 212
Torres Vedras, The Lines of 33
Toulouse 113, 115
Tourism, Swiss 173-4
Travasso, The Good Ladies of 30
Triptolemus 256
Trulli 276
Trummelbach Falls 177
Tuscany 222-8
Turza 83

Turpin, Archbishop 92
Tyrol, Southern

Uncle Tom's Cabin 230-31
Uri, Canton 167, 187

Valcarlos 92
Val di Chiana 231, 234
Vale da Lama 25
Vale de Boi 21
Vale de Guiso 18-19
Vallon-Pont-d'Arc 140
Valmala 81

Vandals 44
Vasco da Gama 1
Vaugelas 144
Vendas Novas 21
Verchiano 242
Vercors, Park 143, 145
    Republic of 149-50
Viana 86
Vigo 53
Vila de Rei 29
Villefort 139
Vinho Verde 47
Viriato (Viriathus) 43
Visigoths 44, 60
Visso 243

Viviers 141
Volturno, River 254

Wellington, Duke of 27, 32-3
Wetterhorn Mountain 180, 181,
    182, 184
Wilde Frau Glacier 175
Wilde, Oscar 180
William the Conqueror 271
Wordsworth, Mr and Mrs 177

Yuso Monastery 85